# Software Design Techniques

## for Large Ada Systems

William E. Byrne

Digital Press

9 8 7 6 5 4 3 2 1

Printed in the United States of America.

Order number EY-E761E-DP
Design and Production: Editorial Services of New England, Inc.
Printing and Binding: Arcata/Halliday

**Library of Congress Cataloging-in-Publication Data**

Byrne, William E.
    Software design techniques for large Ada systems / William E. Byrne.
        p.      cm.
    Includes bibliographical references and index.
    ISBN 1-55558-053-X
    1. Ada (Computer program language)      2. Computer software-
Development.      I. Title.
QA76.73. A35B96    1991
005.13'3--dc20                                              90-3930
                                                              CIP

# Contents

# Preface

Through the years, the growth in the processing power and memory capacity of computers has led to the development of ever larger and larger computer programs. As the size of computer programs has grown, however, inherent software design and implementation problems have also appeared. In response, design techniques have emerged to resolve the problems, and many different programming languages have been developed to support implementation of these designs. Recognizing the need for a general purpose programming language and the cost savings that could be realized by standardizing to a single contemporary language, the U.S. Department of Defense sponsored development of the general purpose programming language Ada. Within the three U.S. services, Ada is now being applied in the implementation of software for large, real-time, embedded computer systems. As a general purpose language, Ada is also being used to implement software for many other application areas within industry, both in the United States and in Europe. Ada reflects the results of the evolutionary changes in the development of large computer programs. In fact, development of large computer programs is where Ada is most useful.

Teaching programmers to program in Ada is not particularly difficult. Learning the syntax of Ada is easy enough. But taking advantage of the power of Ada is a different matter. Programmers may apply the proper syntax of Ada, but with outdated design techniques applicable to older languages which were developed years before extensive processing capacity was available. The result is sometimes called "Adatran" or "Fortrada"—programs written in the syntax of Ada but for a deficient design. Applying Ada in this manner, in ways more appropriate for small computer programs, does not take advantage of the power of Ada.

At the other extreme, the power of Ada is often used in ways that are counterproductive. In attempts to be technically unique and elegant, programmers may introduce extra complexity into the designs for large computer programs, producing systems that are difficult to develop and even more difficult to maintain.

The objective of this book is to introduce design strategies for controlling the complexity inherent in large computer programs and in software systems as groups of large computer programs executing concurrently. The design strategies are meant to reduce complexity at a global level in the transformation of a large problem to a form that is manageable and more readily solvable. This book addresses the subject of software engineering in Ada at a higher level than books on programming with Ada. It focuses on issues associated with the design of software systems as a whole, in contrast with textbooks on programming that focus on localized design and coding issues. It is especially applicable to managers, professional engineers, and college students who have not been exposed to the development of large and complex software systems and who may or may not be proficient in the use of programming languages to implement design.

What is needed in practice is design of large and complex computer programs to be implemented in Ada to help control complexity and risk, implementation problems, and life cycle costs. An understandable program design notation is also needed. With this in mind, I have delineated specific steps of an engineering solution to the designing of a system of Ada computer programs, and have defined a design notation for representing the design in a clear and concise manner as an abstraction of Ada itself. This approach, termed an "engineering approach," is not based solely on theoretical considerations of how to design a large computer program. Instead, a set of systematic and easily understood steps are delineated based on experience and the pragmatic application of Ada. Such an approach promotes conservative designs that limit the use of certain features of Ada that might lead to trouble if overused. To help represent the bulk and complexity of a design, different design views are suggested, corresponding to blueprints and schematic diagrams used in other fields of engineering.

This book presents a coordinated engineering approach to establishing a design for a large and complex computer program to be implemented in Ada. Design issues are identified, and conceptual approaches to resolving these issues are presented, both generically and in the context of Ada. Selected examples of Ada syntax associated with the concepts presented are provided in footnotes and figures. However, to limit the amount of information presented and not cloud design considerations with syntax detail, the implementation of several aspects of a design with Ada source code is not covered. That is left for books on programming with Ada. In this book, the explanations of Ada are meant to provide a designer with sufficient knowledge to formulate an Ada design in a relatively straightforward and abstracted manner. By "abstracted," I mean that a design should avoid implementation detail in specifying the architectural structure, data structures, and operations of a large and complex computer program. Thus, this book can be used to present design technology and the ramifications of Ada to project managers and system engineers, who do not need to learn all the syntax of a complicated programming language like Ada. At the same time, college students and practicing programmers can also use this book to learn the basic concepts of Ada.

The material presented here has been separated into four parts. Part I addresses the scope of software systems to be implemented in Ada. For example, Chapter 1 describes the bulk and complexity inherent in large software systems, which can lead to significant development and maintenance problems and, in some cases, disaster. Chapter 1 also discusses progress in the development of large software systems, which typically has been erratic. It is pointed out that this is consistent with the development of large and complex physical products, and contrasts with relatively small software efforts, where progress typically has been smooth and the risks low. It is important for readers, regardless of their technical background, to be aware of the problems inherent in largeness and the need for proper design techniques in order to lay the groundwork for cost-effective, low-risk system development. Chapter 2 presents an overview of the software process in general, and takes a closer look at requirements definition. Chapter 2 also presents a brief historical overview of design approaches, in the context of software development problems that emerged as the size of software systems grew, and the basic techniques that were introduced to resolve those problems.

Part II addresses basic considerations relevant to designing large computer programs in Ada. These considerations, when taken together, form the basis for design strategy. Chapter 3 discusses design for flexible computer programs that are responsive to change. Chapter 4 examines design for concurrency in response to multiple events that may occur simultaneously. Chapter 5 focuses on the fundamentals of design for data structures, and Chapter 6 examines fundamentals of design for operations in a program. Chapter 7 analyzes commonality in services and attributes possible in requirements for a large computer program. This commonality can be organized in a class-member relationship, in a manner analogous to object-oriented analysis. Chapter 7 then analyzes different design approaches for class-member relationships in the context of Ada.

Part III presents a general design approach for transforming a large software problem into a simpler form to help control development and maintenance risks. The approach is presented as a set of specific engineering steps to design a large computer program as a set of independent and self-sufficient parts and a software system as a set of large programs that are to execute in a distributed manner. The steps are meant to reduce pragmatically the complexity inherent in a software system. Chapter 8 introduces a design notation that can be used to represent the results of each design step, accounting for bulk through a series of different design views. The assumption is that no one view can be abstracted sufficiently to represent design information. Rather, a series of abstracted views is needed, each view providing a certain amount of comprehensible design information. This is consistent with other engineering disciplines (e.g., mechanical, civil, and electrical engineering), where different drawings and tables are commonly used to help represent a design. Chapter 9 introduces steps for designing a large computer program, and Chapter 10 presents specific steps for designing a software system as a set of computer programs. In both cases, a design example applies these steps, the results of which are represented by the different design views.

Finally, Part IV focuses on risks, implementation issues, and life cycle costs for large software systems that have been derived from designs specified using the design steps presented in Part III. Chapter 11 assesses the extent to which those designs help control risk and potential implementation problems and how the misuse of Ada capabilities can introduce exactly the opposite effects. Chapter 12 examines the economics of applying the design strategy discussed in this book. In the final analysis, in the real world of engineering an important bottom-line consideration for judging the merit of a design technique is risk control and economics—not technical elegance or uniqueness.

W. E. Byrne

# Large Software Systems and Design

*This book addresses techniques for designing software systems to be implemented in Ada. The objective is to delineate and describe specific steps on the design of a software system that can be used to help control risk and life cycle costs in the implementation and maintenance of that system. In essence, the design steps are to reflect strategy for transforming complex system requirements into a form that can be readily implemented with Ada.*

*Part I of this book deals with the bulk and complexity of requirements for large software systems. Such bulk and complexity can lead to significant software development and maintenance problems and, in some cases, disaster. In Chapter 1 progress in the development of large software systems is compared to progress in the development of large physical systems. Characteristics of a large software effort are also contrasted with characteristics of relatively small software projects. It is important that readers, whether technically proficient in software development or not, recognize the problems inherent in largeness and the possibilities for cost-effective, low-risk development if proper design techniques are used. Chapter 2 provides an overview of the software development process and takes a closer look at the requirements specification part of the process. It also presents a brief historical overview of selected basic design techniques in the context of software development problems that emerged as the size of software systems grew.*

*The basic point made in Part I is that an average programmer can successfully implement programs of a certain size and complexity. Classical design techniques of the past (e.g., structured top-down design) have worked well for such programs. However, with the explosive increase in processing capacity, larger and larger programs are being developed, programs well beyond the capabilities of average programmers, and of a size and complexity not known when the classical design techniques were invented. Managers, system engineers, software engineers, and others involved in a large software effort must recognize this problem and devise strategies that will resolve the problems inherent in largeness.*

# CHAPTER 1

# Large Software Systems

The rapid advancement in computing technology since the 1950s might be considered part of an information processing revolution. Just as the industrial revolution was concerned with harnessing energy to serve society, the information processing revolution might be considered as the harnessing of information for society. Both revolutions have enhanced and amplified our ability to control the environment. In fact, the information processing revolution has expanded the industrial revolution, as evidenced by the use of robotics.

Advancements in computing hardware since the 1950s have accelerated progress in the information processing revolution, with memory capacity and processing speed increasing at a rapid rate. This progress has resulted in the development of ever larger computer programs and software systems as sets of large computer programs. Software systems have undertaken more and more complex tasks, but at a price. Today, a large amount of the cost of a computing system may be due to the development of software. Moreover, the cost to maintain the software when the computing system is in operation has at times exceeded the original development cost by two to five times.

In reaction to the software development and maintenance costs incurred for military systems (which have been perceived as high), the U.S. Department of Defense sponsored the development of the programming language Ada. Ada brings together in one language mechanisms for implementing designs for software systems that can help control life cycle costs and lower risks. By itself, Ada accomplishes little, but when used in conjunction with proper design strategy, it can accomplish much.

What we need, therefore, is design strategy in the context of Ada to gain control over costs and to lower risks. The design strategy must be delineated in specific steps that are easy to understand and to apply. A design approach will be applied only if it is easier to use than not to use. To know how to devise such a strategy, we need to understand the nature of software engineering to realize factors that contribute to high software costs.

## 1.1 Introduction

### 1.1.1 Objective

This chapter defines software engineering, characterizes large software systems, and addresses considerations relevant to the design of large software systems. As you read this chapter, ask yourself why small software efforts have been accomplished in a relatively timely and cost-effective manner with smooth progress toward stated goals, while larger efforts have often run into significant trouble. You should consider these reasons when you formulate design strategies to be used with Ada in controlling software life cycle costs.

### 1.1.2 Software Engineering

#### Basic Concepts and Objectives

As a general engineering process, a problem is initially described in broad terms and then defined in terms of essential detail. A set of potential solutions to the problem is established, and each potential solution is evaluated with respect to both the expected performance and the cost to achieve that performance. Tradeoffs between cost and performance are central to the general engineering process.

In this book, software engineering is addressed in the context of such engineering practice, as opposed to such disciplines as applied mathematics or the theory of programming languages. Specifically, let us adopt the following definition of software engineering as proposed by F. L. Bauer of the Technical University, Munich, Germany: "The establishment and use of sound engineering principles (methods) in order to obtain economically software that is reliable and works on real machines."

Jeffrey and Linden of the National Bureau of Standards reinforce the Bauer definition: "Software engineering is not just a collection of tools and techniques, it is engineering . . . software engineering has more in common with other kinds of engineering than is usually appreciated. Software engineers can learn from other engineering disciplines."

When adopting the idea that software engineers can learn from other engineering disciplines, we must take into account a major difference between software engineering and other branches of engineering. Unlike other engineers, software engineers deal with conceptual objects, not tangible objects. Nevertheless, like material objects, software objects can be designed as independent entities that interface with other objects. Accordingly, like material objects, software objects can be designed to have unique operations that determine their behavior, and internal states that are hidden from users. Material objects (e.g., alarm clocks and telephones) allow users only a small number of basic inputs (e.g., setting the time, enabling and disabling the alarm, dialing a number) and do not permit access to internal implementation detail. Again, software objects can be designed in the same way. Such restrictions are good for material objects, minimizing the number of places to look when something goes wrong (e.g., we don't disassemble an alarm clock when the telephone fails to ring). The same restrictions are useful in the development and maintenance of software systems as a set of objects.

In this book, we view software engineering as problem solving and seek a pragmatic solution to the software design problem. The solution may appear to some to be complex, while to others it may seem to be straightforward. Regardless, do not forget our objective: establishing design in a pragmatic manner that helps promote the development and maintenance of software systems economically using steps that are easy to understand and to apply in practice.

### Terminology

We must choose a term to describe a software object in the context of Ada. Some may consider the term "object," strictly speaking, inappropriate, since it is used in object-oriented programming with languages like C++ and Smalltalk. Although a design approach in the context of Ada may be similar to a design associated with object-oriented programming, there is not a complete one-to-one correspondence. We could use the term "software module," but this term means different things to different people and has been widely used in conjunction with design techniques of the past (e.g., structured top-down design). For a term closer to Ada terminology, let us use the term *independent package* to name a software object. This term indicates that objects are independent and self-sufficient, a basic criterion for the design strategy to follow.

### 1.1.3  Developing Complicated Products

Consistent with the idea that we can learn from other branches of engineering, let's look at the progress realized in the development of complicated material systems. The main point here is that the development of complicated products, whether material or conceptual, is not necessarily easy to accomplish. Our first lesson is that we are not dealing with a simple problem that is easy to solve. The time and money expended to develop a large and complex product (or system) tends to be considerably greater than those initially predicted. The cycle of progress incurred in the development effort often is characterized by both advances and setbacks, as illustrated by the *S*-curve shown in Figure 1-1.

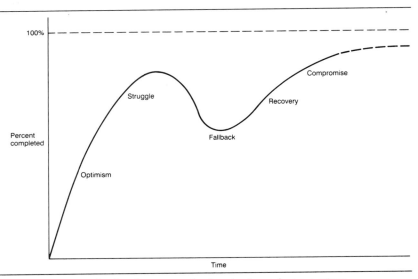

*FIGURE 1-1.*  Cycle of progress in developing a large system

Early in the development life cycle, development personnel tend to be optimistic, with considerable energy and enthusiasm for the project. Schedules and budgets appear reasonable. As the project proceeds, obstacles appear and the rate of progress slows down. Although in a struggle, the project still seems to be on track, but the goal is now being approached slower than expected. Project members notice problems, but they still feel that the deadline can be reached within the time and money allotted in project plans.

Then unanticipated problems in the development of the product begin to emerge. Requirements changes in the definition of the product may increase its complexity and disrupt the smooth flow of its development. The goal of the project appears more difficult to achieve than originally envisioned. As the possibility of disaster enters the minds of the project members, their morale decreases. Some project workers may quit, and second-guessing becomes prevalent among those remaining. Higher levels of management may become aware of the situation and question the competency of the project staff.

Upon reaching a critical low in the project, attempts to recoup follow. The crisis in meeting the original deadline is over, and the original budget may have been used up. The recovery may be undertaken by a new project manager and a "tiger team" of new personnel. The goals of the project are reexamined and changed, and a new and more realistic set of plans established. The new goals set for the project appear to be within reach. As time goes on, progress is made but not without compromise. There is recognition that progress toward the newly defined set of goals is also slowing down, and doubt prevails as to whether those goals can be reached within the new schedule and budget. A final burst of personnel may be added to the project, while negotiations are under way for defining what might be acceptable product performance and reliability, typically lower than that delineated in the requirements specifications.

This scenario is common in the development of large physical systems. Experience has shown that it also applies to the development of large and complex computer programs. The following paragraphs describe characteristics of large software projects and discuss the extent to which their development proceeds in the context of the $S$-curve phenomenon shown in Figure 1-1. First, as an important contrast, let us assess why a small software project is straightforward and easy to accomplish. This is important since several people may have taken a programming course and written a small simple program. We must not generalize that the lack of trouble encountered with such a simple task applies to a large software project.

## 1.2   Characterization of a Small Computer Program

A small computer program might be defined as a sequence of source statements for computer processing that can be readily developed and easily comprehended by a single programmer. A small computer program typically can be developed in an informal manner and easily iterated. In some cases, requirements for a small program may be provided verbally to a programmer. The programmer may then directly map the requirements to source statements of a programming language. In some cases, the entire mapping process may be accomplished in the mind of the programmer. In other cases, requirements for the small program may be specified with written text, and a design for the computer program developed as an intermediate representation of the computer program. A design can be thought of as lying somewhere between the program's requirements specification and its implementing source statements.

A small computer program is not necessarily easy to implement to the satisfaction of a customer. For example, there may be errors in the specification of requirements for the small program, which lead to erroneous program results. When this happens, it may be cumbersome for the programmer to determine whether the erroneous results are due to errors in the program implementation or to the requirements. Even if the requirements have been specified and interpreted correctly, the small program may still be difficult to implement because of, for example, complex logic and multiple iterations through loops. Therefore, there may be some risk in the development of a small computer program. Thus, actual progress may lag behind planned progress, as shown in Figure 1-2. As a general rule, however, progress tends to move smoothly toward the desired goal.

In the past, a small computer program may have been implemented as a main sequence of statements and statements grouped together in callable program units. The called program units may have been used to accomplish processing that is repeated at different points in the small program. For example, program units may have implemented libraries of trigonometric and other mathematical functions.

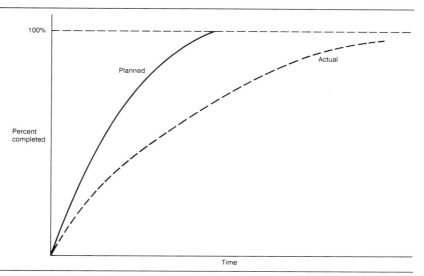

*FIGURE 1-2.* Cycle of progress in developing a small computer program

When a given program unit in a small program is changed, the modification tends to have minimal and understandable effects on the other program units used to construct the small program. When changes are made, the small computer program can be recompiled and reexecuted in a matter of minutes. In a small program, there are not a great number of program units to change, and each program unit tends to be unique, self-sufficient, and therefore independent of the other program units. Thus, the ramifications of a change to a small program typically can be understood and minimal trouble encountered. Small computer programs generally tend to be flexible and can be readily changed without any adverse effects on overall performance. Because of this, the development of a small computer program typically proceeds smoothly, as is generally the case for the development of a small physical product.

## 1.3   Characterization of a Software System and Its Development

### 1.3.1   Development Activity and Personnel Types

Unlike a small computer program, a software system as a collection of large computer programs cannot be developed in a reasonable period of time by any one person. Rather, a software system is developed by a large number of people involved in several different specific activities, including

- requirements definition
- preliminary design
- detailed design
- coding and testing of individual program units
- program unit integration
- computer program acceptance testing

Other project activities encompass project and configuration management, quality assurance, and independent verification and validation.

In practice, development activities do not necessarily take place in a neat sequence, as illustrated in Figure 1-3. For example, the design, coding, and testing activities typically are undertaken for different software components at different times (e.g., program unit A may be in the coding phase while program unit B is still in the design phase). Also, changes in requirements may necessitate halts and rollbacks to requirements analysis from other activities, resulting in extensive changes and reworking of the requirements, the design, and the source code.

In contrast with the development of a small computer program, several people with different capabilities and responsibilities are

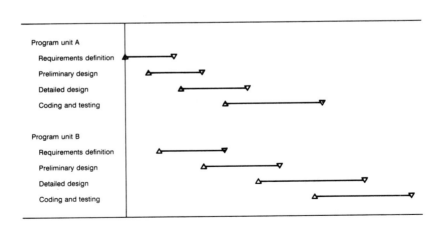

*FIGURE 1-3.* Sequence of development activities for two different program units

associated with the development of a large computer program, including project managers, system engineers, software engineers, programmers, and test engineers. Project managers coordinate the activities associated with the development of a large computer program. System engineers are responsible for requirements definition and may become involved in preliminary design. Software engineers work on preliminary design and become involved in detailed design. Programmers are responsible for design detail, coding, testing of program units, and program unit integration. Test engineers perform final acceptance testing of the computer program as a whole. Quality assurance and independent verification and validation (IV&V) personnel review and check these activities, and configuration management personnel control changes to products produced as a result of these activities.

## 1.3.2 Pace of Development Progress

Early in the development life cycle of a large computer program, several problems may have to be addressed. For example, the functional requirements for the software product may be incomplete, and specified requirements may not comply with all the needs and desires of the customer. If this is the case, the requirements will have to change and be expanded during the development life cycle of the computer program. In spite of this, optimism for project success may well prevail among the members of the development team.

Using questionable requirements as a baseline, project managers typically establish a budget and a schedule for development of the software product. They may project the budget and schedule using estimating algorithms that take into account several factors, such as required reliability, product complexity, execution time, and storage constraints. Typically, however, the most important cost driver in such an estimating algorithm is the number of source statements required to implement the large computer program. Unfortunately, this number has to be projected based on the incomplete requirements.

This situation brings to mind the story of the farmer who is going to weigh his pigs before bringing them to market. He places the pigs on one side of a scale and loads rocks on the other side until the scale balances perfectly. He then establishes the weight of the pigs by guessing the weight of the rocks. In the same manner, the project manager of a large software development project may be forced to base the development budget and schedule on only a guess of the number of source statements needed to construct the large computer program. Because of this, the original budget and schedule for a project may be of questionable accuracy, often based on overly optimistic projections (i.e., the lowest guess may well win the job).

As the project proceeds, the computer program requirements are assessed by development personnel, who fill in the holes in the original requirements. The evolving set of requirements may have to be extensively modified. The project may get bogged down just getting out of the gate while an agreement is reached between the development organization and the customer as to exactly what the computer program is supposed to do. Eventually, the customer will have to agree with some version of the software requirements, and computer program development will begin.

Once the requirements have been specified, the design and implementation of the large computer program can commence. These efforts may run into unforeseen roadblocks, with certain program units proving difficult to construct and implement efficiently. Nevertheless, the struggle proceeds, obstacles are overcome, and the development organization assures the customer that all is well. Testing of individual program units may appear to be going well, and overall the project still seems to be on track.

When the individual program units finally are integrated (i.e., brought together to execute as a whole large program), implementation problems may surface. Several interfaces between interacting program units may be incompatible. Outputs produced by some of the program units may prove to be different from those expected by the calling program units. To correct these and other deficiencies, several changes are made to individual program units, causing additional program units to be deficient. Project team members begin to realize that the project may be in trouble, and the project manager soon recognizes the possibility of disaster.

In an attempt to recoup, the software project may now be reorganized, new project personnel may be added to the development team, and recovery is attempted. However, progress may still proceed slowly. To make matters worse, the customer may direct several changes to the baseline requirements. Attempts at introducing these changes slow down progress even further, which may result in even slower progress than the rate typical for the development of a large physical system, as shown in Figure 1-4.

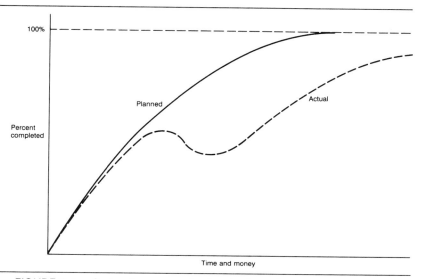

*FIGURE 1-4.* Cycle of progress in developing a large computer program

### 1.3.3 Characterization of the Size of a Software System

Let's now characterize the size of a software system encompassing a set of application programs, each of which may consist of, say, 50,000 to 100,000 source statements. For example, assume a software system consists of 10 large computer programs averaging 100,000 source statements each. The number of pages in a source statement listing for all of this application software might exceed 20,000 pages. If strung out side by side, this list would stretch over 3 miles.

During development of a software system, a great deal of documentation has to be produced by a large number of different people. Usually, the software system is divided into parts that are put under configuration control. The parts, called configuration items, typically are programs of the system that can be developed by a small team of programmers. Once under configuration control, changes cannot be made without approval of a configuration management board. For each configuration item, the following documents may be prepared:

- a software requirements specification
- a software design document

- a software test plan to describe the resources to be used for testing and the test schedules to be followed
- a software test description to specify the test cases and procedures to be followed
- a software test report to document the results of the testing

In addition, for the software system as a whole, the following additional documents may be prepared:

- a computer system operator's manual to provide information and procedures for initiating, operating, monitoring, and shutting down computers in which application programs of the software system execute
- a software user's manual to provide operators with instructions on how to load and execute software configuration items
- planning and other documentation to be used by managers to control the development of the software

In our example of a software system that consists of 10 large computer programs averaging 100,000 source statements each, there might be 40 or more different configuration items. Since each configuration item would typically be described in the documents listed above, the software system as a whole would be described in more than 200 different documents, each containing detailed technical information. If those documents averaged about 200 pages each, the entire documentation would include over 40,000 pages. The point is that a software system is large in scope, as illustrated in Figure 1-5.

## 1.4 Design Considerations and Ada

In the following chapters, we will investigate how design considerations in the context of Ada can be used to address fundamental problems in the development and maintenance of large software systems that consist of multiple computer programs. Our objectives are to explain:

1. how design methodologies appropriate for Ada can be used to organize a large computer program as a set of relatively independent parts that are responsive to the needs of multiple users, small enough to be easily implemented, and sufficiently independent to be integrated and maintained

*FIGURE 1-5.* Documentation for a software system can be extensive.

2. how the software design can be represented in a concise and understandable manner as an abstraction of Ada itself, forming the basis for efficient implementation with Ada source statements

In this way, we will attempt to reach our goal of establishing a mechanism for transforming a complex problem into a form that can be readily implemented in Ada.

## 1.4.1 The Need for Design

In other fields of engineering, design is fundamental in the development of engineering systems. Blueprints are used in civil engineering projects, mechanical drawings in the development of mechanical systems, and schematic and wiring diagrams in the development of electrical systems. Such designs and their representation for complex systems are developed at great expense over a significant period of time.

With respect to software, design and its representation should be understandable by management personnel as well as programmers and software engineers. A design will be widely used only if it is

comprehensible and understood by a wide range of project partici-
pants. Managers need to grasp intellectually the problem they must
manage—misunderstood projects tend to go astray. In addition,
initial budgets tend to be insufficient, initial schedules too short, and
resource allocation during the course of the project inappropriate.
For a manager, the design should establish manageable components
that can be developed and integrated smoothly. The components
should be appropriate for monitoring, using both cost/schedule
control systems and software metrics (i.e., parameters that characterize a software component and its development).

Of course, technical personnel also need to understand a design.
Software engineers derive a design from the customer's requirements. The derived design can be thought of as the representation of
a computer program that lies somewhere between its requirements
and the implementing code. The design should address and provide
the basis for resolving basic software development problems. Programmers should be able to grasp the architectural considerations
inherent in the design. In this respect, the programmers might be
considered engineers, who must understand the methodology and
principles used to establish a computer program's architecture. The
programmers then establish detailed source code for the architectural components. In doing so, the programmers must adhere to
lower-level design requirements. When they are developing the details of the source code, programmers can be thought of as artists—
they "paint" the architectural components of a design with source
code using the "colors" permitted by the design (i.e., in accordance
with data structures and operations that the design specifies).

## 1.4.2 Large Computer Programs and Ada

The source statements of the programming language used for a large
computer program should facilitate implementation of the design.
The most popular languages of the past (e.g., FORTRAN and COBOL)
were created long before computer memory and execution speed
allowed construction of large and complex computer programs.
Thus, some software engineers and programmers feel that these
older languages lack the capabilities to efficiently map the design of
a large computer program into high-level source statements.

Recognizing the need for a contemporary programming language
that could be used as a standard in the development of computer
systems for the three U.S. military services, the U.S. Department of
Defense sponsored development of the high-order language Ada. Ada

provides features consistent with design approaches of the past (e.g., structured top-down design) and also reflects recent software technology used to design large and complex computer programs. Because of its complexity, the details of Ada are not as easy to learn as older languages. This should not be viewed as a weakness of Ada, however, since a certain amount of complexity is necessary in the development of large and complex computer programs. In fact, development of large computer programs is where Ada is most useful. Applying Ada outside this culture, in ways appropriate only for small computer programs, does not take full advantage of the power of Ada.

## 1.4.3 Design Representation

This book focuses on the fundamentals of Ada technology associated with the design of a large computer program and a software system. Because these fundamentals are intended to be understood by users who may or may not know the syntax of Ada, an Ada-unique design notation is necessary.

You may ask, "Wasn't Ada meant to be readable?" Most programmers familiar with Ada feel it is locally readable when written with reasonable style. If we examine a fragment of Ada code, we can see the design of that fragment. However, understanding the overall design of a software system as a set of large computer programs means more than just recognizing the parts. It is critically important to readily recognize the relationship of a fragment to the whole.

In the past, hierarchical block diagrams have been used to represent the declaration relationship between program units, as shown in Figure 1-6. In this diagram, a program unit shown at level $n + 1$ is connected to a program unit at level $n$. Such diagrams are not adequate with Ada, however, because they do not distinguish between different kinds of Ada program units that serve different purposes. They do not represent the concurrent program unit execution that can take place in Ada, nor can they represent the unique capabilities of Ada to partition a large and complex computer program into relatively independent sets of program units. Also, block diagrams do not express relationships between Ada library units. All of these features are fundamental to the design of a software system.

Accordingly, we need to establish a notation for representing the design of large computer programs as a generalized abstraction of Ada, facilitating implementation with the proper linguistic constructs. Again, we emphasize that Ada, the design methodology, and

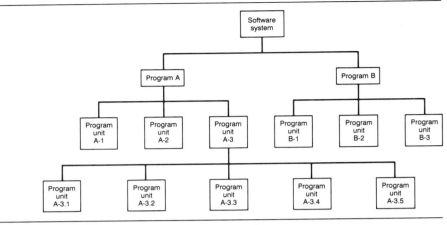

*FIGURE 1-6.* Hierarchy of program units

this notation should apply to software systems as sets of large computer programs. To illustrate this point, compare an architect, who designs large buildings, to a home handyman, who may add a room to his home. The home handyman can proceed with minimal design information, making fragmented design decisions as he proceeds. A large architectural construction project, on the other hand, needs blueprints and other design documentation. The construction of a building is undertaken by many people (e.g., plumbers, electricians, metal workers, and brick layers), who divide the project into a set of manageable parts and communicate using blueprints. The blueprints present design information in a series of pictorial abstracts. In the same manner, small software efforts undertaken by a single person can proceed without partitioning or design structure information. However, as in construction, a plateau of project size and complexity is reached where it is not cost effective to proceed without explicit manageable parts and blueprints that represent those manageable parts.

## 1.5    What Is the Bottom Line?

The following chapters analyze what has led to problems in the development of large and complex software products and discuss how design approaches can address issues critical to the development of large computer programs. The material in this book should not be interpreted as "new religion." Rather, the material takes advantage of existing design techniques that have evolved over the years and examines the role of each technique in the design of a large computer program. Specifically, the following information is presented:

1. systematic design steps, taking advantage of the concurrency inherent in Ada and design techniques that can be used to resolve critical problems associated with large computer programs
2. fundamentals of Ada technology and the relationship of these fundamentals to the design of a software system and the large computer programs that make up the software system
3. a notation for representing systematic Ada designs in a manner understandable to those with or without knowledge of Ada syntax
4. issues associated with the implementation of a design with Ada and how design can help control problems inherent in this process

If we go back to the definition of software engineering as a method for obtaining software economically, the bottom line for our efforts will be the establishment of design approaches that will control risk and cost in the development and maintenance of large Ada computer programs.

## 1.6    Key Concepts

- Progress in the development of a large physical system typically suffers at least one major setback before the project reaches completion.
- Progress in the development of a small computer program may lag behind planned progress, but as a general rule the project tends to move smoothly toward the planned goal.
- Progress in the development of a large computer program often suffers major setbacks, much like the progress in the development of a large physical system.
- As in other system development efforts, design and its representation are important to the successful development of a software system as a set of large computer programs.
- Design techniques appropriate to the development of a software system should not be interpreted as "new religion." Rather, such design techniques have evolved in response to the problems inherent in the development and maintenance of ever larger and larger software systems.

## 1.7    Exercises

1. What is the sequence of human emotions typically encountered in the development of a large physical system?
2. What are the characteristics of a small computer program?
3. What problems can be encountered in the development of a small computer program?
4. How can we characterize progress expected during the development of a small computer program?
5. What are the characteristics of a large computer program?
6. What kinds of specific activities are typically undertaken in the development of a large computer program?
7. What are the major pitfalls that have to be overcome in the development of a large computer program?
8. Why do we need a design for a large computer program?
9. What should characterize the design representation for a large computer program?
10. How should we measure the effectiveness of a design methodology?

# CHAPTER 2

# Requirements and Traditional Design Considerations

The software enigma has been caused, in a sense, by technology overtaking events. Computer hardware has advanced so rapidly that requirements for software systems have become extremely demanding. Software complexity has steadily grown over the last two decades as the computing power of hardware increased at an exponential rate. However, as processing capacity has grown, software development methodology has not always evolved fast enough to satisfy customer needs. As computer hardware has become more powerful, more sophisticated requirements for software systems have been defined. Traditional design approaches have reached the point where they are no longer adequate for the size and complexity of the software systems needed to implement the sophisticated requirements.

To further understand the nature of the software development and maintenance problem and as a prerequisite to formulating design strategy for the control of software costs, we need to take a look at the software development process, examine the scope of sophisticated requirements for a software system and review some of the traditional approaches that have been used to implement those requirements.

## 2.1    Introduction

This chapter provides an overview of the software development process and takes a closer look at the requirements definition part of this process. Specific examples are given of basic software development problems that have been encountered as the size and complexity of computer programs grew, as well as a historical overview of some basic techniques that evolved in response to those problems. For example, we will look at structured programming, which emerged in the late 1960s, and top-down design, which emerged in the 1970s. The application of these techniques has resulted in organized and understandable designs, but the software systems derived from these designs have proved to be inadequate. This has led to object-oriented techniques, and other software design technology of today.

## 2.2     Software Engineering and Requirements Specification

There is a process used by software engineers to obtain solutions to problems as practical software systems. As shown in Figure 2-1(a), this process includes problem definition and analysis, requirements specification, design, implementation, testing, integration, installation, and maintenance. The engineering process shown here is an idealistic view—when one activity ends, the next activity immediately follows. Unfortunately, the process is not so simple in practice. For example, the activities may overlap rather than take place in a neat, sequential manner. Also, there may be considerable feedback and interaction among the different activities of the process. Any one activity can affect any other activity. From a design perspective, there may be interaction between design and any of the other activities, as shown in Figure 2-1(b). For example, design issues can affect requirements specification and problem definition. Design can also affect and be affected by implementation, testing, integration, installation, and maintenance.

This book focuses on the design part of this engineering process as it relates to building software systems in the context of Ada. However, we cannot completely ignore the other activities in this engineering process, especially requirements specification. The success of design for software systems—in fact, even the *approach* to design—is driven by the nature of requirements, both their scope and stability. Further, the design approach should not only facilitate the implementation activity but also lay the foundation for effective testing, system integration, site installation, and maintenance.

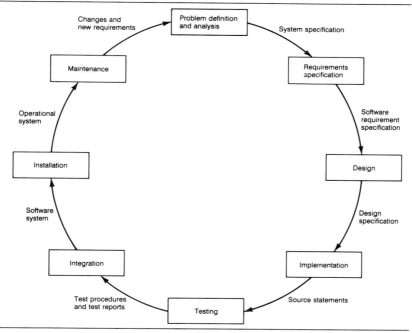

*FIGURE 2-1(a).* Activities in the software life cycle

## 2.2.1 Scope of Software Requirements

Basically, requirements specify what a computer program is to do, while design establishes a "blueprint" of how the requirements are to be implemented using software source statements. Requirements for a software system are derived from the customer's definition of what the system should do and the analysis to follow. The problem is initially defined and described in broad terms without detail. During analysis, the problem definition is expanded with essential detail, and potential solutions to the problem are formulated. Each solution is evaluated and compared to alternatives. The solution considered the best is chosen and specified in detail as a set of requirements. The requirements define in specific terms what the system is to do and define the roles of hardware and software in the operation of the system. Software requirements should include the following:

- a description of program functionality
- a concept of operation
- performance constraints (e.g., constraints on the use of memory and processing time)

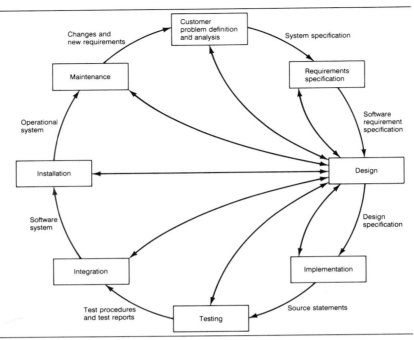

*FIGURE 2-1(b).* Design perspective of activities in the software life cycle

- policy considerations (e.g., for software reliability, maintainability, and portability)

For certain classes of computer programs, the requirements may emphasize algorithms and the precision of the algorithms' results. For other classes of programs, the requirements may emphasize the rate of data flow into or out of the program and the details of interfaces with external entities. For other classes of computer programs, the requirements may emphasize the collection, storage, and retrieval of large amounts of data. For yet other classes of programs, the requirements may specify allowable program states (e.g., on, off, normal, degraded) and permissible transitions from one state to another. A comprehensive set of requirements for a large software system can include all of these aspects.

## 2.2.2  Representing Software Requirements

Requirements can be represented in different ways. In practice, they can be specified exclusively with text or by various combinations of text, tables, and graphics. For example, a combination of data flow diagrams, a data dictionary, structured English, and state-transition diagrams can supplement an English language description of functionality, concept of operation, performance, and policy.

To illustrate each of these representations and present a sample problem, let us consider the requirements for software to be used in an interface control unit (ICU) consisting of a CPU, monitor, console, and I/O board. The ICU is to link an operations center A and an operations center B with a radar station and communication lines (see Figure 2-2). Specifically, the ICU is to route messages received from the communications channels and the radar station to the operations center. As specified in Table 2-1, it is also to respond to operator requests for the display of messages, which account for the position and velocity of aircraft and their flight path identifiers. Such systems are used to collect information that can be processed to track and identify aircraft. For example, in North America several radar sites exist around the United States and Canada. The information provided by these sites needs to be distributed to locations where it can be analyzed. In the United States, data can be forwarded to the U.S. Air Force, U.S. Customs centers, and the U.S. Coast Guard, where it can be analyzed to identify possible hostile threats and drug smugglers.

### Data Flow Diagrams

As a mechanism for representing software requirements for ICU software, data flow diagrams could be used to indicate sources of data, the transformation of data into different forms, the storage of data, and the final destination of data (system outputs). Figure 2-3(a) is an example of a data flow diagram used to represent ICU processing at a high level. As the figure indicates, the ICU software is to receive messages, process the messages (e.g., to strip off header and trailer fields), and make a record of the information that has been received. Also, the software is to determine the destination of each message received, attach appropriate control fields to the message in preparation for its distribution, record all the fields of resulting output messages (i.e., data and control fields), and forward the message for distribution. Furthermore, the software is to provide capabilities to generate message displays.

### Structured English

At a yet lower level of detail in our sample problem, the requirements can specify data and operations in more detail. Figure 2-3(b) is an example of a more detailed data flow diagram used to specify

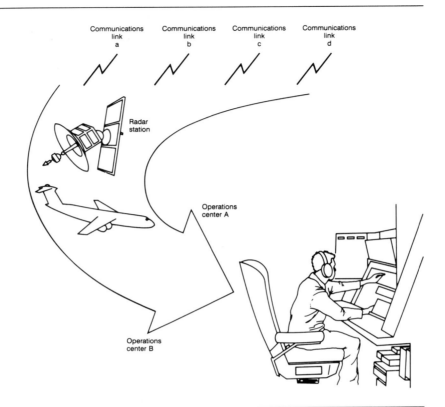

FIGURE 2-2(a).   Interface control unit: moving information from a radar station and communication lines to operations centers

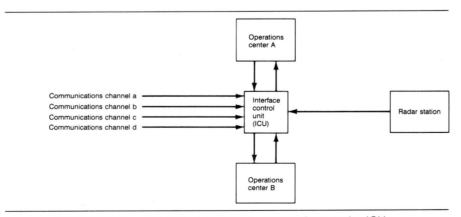

FIGURE 2-2(b).   Interface control unit: connections to the ICU

*TABLE 2-1.*   ICU System-Level Requirements

| Items | Requirements |
|-------|--------------|
| Interfaces | The ICU shall establish a communications link between operations center A, operations center B, a radar station, and communications channels a, b, c, and d. |
| Message routing | The ICU shall route messages received from the radar station to both operations centers. The ICU shall route messages received over communications channel a to operations center A. The ICU shall route messages received over communication channel b to operations center B. The ICU shall route messages received over communication channels c and d to both operations centers. |
| Message assignments | Messages in format X are received from the radar station. Messages in format Z are received over communications channels a, b, c, and d. Messages to be routed to the operations centers are to be in format Y. |
| Format X | Messages received from the radar station are formatted as follows:<br>■ Byte 1 is a frame-start flag.<br>■ Byte 2 is the X coordinate in meters.<br>■ Byte 3 is the Y coordinate in meters.<br>■ Byte 4 is the Z coordinate in meters.<br>■ Byte 5 is the velocity in kilometers per hour.<br>■ Byte 6 is an aircraft identifier.<br>■ Byte 7 is a flight path identifier.<br>■ Byte 8 is a frame-end flag. |
| Format Z | Messages received over communication channels are formatted as follows:<br>■ Byte 1 is a frame-start flag.<br>■ Byte 2 is a flight path identifier.<br>■ Byte 3 is an aircraft identifier.<br>■ Byte 4 is the velocity in kilometers per hour.<br>■ Byte 5 is the X coordinate in meters.<br>■ Byte 6 is the Y coordinate in meters.<br>■ Byte 7 is the Z coordinate in meters.<br>■ Byte 8 is a frame-end flag. |
| Format Y | Messages routed to one or both of the operations centers shall be formatted as follows:<br>■ Byte 1 is a frame-start flag set to 111.<br>■ Byte 2 is the aircraft identifier.<br>■ Byte 3 is the flight path identifier.<br>■ Byte 4 is the X coordinate in feet.<br>■ Byte 5 is the Y coordinate in feet.<br>■ Byte 6 is the Z coordinate in feet.<br>■ Byte 7 is the velocity in miles per hour.<br>■ Byte 8 is an end-frame flag set equal to 1001. |

TABLE 2-1.   (continued)

| Items | Requirements |
|---|---|
| Displays | The ICU shall display received messages immediately after their arrival. Upon operator request, the ICU shall display recorded messages keyed by time, date, message, source, or message destination. |
| Message recording | The ICU shall record every message received and every message to be routed. The recorded messages shall be entered into a historical database along with the date and time of the message transaction. |
| Coordinates and velocity | For messages received in format X and format Z, coordinate values are to the nearest meter and velocity to the nearest kilometer per hour. |

operations on the message's source to determine its destination. A description of specific operations might be presented in concise, crisp, structured English describing precisely the actions to be performed. Structure can be introduced to specify major logical decisions to be made. If properly written, concise structured English would indicate what the operations are without saying how the operations eventually will be implemented. Alternatively, tables, mathematical algorithms, graphs, or textual narrative may be appropriate to represent operations in detail.

### State Transition Diagrams

States of a computer program can be specified in conjunction with the performance requirements specified in data flow diagrams, tables, graphs, and a data dictionary. States can be thought of as distinct and independent modes of operation that do not occur at the same time. For example, at a high level a word processor could be either in the on or off state. While on, the word processor could be in one of many different substates of operation for editing, page numbering, printing, or checking spelling.

A system's dynamic performance is governed by transitions from one state to another. The transitions may be triggered by operator action, or they may take place if certain conditions are met. For example, in a digital watch, when the time of day hits the alarm time setting, the watch makes a transition from its display state to its alarm state. Certain actions may take place at the time of state transition. For example, in the transitions from the display state to the alarm state, a signal is sent to the watch's beeper.

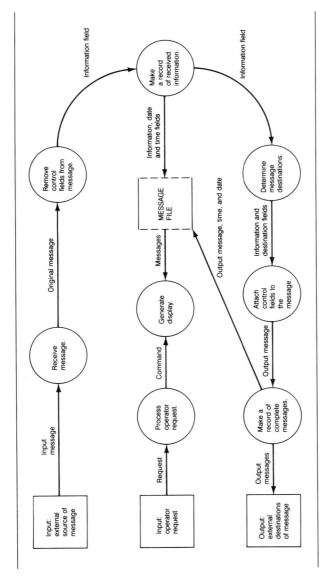

*FIGURE 2-3(a).* Data flow diagram: high-level view

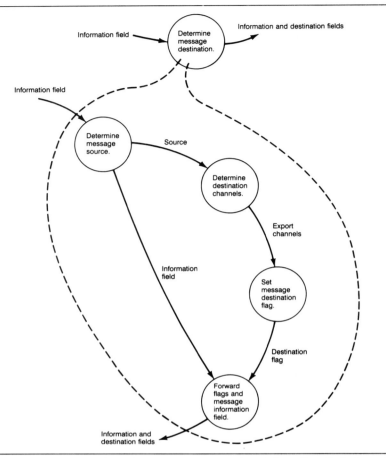

FIGURE 2-3(b). Data flow diagram: lower-level view (Detailed view of "determine message destinations")

State transition diagrams can be used to graphically represent states and transitions between states. For example, as shown in Figure 2-4(a), rectangles can represent states, and arrows between the rectangles can represent transition from one state to another. As shown in Figure 2-4(a), when a system is in state A and event b occurs, the system makes a transition to state B. When it is in state B and event a or c occurs, the system makes a transition to state A. For a large and complex system, substates of a given state can also be represented graphically. For example, as shown in Figure 2-4(b), rectangles can represent subsets and can be placed within the larger rectangles that represent states. Again, arrows to and from the substates can represent state transition. As shown, when the system

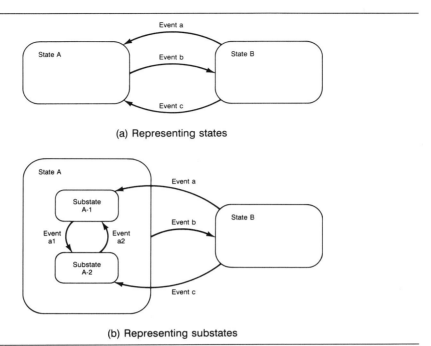

(a) Representing states

(b) Representing substates

*FIGURE 2-4.* State transition diagrams

is in state B and event a occurs, the system makes a transition to substate A-1 of state A. If the system is in state B and event c occurs, the system makes a transition to substate A-2.

Figure 2-5 suggests states applicable to the ICU example and the events that trigger state transition. In this figure, the ICU is in the OFF state, the INITIALIZATION state, or the STANDARD OPERATIONAL state. To make the transition to the INITIALIZATION state, power is turned on. While in the INITIALIZATION state, the software system is loaded and initial values of the program's unique parameters are established. Upon completion of initialization, the software system makes the transition to the STANDARD OPERATIONAL state in which messages are received and routed and operator requests are responded to. To make the transition to the OFF state, power is turned off.

## 2.2.3 Documenting Software Requirements

Requirements for a computer program can be organized and formally documented in a software requirements specification. This document

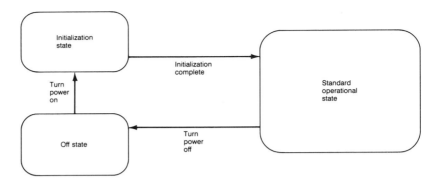

FIGURE 2-5. State transition diagram for the ICU

utilizes English text, data flow diagrams, data dictionaries, structured English, state transition diagrams, and other mechanisms to present computer program requirements. The software requirements specification can include sections to describe functionality, and requirements for such things as concept of operation, performance constraints, and policy.

A *functionality section* provides a complete and detailed description of data and the operations that the software is to implement. It might include subsections on states, processing capabilities, and external interfaces. The *states* subsection can specify required states of operation and any substates. This subsection may contain a high-level state transition diagram, showing all the major states, the transitions between them, and the events that must be met for each transition. For each major state, a paragraph can identify and describe that state. If a state encompasses substates, subparagraphs can be provided to describe them. Each subparagraph may make reference to a state transition diagram that shows the interrelationship among substates within the subject major state. This subsection can also describe operator actions and the state transitions caused by those actions. The *processing capabilities* subsection can specify required processing capabilities and their relationship to the states/ substates of operation. This subsection may refer to a data flow diagram that shows data movement between various processing operations and a data dictionary that defines elements shown in the diagram. This subsection should account for each required processing operation specifying, for example, mathematical algorithms and the precision of algorithm results. The *external interfaces* subsection can specify requirements for interfaces with other systems. This subsection can refer to a block diagram that shows the processing system in which the large computer program is to execute and the interfacing of the hardware with the processing system. Such hardware could include peripherals, other processors, and communications links. A separate paragraph might describe each external hardware interface. This subsection can also identify the purpose of each interface, the relationship of the interface to the states of operation, and the relationship of the interface to general processing capabilities. The interface requirements might specify rates of data flow and other interface details considered necessary or important to the implementation of software (e.g., communication protocols).

Several other sections can be used to expand and qualify a system's requirements. A *concept of operation* section provides a complete description of operator commands and the response of the software system to each command. A *performance constraints* section specifies such things as the time required to complete certain operations and the amount of data that is to be generated, accessed, or stored. This section might describe specific algorithms and the accuracy associated with the results of calculations. It can specify the range of permissible values for data entities. A *policy* section specifies requirements for such quality factors as reliability, maintainability, and portability. Reliability requirements should be stated in quantitative terms, including the conditions under which they are to be met. For example, we might specify that a computer program shall operate without error for 24 hours under normal input data flow. Maintainability requirements should also be stated in quantitative terms. For example, these requirements may specify the mean time required to undertake specific maintenance actions. Portability requirements should state the extent to which the large computer program can be moved from one processor to another.

Other sections in a software requirements specification can address such things as *training, quality assurance, testing, preparation for delivery, documentation requirements*, and *design standards*. The requirements for quality assurance, testing, and design standards should be related to requirements for reliability, maintainability, and portability.

## 2.3 Historical Overview of Traditional Design Considerations

The size and complexity of computer programs have grown over the years as processing capacities have increased, but not without problems. This section provides a historical overview of basic design techniques that evolved to solve those problems as the sophistication of requirements for software systems increased. First, let us briefly examine the scope of a software design.

### 2.3.1 Scope of Design

The software design of a large and complex computer program facilitates transition from requirements for the computer program to an executable processing system. The design can be thought of as the representation of a software system that lies somewhere between the requirements specification and the implementing code. At a *high level*, design specifies subsystems to be used in the architectural composition of the software system and the flow of data entities between the subsystems. It also typically specifies policy choices made for such things as reliability, maintainability, and portability.

At *lower levels*, design specifies the mechanisms to be used to implement the software subsystems and policy choices. It specifies the software entities to be used to compose the subsystems, specifies and organizes data elements, and specifies operations to be performed. For each data element, the design may indicate its purpose, whether it is a variable or a constant, its type (e.g., fixed point or floating point), units of measure required (e.g., seconds, feet, meters), the range of permissible values, and the accuracy required (e.g., an approximation for a variable might have to be correct within 1 percent of its exact value). Furthermore, a design may specify the extent to which data elements are to be used. For example, the design may dictate the program entities that may have access to a given data element and those that may not. For data elements to be received from or sent to entities external to the computer program, the design may specify the external source of the data element or the external entity to which the data element may be sent.

### 2.3.2 Design in the Early Years

In the early 1960s, the design of a computer program was relatively simple, basically only accounting for such things as the input and output of parameters, calculations performed, comparisons between variables, and alternative actions taken based on those comparisons. As a graphical aid, design was often represented with flowcharts, which used various geometric figures to represent the processing to be performed. For example, diamonds represented decisions, rectangles represented mathematical calculations or other sets of operations to be performed, and parallelograms represented the input or output of information (see Figure 2-6). Within each geometric figure, a small amount of mathematics or text specified the processing to be accomplished. The icons were connected by arrows to signify the sequence of processing to be performed. For reasonably conceived programs with limited sets of operations, the design representation in a flowchart would be understandable, as illustrated in Figure 2-7. An ill-conceived design might include awkward sequences of operations characterized by erratic jumps.

As part of the design process in those days, flowcharts could be used to identify redundant processing. Such redundancy typically was eliminated to conserve limited memory capacity. This measure

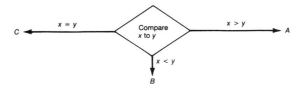

(a) Diamond for decision making

(b) Rectangle for processing to be performed

(c) Parallelogram for signifying input and output operations

FIGURE 2-6.  Example of icons used in a flowchart

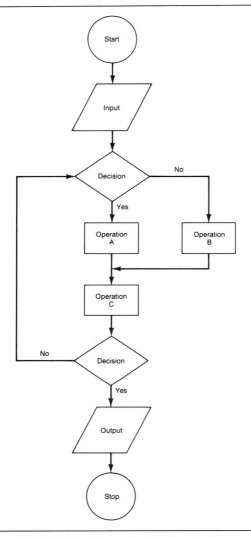

*FIGURE 2-7.* Example of a flowchart

was accomplished by inserting the redundant processing into a subroutine, a program unit that could be established at one place, and then linked to two or more calling locations in the sequence of source statements. Upon being called, the subroutine assumed program control, performed its programmed operations, and then returned to the caller. The caller might pass input parameters to the subroutine and in return receive output parameters from the subroutine.

## 2.3.3 Structured Programming

The designs of the early days were an art form in the sense that programmers used their imaginations to come up with the structure of routines and subroutines used to construct a computer program. There was no widespread basis for how to lay out the structure of routines and subroutines. Rather, design often evolved in a patchwork manner. There was no standard requirement for an organized structure to the program nor a method used to reach that structure. Programmers could pass control to any part of the program in any way they deemed necessary. For very small programs whose flowcharts were only a few pages, the art form could work well if the programmer was ingenious. However, as the size of the program grew, it became difficult, if not impossible, to follow the complexity and multiple jumps used to implement the program. Accordingly, such programs were often difficult to modify and expand.

In response to these problems, the concept of structured programming evolved in the late 1960s. This approach to programming is based on the premise that basic control structures with one entry and one exit point can be used to express the processing undertaken in a computer program, no matter how complex. These basic control structures are *Sequence*, *If-Then-Else*, and *Do While*. The *Sequence* control structure establishes a sequence of events, one immediately after the other, as shown in Figure 2-8(a). The *If-Then-Else* structure establishes conditional statements, as shown in Figure 2-8(b). The *If* part tests a given condition. The *Then* part is executed when the condition tested is true, and the *Else* part is executed when the condition is not true. The *Do-While* structure establishes program looping, where one or more events occur as long as a given condition remains true, as shown in Figure 2-8(c). As shown by the example in Figure 2-9, with this structure an event may occur over and over until a parameter $n$ reaches its maximum value, $Nmax$. In this figure, the event encompasses the algorithm $y(n) = y(n-1) + f(n) \, (y(0) = 0)$, so that the results of the loop would be $y(Nmax) = f(1) + f(2) + \ldots + f(Nmax)$.

Figure 2-10 is an example of design requirements for a structured program. The requirements are presented in pseudocode, a form of

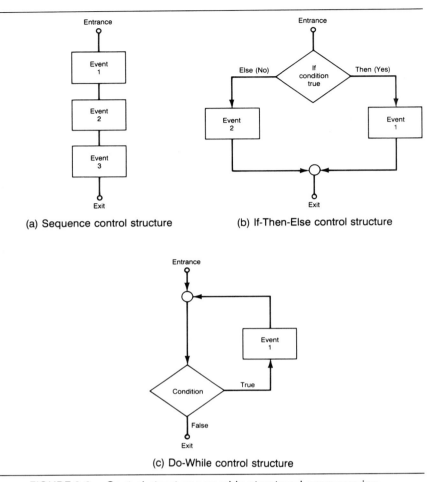

(a) Sequence control structure      (b) If-Then-Else control structure

(c) Do-While control structure

*FIGURE 2-8.*    Control structures used in structured programming

structured English. The pseudocode specifies how the computer program is to be implemented. This contrasts with structured English presented in computer program requirements specifications, which specifies what a program is to do but not how it is to be done. Pseudocode clearly identifies control structures through the use of DO WHILE and ENDDO to bracket a Do-While structure and IF and ENDIF to bracket an If-Then-Else structure. For the same computer program, a flow diagram does not identify each individual control structure as clearly as pseudocode. In the 1970s, flow diagrams also were more expensive to prepare and maintain than pseudocode. Text editors were available to prepare and maintain pseudocode, but

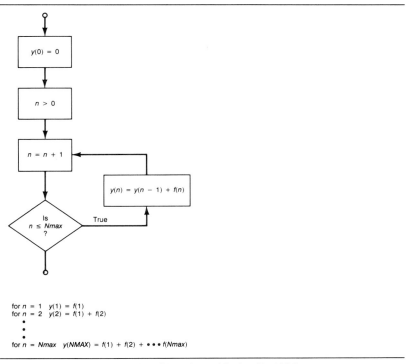

for $n = 1$   $y(1) = f(1)$
for $n = 2$   $y(2) = f(1) + f(2)$
   .
   .
   .
for $n = Nmax$   $y(NMAX) = f(1) + f(2) + \bullet \bullet \bullet f(Nmax)$

*FIGURE 2-9.*   An example of looping with the Do-While structure

graphics packages were not yet widely available to prepare and maintain graphical design representations.

In general, the reader of a structured program can recognize the general kind of operation inherent in each control structure (be it an event, a decision, or a loop), thereby making the computer program easier to read and understand. Furthermore, the reader knows that whatever happens within the control structure, it will always exit from a common point. This eliminates the possibility of "tricky" branching to remote parts of the program in the middle of a control structure.

### 2.3.4   The Top-Down Design Technique

Although structured programming and its representation with pseudocode were a step forward, critical software development problems resulted as the size of computer programs grew. For example, it was difficult, if not impossible, to comprehend in its

Start RUNNING AVERAGE

Input number of readings in running average ($NR$)
Set parameter value $V = 1$
Set count index $i = 0$

DO WHILE $V \neq 0$
   Set $i = i + 1$
   Input $V$ and set $VS(i) = V$
   Input month $M$ and set $MS(i) = M$
   Input day $D$ and set $DS(i) = D$
ENDDO

Set Maximum Number of Readings $IMAX = i$
Set $i = NR$

DO WHILE $i < IMAX$
   Set $i = i + 1$
   Calculate $AVS(i) = \left\{ \sum_{id = i - NR}^{i - 1} VS(i) \right\} / NR$
ENDDO

Print the text NUMBER OF READINGS IN RUNNING AVERAGE =
Output $NR$ immediately after text
Print the text PERCENT DIFFERENCE WANTED, YES OR NO
Input % DIF

IF % DIF = yes
   THEN set $i = NR$

      DO WHILE $i < IMAX$
         Set $i = i + 1$
         Calculate $DIFS(i) = \{[VS(i) - AVS(i)]/AVS(i)\} * 100$
      ENDDO

   ELSE continue
ENDIF

IF % DIF = yes
   THEN Print the heading DAY   MONTH  %  DIFFERENCE
   Set $i = NO\_READING - 1$

      DO WHILE $i < Imax$
         Set $i = i + 1$
         Output $DS(i)$, $MS(i)$, $DIFS(i)$
      ENDDO

   ELSE Print the heading DAY   MONTH   VALUE   AV.VALUE
   Set $i = NR - 1$

      DO WHILE $i < Imax$
         Set $i = i + 1$
         Output $DS(i)$, $MS(i)$, $VS(i)$, $AVS(i)$
      ENDDO

ENDIF

FIGURE 2-10.   Detailed design for a structured program

totality a large computer program designed exclusively with structured pseudocode. To help resolve this problem, the concept of top-down design emerged.

### Top-Down Design Considerations

With top-down design, a large and complex computer program is composed of small and comprehensible program units, with processing activity distributed among the units. With this technique, a relatively small and easily comprehended number of requirements are to be implemented within program units at one level, with the rest of the requirements implemented in called program units at lower levels. At each lower level, the process is repeated until all processing capabilities are accounted for.

To establish a top-down hierarchy of program units, the designer may start at the top of the hierarchy and work down, at the bottom of the hierarchy and work up, or even in the middle of the hierarchy. In the first case, the designer can identify user and other external needs at the start, and then specify a hierarchy of program units needed to satisfy those needs. In some cases, however, the designer may have other information that affects how to establish the program unit hierarchy. For example, the bottom-level components may be known in advance, and the designer may utilize, to a certain extent, bottom-up component composition. The designer develops higher- and higher-level components until the top of the software structure is reached. In other cases, the designer may initially identify components in the middle of a software structure. Then the designer works in a bottom-up manner from the middle to the top and in a top-down manner from the middle to the bottom to establish the program unit hierarchy. In all cases, however, when the design has been completed, a top-down hierarchy of program units has been established.

With the top-down approach to software design, the hierarchical structure of program units can be derived, taking into account both data flow and the implementation of functions. The designer is concerned with the major functions that are to be implemented to satisfy user requests and with data flow within the software system. For each function, the designer must address the input data required and the transformation of this data into output data within implementing program units. In some cases, the program units may utilize relatively complex sets of data elements and may establish databases to store the input and output data, from which data element values can be retrieved by use of specified keys. For those readers without experience in the development of a top-down design, an example is presented next. Those readers familiar with top-down design may want to proceed to Section 2.3.5, "The Use of Logical Concurrency in Design."

### An Example of Top-Down Design

For an example of top-down design, let us consider a possible hierarchy of program units that a designer specifies to satisfy requirements for the ICU discussed in Section 2.2. As shown in Figure 2-11, the designer establishes an executive program unit at the highest level. The purpose of the executive unit is to coordinate the execution of lower-level program units that enable processing for message routing. At level 2, the designer establishes a communications, or COMM, program unit (PU), a RECORD PU, a ROUTER PU, and a CONSOLE PU.

For the level-2 COMM PU, the designer specifies that it is to fetch and process messages when they arrive at the system's I/O board and place the messages in memory for subsequent processing. The designer indicates that the COMM PU is to call two level-3 program units, the I/O BOARD PU and the PROTOCOL PU. The I/O BOARD PU is to check each communications line for the presence of a message. It is to detect a valid beginning message frame when a message appears at a given channel, fetch the message, strip off its opening flag, and place it in a buffer. The PROTOCOL PU is to send out a control message over the communications channel when the message has been received indicating that the reception was successful. Then it is to identify the control fields of the message, strip them off, and store the result in a second buffer.

For the level-2 RECORD PU, the designer specifies that it is to record messages when they are received and prior to their distribution. The designer indicates that the RECORD PU is to call two level-3 program units, the FILE PU and the CONSOLE PU. The FILE PU is to add the date and time to a received message or to a message to be distributed. It is then to record the message on a disk, along with an indication of its source or destinations. When the disk is full, the RECORD PU is to notify the system operator for subsequent storage on tape. The CONSOLE PU is to implement the display of stored messages keyed by time, date, message source, or message destination.

For the level-2 ROUTER PU, the designer specifies that it is to distribute messages in accordance with routing destinations programmed into a routing table. Specifically, this PU is to determine the

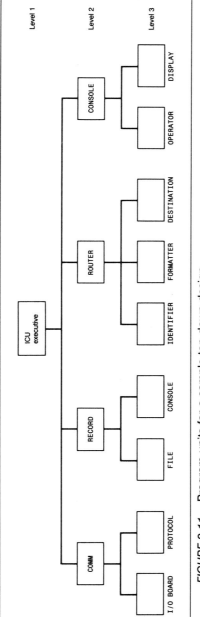

*FIGURE 2-11.* Program units for a sample top-down design

destination of a message received from the COMM PU, create the proper message format, send a copy of the message to the RECORD PU for recording, and return a copy to the COMM PU for subsequent distribution. The designer indicates that the ROUTER PU is to call three level-3 program units, the IDENTIFIER PU, the FORMATTER PU, and the DESTINATION PU. The IDENTIFIER PU is to determine the type and format of a message, which is to be inserted into the message's header. The FORMATTER PU is to establish the proper control fields for different versions of the message as a function of the protocols applicable to the various distribution points (i.e., format X for the radar station, format Y for the operations centers, and format Z for the communications channels). The ROUTER PU is to use the routing table to determine the destinations of the message based on its source and type. It is to place each message to be exported into an appropriate destination queue.

For the level-2 CONSOLE PU, the designer specifies that it is to establish operator interfaces. Upon operator command this PU is to display recorded messages keyed by date, time, and the source or destination of the message. Also, it is to display messages immediately after they are received. The designer indicates that the CONSOLE PU is to call two level-3 program units, the OPERATOR PU and the DISPLAY PU. The OPERATOR PU is to facilitate interaction with the system operator, including the initiation of appropriate responses to mouse and keyboard inputs. The DISPLAY PU is to generate requested displays.

The designer could then establish any lower-level program units deemed necessary. For example, the designer could specify that the OPERATOR PU is to call a KEYBOARD PU and a MOUSE PU and that the DISPLAY PU is to call the TEXT PU, the GRAPHIC PU and the TABLE PU. The KEYBOARD PU is to interpret operator commands made via the keyboard. The MOUSE PU is to receive and process operator actions made via the system mouse. The TEXT PU is to display free text received from the operator keyboard. The GRAPHIC PU is to generate plots and other graphics requested by the operator (e.g., a plot of parameters versus the time of day). The TABLE PU is to generate tables requested by the operator (e.g., a list of all messages received between specified times on a specified day).

## 2.3.5 The Use of Logical Concurrency in Design

The combination of top-down design and structured programming was a major step forward in software design methodology. Yet, with the increasing power of processors and their operating systems, new concepts in software design continued to emerge in the 1970s, including designs that can respond to multiple demands that may occur simultaneously.

In many processing problems and application programs, there are parts of a program that logically should execute concurrently. In a computer system, resident software typically has to satisfy multiple demands. For example, user commands and communications interface requests may compete simultaneously for a computer's processing time. A computer program must respond in a timely manner to commands and requests, even when they are received at about the same instant. Software can be written to implement the data and operations on the data needed to respond to each user command and communications interface request. In addition, software may have to be written to automatically initiate processing within a computer program on a periodic or other basis. For example, a software built-in test of equipment may be initiated periodically, or processing may start automatically when a sensor value reaches a critical value.

For the ICU example, the resident computer program interacts with the operations centers, the radar system, and the communications channels, as shown in Figure 2-12(a). It is possible that messages may arrive at the system at essentially the same time the system operator is requesting the display of previously received messages. Accordingly, the design of the ICU's computer program could call for logical concurrency, as shown in Figure 2-12(b). One concurrent thread of processing is to receive messages from the communications channels and the radar station and distribute them appropriately. A second thread concurrent with the first thread is to receive operator requests from operations centers A and B for displays of recorded messages. These logically concurrent parts of the program are always active, waiting for a message or an operator request. In general, a concurrent part of a program may spend most of the time waiting for an event to occur, execute only a few microseconds upon the occurrence of the event, and then return to a waiting state.

## 2.3.6 Object-Oriented Design

In the 1980s, data-driven design emerged in the context of object-oriented design. In the early years, software design often focused on the representation of operations and services to be performed.

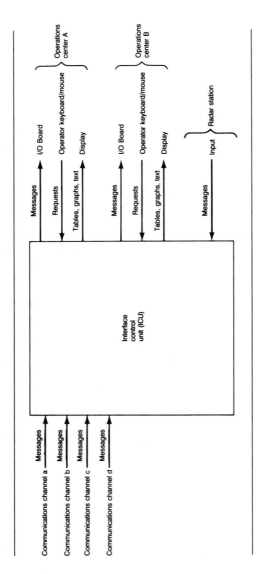

*FIGURE 2-12(a).* Multiple ICU demands: interfaces

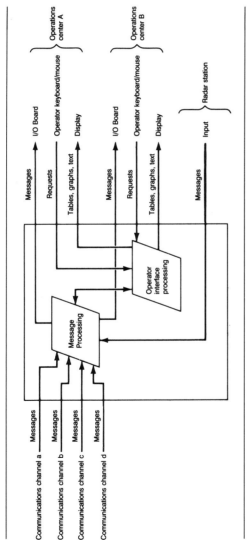

Communications channel a — Messages

Communications channel b — Messages

Communications channel c — Messages

Communications channel d — Messages

Message Processing

Operator interface processing

Messages — I/O Board

Requests — Operator keyboard/mouse ⎱ Operations center A

Tables, graphs, text — Display

Messages — I/O Board

Requests — Operator keyboard/mouse ⎱ Operations center B

Tables, graphs, text — Display

Messages — Input ⎱ Radar station

FIGURE 2-12(b). Multiple ICU demands: logical concurrency

During the 1970s, data-driven design methods began to emerge with new high-order languages (e.g., PASCAL), providing a variety of ways to organize and characterize data in data structures. During the 1980s, data structures were emphasized in design approaches, and object-oriented design evolved in the context of languages like SMALLTALK.

There are various conceptual dimensions to object-oriented design and the analysis required to apply it. One basic concept holds that requirements for a large computer program can be grouped around a set of real-world objects. A software design can directly reflect the real-world objects in the architectural structure for a computer program.

A second basic concept views the software design for each object as a data structure to which operations can be attached. Objects are then selected on a data-first, not functional, basis. This approach tends to add continuity to a software system if the data structures for the objects selected do not change over time, but the functional operations do (which, some software engineers and analysts argue, is the case over the life cycle of many software systems).

A third concept in object-oriented design requires that the implementation of each object be encapsulated. The data structure and operations in the encapsulation are hidden and not accessible by other object implementations. In this way, the object implementations are made independent and self-sufficient (i.e., a change to one object implementation does not affect another).

Other basic conceptual dimensions to object-oriented design include such things as classes, instances of classes, and inheritance. Many different objects in a problem space may have similar attributes and perform similar services. In object-oriented analysis, attributes and services common to a set of objects are said to form a class of attributes and services, which can be inherited by the objects as members of the class.

There are different ramifications to applying such concepts of object-oriented design when developing a large software system. For example, some software engineers and analysts maintain that an object-oriented design tends to produce reusable and extendable software objects, a factor that is relevant to the design of a large and complex software system. Various companies have developed software objects for use in programming "construction sets." A programmer can implement the design for a large program with the prefabricated objects, rather than rewriting them from scratch. Since each object tends to be independent and self-sufficient, they can be introduced into a system without interfering with other parts of the system.

Although not strictly an object-oriented language, Ada facilitates implementing some of the aspects of an object-oriented design important to the development of large software systems. For example, Bertrand Meyer categorizes Ada with other languages with respect to object-oriented programming in his book *Object-Oriented Software Construction*, as follows:

> In its most simple form, object-oriented programming is just "programming with abstract data types." A primitive implementation of the idea is to constrain all accesses to a data structure, in any module not owning the structure, to use routines rather than access the fields directly. In the absence of special language support, this is a purely methodological rule, which can be implemented in any language having the notion of routine; it may be called disciplined data structure access. But of course this is not object-oriented programming—just a form of information hiding.
>
> The second category includes languages that offer a form of modularity based on data structures. These languages allow the definition of modules that encapsulate a data structure description with routines that manipulate the data structure. This may be called encapsulation. Typical of this category are Ada and Modula-2. A module in such languages may be associated with an abstract data type implementation. However, the notions of type and module remain distinct; inheritance is not offered.
>
> The next category . . . covers true object-oriented languages. Classes are used as both modules and types. This opens the way to inheritance, polymorphism, redefinition and dynamic binding.

Grady Booch, in his book *System Engineering with Ada*, popularized the idea of using encapsulation aspects of an object-oriented design in the context of Ada. He promotes the analysis of an English language description stating the solution to a software problem to identify objects and attributes of the objects, operations that may be applied to the objects, and interfaces between the objects. In the context of a large software system, this would require analysis of the formal specification of requirements for that system. Roger Pressman argues in his book *Software Engineering—A Practitioner's Approach* that object-oriented design currently combines elements of data design, architectural design, and procedural design. He states "by identifying objects, data abstractions are created. By defining operations, modules are specified and a structure for the software is established. By developing a mechanism for using (e.g., generating messages) the objects, interfaces are described."

### 2.3.7 Application of Design Technology

Through the 1960s and 1970s, systems evolved into sophisticated architectural combinations of hardware and concurrently executing threads of program units in response to the ever increasing sophistication of processing requirements. However, despite seemingly brilliant architectural designs, progress in the development of large software systems was often erratic, and maintenance problems were at times formidable. Because of this, object-oriented and other new software design technology continued to emerge in the 1980s.

Our job is to assess both the older and newer techniques, and devise an overall design approach that takes advantage of the techniques, when and where each is appropriate.

## 2.4 Key Concepts

- Requirements for a large computer program can be varied and complex, specifying such things as operator commands, algorithms, data flow, interfaces, management of data, and states of operation. These requirements are represented by various combinations of text, tables, and graphics (e.g., data flow diagrams, data dictionaries, structured English, and state transition diagrams).

- A software design facilitates transition from requirements to an executable processing system. A design can be thought of as a representation of a computer program that lies somewhere between its requirements specification and the implementing code.

- With the evolution of larger and larger processing capacity, the size and complexity of computer programs have grown; with this increase in size, associated development problems have cropped up. In response to these problems, design techniques have evolved over the years.

- In the early years, computer programs were relatively small, and design had to account for only a limited number of inputs, outputs, and processing operations. Subroutines were used to eliminate redundant processing and to conserve the limited memory capacity available. There was no widespread system to establish the organization and structure of these programs, and control was often transferred to and from any part of a program in any way deemed necessary.

- By the late 1960s, as the size of programs grew, it became difficult to follow the path of multiple jumps, making such programs difficult to modify and expand. One response to these problems was the concept of structured programming, where a series of control structures (each with one entry point and one exit point) were used to implement programs.

- In the 1970s, as the size of programs grew even more, it became difficult to comprehend in its totality a computer program designed exclusively with control structures. In response to this problem, the concept of top-down design emerged, where a computer program is constructed with a set of small and easily understood program units arranged in a hierarchical manner.

- With the evolution of operating systems, the architecture of large computer programs included logical concurrency to service multiple demands that may occur at the same time.

- In the 1980s, data-driven design emerged in the context of object-oriented design. Object-oriented design tends to produce reusable and extendable software objects, which is relevant to the design of a large computer program.

## 2.5    Exercises

1. What factors should you address in specifying requirements for a computer program?
2. What mechanisms can be used to present requirements in a software requirements specification?
3. What is the purpose of a design for a computer program?
4. What problems have been encountered in the development of computer programs as processing capacity has increased and computer programs have grown larger?
5. In a problem space, the standard deviation ($\sigma$) of a set of numbers $x_i$ ($i = 1, 2, \ldots, Imax$) is to be calculated using the algorithm

$$\sigma \neq \frac{1}{N} \sum_{i=1}^{Imax} (x_i - \mu)^2,$$

where $\mu$ is the mean value of the set of numbers given by

$$\mu = \frac{1}{N} \sum_{i=1}^{Imax} x_i$$

Prepare a flow diagram for a set of operations that could be used to calculate $\sigma$ for a given set of numbers $x_i$, $i + 1, 2, \ldots, N$. Represent these operations with structured pseudocode.

6. The top-down design for a computer program consists of 25 program units. Draw a possible hierarchy of program units in two levels. Draw a possible hierarchy of program units in four levels. What are the advantages of the first hierarchy versus the second hierarchy? The disadvantages?

7. How does an object-oriented design differ from a top-down design? Draw a diagram that represents the architectural aspects of an object-oriented design for a computer program, where the design specifies the use of three data structures and 25 program units.

# Basic Design
# Considerations

*The second part of this book addresses basic considerations relevant to the designing of large computer programs and software systems to be implemented in Ada. The basic considerations include design for flexibility, so the software will be responsive to change, and design for concurrency, so the software can respond to multiple events that may occur at the same time. In addition, the chapters in Part II examine design for data structures, operations, and class-member relationships, all in the context of Ada.*

*As a general approach, the second part of this book presents a basic design issue and then suggests conceptually how the issue can be resolved both generally and within the context of Ada. In solving a design problem, you should not idolize one specific technique or interpret one technique as "religion." Rather, you should consider various techniques, the advantages and disadvantages of each technique, and the role each can play in the difficult task of designing a large and complex software system. In practice, a specific technique or set of techniques applied in the design of a software system is driven by the problem at hand and the designer's choice in how to solve that problem in a low-risk and cost-effective manner.*

CHAPTER **3**

# Design for Flexible Software

Over the life cycle of a software system, requirements for the system are always in a state of flux. The changing requirements necessitate continual changes to the design and implementation of the software system. For large systems with complex requirements, changes can be difficult and costly to make, and can adversely affect the performance of parts of the system that seemingly are not associated with the change. This phenomenon has been part of the price for the increased sophistication of system requirements and the software that implement those requirements. Because this problem is fundamental to the development and maintenance of software, its resolution is basic to design strategy that supports the control of costs over the life cycle of a software system.

## 3.1 Introduction

This chapter addresses problems that can be encountered when changes are made to a large and complex software system. Since change is an inherent part of software development and the essence of maintenance, design should support the development of flexible software that is responsive to change. This chapter describes how such design can be accomplished in the context of Ada.

## 3.2 Changing a Computer Program

### 3.2.1 Adverse Effects

The first part of this book noted that computing systems have evolved into aggregations of hardware and concurrently executing programs that implement sophisticated and complex requirements. Despite seemingly brilliant software designs for the requirements, progress in implementing large and complex sets of programs has often been erratic, and problems in maintaining the resulting software systems have been formidable. Even after attempts to recover from setbacks encountered in a large development project, progress has been found to be slow, and further setbacks have been realized.

What is the reason for this? Why have setbacks so often occurred and recoup failed? In general, it is much more difficult to build a large software system than most people realize. Thousands of interacting program units must be designed, constructed, monitored, and controlled. This significant technical and management task is prey to a wide spectrum of problems. For one thing, several people are involved in the project, which introduces significant communication and coordination problems. To understand the others' efforts, they must deal with volumes of documentation, which always are a version or more behind the current version of the source code.

A large computer program is always in a state of flux, with changes being introduced to correct known errors and in response to changing requirements. A programmer who is asked how the program units under his or her responsibility are performing might indicate that the changes introduced into the latest version of the large computer program have caused strange side effects in the performance of some of the program units upon their execution. One of the fundamental enemies of a large computer program is change.

But why is change so bad? The adverse effects of change on the performance of a large computer program are in direct conflict with the experience gained in the development of small computer programs. Small computer programs typically are malleable—responsive to changes introduced by programmers. Many managers and other project personnel may have taken a course in programming and perhaps even written a small computer program. When changes are introduced into a small computer program, the modified program can be recompiled and reexecuted in a matter of minutes. And all usually works well. Based on these experiences, it is easy to generalize that software is flexible and easily changed. This generalization can lead to disaster, however, when it is applied to the development of a large computer program.

Why is this? What is the problem? First, let us say that each development effort will have its own unique problems, and the competency of personnel obviously will vary from one development effort to another. Second, as a general condition, a large computer program may include a large number of program units. For example, a program with 100,000 source statements might include 500 to 1,000 program units. Each of these program units must be individually designed, coded, tested, and then integrated with the other program units. If appropriate steps have not been taken, all the program units potentially are dependent on one another. Because of this, a change made to one program unit may have surprising and undesirable side effects on other program units. A change made to a global variable, type, or program unit, introduced to satisfy the needs of one aspect of a software system, may disrupt the performance of other aspects.

A change might account for an alternation to a processing algorithm or logic or even a new definition of the meaning of a variable or its type. For example, consider a program unit that is called by several other program units. Assume that, among other things, the program unit receives as input parameters $x_1$, $x_2$, and $x_3$ when called and operates on these parameters to calculate the output parameter y as follows:

$$y = w_1x_1 + w_2x_2 + w_3x_3 + w_4$$

In this relationship, $w_1$, $w_2$, and $w_3$ are weighting constants. Suppose that during operational testing of the large computer program, a specific calling program unit is found to perform better if the weighting factor $w_4$ is increased by the increment $\Delta w_4$ to $w_4 + \Delta w_4$. This improves the performance of the calling program unit and all the program units that depend on it. Accordingly, the programmer responsible for the calling program unit modifies the called program unit. However, this change may not be anticipated by other calling program units. Thus, the performance of these program units and all the program units that depend on them may become suboptimal (if not incorrect) due to the change in the output y to $y + \Delta w_4$. Testing of the large computer program might reveal these problems, and perhaps the following correction could be introduced:

$$y = w_1 x_1 + w_2 x_2 + w_3 x_3 + W$$

where $W = w_4 + \Delta w_4$ for certain calls, while $W = w_4$ for other calls. Although you may think this situation is not likely to occur, remember that in large software efforts several different people are involved in development and maintenance. It is not always easy to track the ramifications of changes made by all the different players involved, and any change or combination of changes is possible.

In general, when program units of a large computer program are interdependent, the modification of one program unit may adversely affect various other program units. These program units, in turn, may affect several other program units. A sort of ripple phenomena or domino effect may set in. As previously noted, a large computer program is always in a state of flux. Because of this flux and because change often leads to trouble, large software systems tend to be difficult to modify and complete.

In practice, the effects of a change may be difficult to detect and correct. In the preceding example, the effect of the change might be critical only over certain small values of $x_1$, $x_2$, and $x_3$. The effect of the change may affect some callers, but not others. Therefore, the effect of the change might, in a sense, move around the program and cause trouble in certain remote locations. When these problems are detected at those remote locations, it may be difficult to trace back to the cause of the problem and make the appropriate correction. The larger the number of program units in a large computer program and the more interdependent they are, the greater the problem becomes.

To illustrate the scope of this problem, let us consider the number of combinations of program units that could interact during the execution of a large computer program consisting of $n$ program units, which is given by the relationship $n(n-1)/2$. Assume that 1 percent of these possible combinations take place in the execution of a large computer program. It then follows that in a small computer program consisting of 100 program units, the number of combinations of two interdependent program units is about 49. In contrast, in a large computer program consisting of 1,000 program units, the number of combinations of two interdependent program units is 4,995—an increase of over 10,000 percent. In practice, the dependencies could be much worse. These circumstances help explain not only the disaster phase that often occurs in a large computer program development effort, but also the limited progress that may take place during the recoup phase. When coupled with other problems unique to the development of a computer program, software development progress can be erratic.

## 3.2.2 Requirements Instability

One major reason for changing a computer program is the instability of requirements, which is in part caused by the inability of customers to define a firm and fixed set of system requirements. In an attempt to help rectify this situation, some project managers and system engineers have proposed the development of a prototype for a software system. The user can operate the prototype system to assess interfaces and to identify missing capabilities. Also, the performance of selected complex algorithms can be assessed. This knowledge can then be used to establish more comprehensive operational requirements. In this way, the number of changes that have to be made to the requirements during full-scale development can be reduced, thus controlling, to a certain extent, the problem of change.

Even after analysis of a prototype, the precise definition of what a large system should do may be difficult, conditions in which the system will be used may change, and the comprehensive transformation of system performance into detailed requirements specifications by system analysts will be difficult. Thus, the initial version of a large software system often does not perform exactly in conformance with eventual customer needs. In the view of some engineering experts, this difficulty is unavoidable. The requirements for a large computer program are extensive, subject to continual change, and just too complex for the human mind to recognize all the details needed to establish a comprehensive set of requirements. (To make matters worse, those responsible for specifying requirements often are not familiar with the implementation ramifications of what they are specifying. This can lead to requirements specifications that put an unnecessary burden on software designers, programmers, and testers.)

Because of these problems, it typically is necessary to expand or modify requirements during the development and maintenance life cycle of large and complex software systems. Changes are introduced to fill in missing requirements and to modify requirements found to be inappropriate. (To add insult to injury, with traditional design approaches the cost to modify software once development is complete [on a per-line-of-code basis] usually is far greater than original development costs.) Because of this, design strategy applicable to Ada has to take into account the fact that a large software system will be in a constant state of flux, even when development is considered complete.

## 3.3 Controlling Change through Packaging

To control the adverse effects of change in a large program, we need to control global dependencies between program units, variables, and types. To meet this end, let us consider not introducing a global data structure into a design and not making program units globally accessible in the design. Rather, let us partition a large computer program into independent packages, each of which is to encapsulate a unique data structure and unique operations.

### 3.3.1 Independent Packages

When a large computer program is designed as a set of independent packages, a change to the data structure or operations in one independent package will not affect the performance of other independent packages. The extent to which this can be accomplished in a design and adhered to during development determines the extent to which the adverse effects of change can be controlled. Ideally, the effect of a change in an independent package is meant to remain trapped within that package and not to ripple beyond the walls of that package.

To maintain independence, an independent package should be designed to encapsulate a unique data structure and operations not to be shared with other independent packages. The unique data structure should account for variables, flags, and constants used in the formulation of operations unique to the independent package.

In the execution of a large computer program, some independent packages will interact. Typically, data entities will be passed between interacting packages. The passed data entities should be selected with care so as not to introduce dependencies; they should not include any of the variables, constants, flags, or types used in the formulation of unique operations. If this approach is followed in a design (and adhered to during implementation of the design), packages can remain independent even when they interact.

### 3.3.2 Coarser Level of Granularity

When designing a computer program, independent packages can be selected to establish a coarser level of granularity in the architectural structure of the program than the structure that would result from a traditional top-down design. Thus, independent packages should be larger than the individual program units associated with a traditional top-down design, which typically are implemented by 100 to 200 source statements.

The question then arises as to how large the independent packages may become. Generally speaking, an independent package should be a major portion of a computer program but constrained in size and complexity so that its design is relatively easy to understand, implement, and maintain. Accordingly, the number of program units and the extent of the data structure used in the design of an independent package should be well within the perception of programmers with average ability.

Although no strict rule can be formulated to cover all cases and categories of problems, a package typically might be implementable with 1,000 to 5,000 source statements depending on the nature of the problem, and the complexity of the package's data structure and operations. Typically, the implementation of a package would not be expected to exceed 10,000 source statements. Packages constrained to these size limits are normally readily developed and maintained. For such packages, the internal dependency relationships among program units, variables, and types usually are not excessive.

### 3.3.3 Modeling the Problem

When selecting a set of independent packages for a design, the designer should consider the kinds of data and operations to be specified for each package. For example, to further increase the understandability of a design, the data structure and operations internal to a package might directly reflect a real-world entity defined in the software requirements. By choosing independent packages in this way, a designer can think of the overall program design as a model of a real-world problem or situation.

The name assigned to an independent package should reflect the real-world entity to be modeled, not the functionality of that entity. For example, the name assigned to a package meant to service a set of communications lines might be called COMMUNICATION_LINES as opposed to MESSAGE_RECEIVER. In practice, the closer the model is to the problem, the less system engineers, programmers, and others have to make a mental transformation from the problem to the design. Thus, designs with independent packages that model the real world can make a large computer program not only more responsive to change but also more understandable to those programmers responsible for implementation or maintenance familiar with the problem defined in requirements. The more directly a design maps to the problem, the more understandable the design. If a design is distant from the problem, the mental transformation from the design to the problem increases complexity.

When we establish a design as a model of a real-world problem, the independent packages can to a certain extent mimic real-world entities they model. Real-world entities (e.g., an alarm clock or a telephone) typically make available to users only a small number of basic inputs (e.g., setting the time, enabling and disabling the alarm, dialing a number), while not permitting them access to internal implementation detail. These restrictions are good for real-world entities in that they minimize the number of places to look when something goes wrong (e.g., you don't disassemble the alarm clock when the telephone fails to ring). In the same way, an independent package as a model of a real-world entity isolates the effect of a change to the requirements for that real-world entity. This makes both development and maintenance easier and more efficient for programmers. They know exactly where to look if a change causes a problem.

## 3.4    Ada Design for Packaging

Ada provides a program unit that can be used to implement an independent package. Appropriately, this program unit is called an Ada package. It can be used to encapsulate the data structure and operations unique to an independent package.

### 3.4.1    Ada Packages

An Ada package can be thought of as a black box containing certain data and services made available to other packages only through an interface. The interface is defined in the specification of the package, the first part of a package's two-part structure. Entities contained in the black box are encompassed by the body of the Ada package, the second part of the two-part structure. These two parts are textually distinct and may be compiled separately. Figure 3-1 exemplifies keywords used to establish an Ada package (double dashed lines indicate comments).[1]

The specification is referred to as the "visible" part of a package. It is used to identify all the facilities in the package that will be available to other packages. This includes program units that can be called to provide access to the services of the package, and variables, constants, and types to be visible to other packages.

The body is referred to as the "hidden" part of an Ada package. It is used to implement the body of visible program units and includes both the specifications and the bodies of hidden program units. The package body can also include other entities not to be visible to users of the package, including data entities used in the implementation of program units.

As a mechanism for encapsulating data and operations, an Ada package is typically a passive program unit. However, the sequence of statements between `begin` and `end` (if provided) are executed after declarations take effect. This sequence could be used to implement initialization operations (e.g., to make the calculations needed to set initial values for variables used in the package).

---

[1]The package's specification is written using the keywords `package`, `is`, and `end`. As shown in Figure 3-1, the first line of the specification consists of the keyword `package` followed by the name of the package and the keyword `is`. The lines immediately following include the declaration of data that are to be accessible to program units external to the package and the specification (and only the specification) of program units that can be called by program units external to the package. The specification of the Ada package is concluded with the keyword `end` and a semicolon, with the name of the package between them.

The package's body is written using the keywords `package body`, `is`, `begin`, and `end`. The first line of the body consists of the keywords `package body` followed by the name of the package and the keyword `is`. The lines immediately following include source statements used to declare data not to be accessible to users, the body of program units to be accessible to users (i.e., program units whose specifications were included in the specification of the package), and declare program units not directly accessible by program units external to the package (i.e., units that were not included in the specification of the package). These lines can be followed by the processing that is to be undertaken by the package, encapsulated by the keywords `begin` and `end`. (The inclusion of such processing is optional and can be completely excluded.) A semicolon after the keyword `end` completes the package, with the name of the package optionally written between `end` and the semicolon.

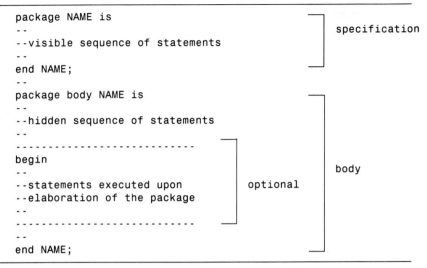

```
package NAME is                                      ┐
--                                                   │ specification
--visible sequence of statements                     │
--                                                   │
end NAME;                                             ┘
--
package body NAME is                                 ┐
--                                                   │
--hidden sequence of statements                      │
--                                                   │
-----------------------------       ┐                │
begin                               │                │
--                                  │ optional       │ body
--statements executed upon          │                │
--elaboration of the package        │                │
--                                  │                │
-----------------------------       ┘                │
--                                                   │
end NAME;                                             ┘
```

*FIGURE 3-1.*  Syntactic structure of an Ada package

## 3.4.2   Design with Independent Packages

For an example of an Ada design with independent packages, let us
return to the ICU problem. The designer might choose to establish
independence by packaging data structures and operations in packages modeling communication lines, data management, messages,
and the operator consoles. In a *package for communications lines*,
the design might specify that messages received from communication lines are to be entered into a queue. Each message in the queue
is to be forwarded to other independent packages for routing and
entrance into a historical database of message transactions. In a
*package for data management*, the design might specify requirements for entering received messages (or messages to be routed)
into a database, along with the date and time of their reception (or
routing). In a *package for messages*, the design might specify that
output messages are to be prepared and forwarded to appropriate
destinations. In a *package for operator consoles*, the design might
specify the processing necessary to respond to requests made by ICU
operators at system consoles. With such a design, four independent
packages would be established, as illustrated in Figure 3-2.

### 3.4.3 Ada Considerations for Packaging

In the ICU example, the design could specify a set of Ada packages named COMMUNICATION_LINES, MESSAGES, DATA_MANAGER, and OPERATOR_CONSOLE. The design might call for the passing of messages from the COMMUNICATION_LINES package to the other packages, and from the MESSAGES package to the DATA_MANAGER package, and back to the COMMUNICATION_LINES package. The design could also require that operator requests for display of message transactions be received via the OPERATOR_CONSOLE package, and that this package is to retrieve historical data from the DATA_MANAGER package. The design would thus require data entities to pass from one package to another, which would be accomplished by program units in one package calling visible program units in another package.

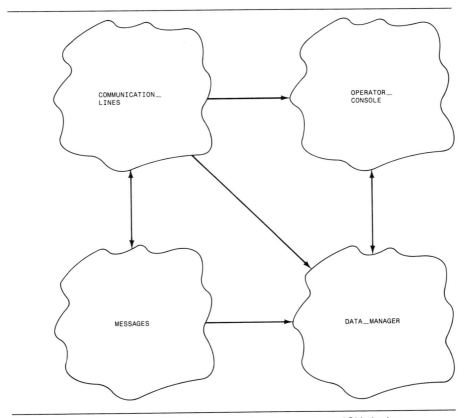

FIGURE 3-2. Possible independent packages in an ICU design

To make the visible program units accessible in Ada, the package containing the calling program units must be preceded by an Ada *with* clause. For example, the Ada package OPERATOR_CONSOLE can gain access to the Ada package DATA_MANAGER as follows:

```
with DATA_MANAGER;
package OPERATOR_CONSOLE is
   .
   .
   .
```

In this way, accessibility can be gained between interacting packages in the ICU design.

The use of the with clause in the ICU example is shown in Figure 3-3. In the design, the COMMUNICATION_LINES package is to access the OPERATOR_CONSOLE, DATA_MANAGER, and MESSAGES packages,

```
-------------------------------------
package DATA_MANAGER is
   ...
end DATA_MANAGER;
package body DATA_MANAGER is
   ...
end DATA_MANAGER;
-------------------------------------
with DATA_MANAGER;
package MESSAGES is
   ...
end MESSAGES;
package body MESSAGES is
   ...
end MESSAGES;
-------------------------------------
with DATA_MANAGER;
package OPERATOR_CONSOLE is
   ...
end OPERATOR_CONSOLE;
package body OPERATOR_CONSOLE is
   ...
end OPERATOR_CONSOLE;
-------------------------------------
with DATA_MANAGER, MESSAGES, OPERATOR_CONSOLE;
package COMMUNICATION_LINES is
   ...
end COMMUNICATION_LINES;
package body COMMUNICATION_LINES is
   ...
end COMMUNICATION_LINES;
```

*FIGURE 3-3.*  Applying the Ada with clause

and the `OPERATOR_CONSOLE` and `MESSAGES` packages are to access the `DATA_MANAGER` package.

## 3.5 Key Concepts

- Large computer programs generally are inflexible, not subject to change without possible degradation in overall performance.
- Some software engineers and analysts feel that the adverse effects of change on a large computer program are due to the dependency relationships among program units, variables, and types inherent in a large computer program.
- To control the adverse effects of change, a design can apply the concept of encapsulating data entities and operations on those entities within packages. To establish independence, the data entities and operations should be unique to that package and not shared with other packages.
- Independent packages partition a large computer program. The independent packages can be thought of as a coarser level of granularity in the architecture structure of a large computer program than that traditionally associated with top-down design.
- Ada packages can be used to encapsulate program units, variables, and types in the implementation of independent packages. The effects of a change to an independent package are trapped within that package and will not affect other packages.
- Independent packages can be thought of as models of real-world entities found in the description of a problem.

## 3.6 Exercises

1. How can a designer make a large computer program flexible?
2. What is the role of a global data structure in the design of a large computer program?
3. How can information be passed from one Ada package to another without affecting the independence of those packages?
4. What is the purpose of the Ada with clause? Give an example.
5. For the ICU example described in Chapter 2, suggest alternative independent packages that might be used to model the problem. What criteria would you apply in making the final selection of a set of independent packages?

# CHAPTER 4

# Design for Concurrency and Interaction among Independent Packages

In the design of a software system, independent packages can be chosen to reflect real-world entities defined in software requirements. When choosing these packages, a designer should think of the design as establishing a model of the real-world problem or situation. In a real-world problem, the real-world entities interact, and in addition, two or more may have to operate at the same time. Therefore, a design as a model of the real-world problem needs to reflect both interaction and concurrency among independent packages.

## 4.1    Introduction

This chapter focuses on introducing interaction and concurrency among independent packages into a software design. Specifically, it addresses design considerations for concurrency in the context of Ada tasks, the Ada program units used to implement concurrency in a computer program. It also discusses package interaction in the context of passing parameters from a task declared in one package to a task declared in another package, and in the context of passing messages between Ada subprograms declared in packages. (An Ada subprogram is the Ada program unit used to segment sequential processing operations into small pieces, each of which achieves a particular effect. Basic examples of syntax for Ada tasks and subprograms are given in footnotes.) For a more detailed discussion, refer to programming books on Ada.

## 4.2    Design for Simultaneous Demands

### 4.2.1    Concurrency among Independent Packages

In a large computer program, it is possible that multiple demands for services may be initiated at about the same time. For example, in the ICU problem, messages may arrive at the ICU at essentially the same time the ICU console operator is requesting a display of previously received messages. In the execution of a computer, the needed concurrency can be accomplished using algorithms to interleave processing so that two or more tasks appear to be executing simultaneously.

When software requirements include different demands on real-world entities that may be made at the same time, the design should specify logical concurrency to service those demands. For example, the design for the ICU could specify that the COMMUNICATION_LINES and the OPERATOR_CONSOLE package are to execute concurrently. Ada provides capabilities for facilitating concurrency directly with Ada source statements.

These capabilities make Ada different from most other high-order languages, which provide little or no support for facilitating such concurrent activity. Instead, concurrent aspects of a design have to be implemented through the facilities of an operating system or through multitasking assembly language routines. In those cases, a programmer has to step outside the high-order language to implement concurrency. The disadvantages are that the resulting software is less portable and the programmer may have to invest a significant and costly effort in learning how to use an operating system, or develop multitasking assembly language routines. The resulting program development may be logically complex and, therefore, difficult for maintenance personnel to comprehend.

### 4.2.2 Ada Tasks

In Ada, the program unit called a "task" establishes concurrency directly through Ada source statements. Ada tasks run concurrently in a multiprocessor or execute concurrently from a logical viewpoint in a single processor. (Ada tasks actually execute in an interleaved manner in a single processor under control of an Ada run-time system.)

#### Structure of an Ada Task

An Ada task consists of a specification and a body, as does an Ada package. The specification of a task is one or more Ada source statements that establish the name of the task and entries to the task that can be called by other tasks to facilitate intertask communication. The body of a task contains a sequence of statements needed to implement operations and accept entry calls (referred to as entry points). Figure 4-1 shows keywords for the structure of an Ada task.[1]

#### Execution of Ada Tasks

An Ada task is activated upon elaboration of the declarative part of its parent. If several tasks are declared by the parent, they all will be activated at the end of the elaboration. Once activated, a task can be constructed to logically run indefinitely using an infinite loop in its body (e.g., to monitor sensors), or it can be constructed so as to be complete when it reaches the end of the Ada source statements that make up its body. A parent task will not terminate until all its children tasks have terminated.

---

[1]The keywords used to establish the structure of an Ada task are task, is, entry, and end. The first line of a task's specification consists of the keyword task followed by the name of the task and the keyword is. The lines immediately following may declare callable entries for the task. The specification is concluded with the keyword end and a semicolon, with the name of the task optionally placed between them.

The task's body uses the keywords task body, is, begin, accept, do, and end. The first line of the body consists of the keywords task body followed by the name of the task and the keyword is. The lines immediately following include source statements that establish processing internal to the task and the acceptance of entry calls to the task. The task's body is concluded with the keyword end and a semicolon, with the name of the task optionally placed between them.

Tasks exist in different states, for example,

- running (concurrently executing)
- blocked (delayed or waiting for execution)
- ready (unblocked but waiting for execution)
- dormant (not yet activated)
- completed (terminated upon execution of a body)
- abnormal

A task can be assigned a priority that indicates the degree of its execution urgency. For example, if two or more tasks with different priorities are in the ready state, the task with the more urgent priority will be selected for running.

```
task CONCURRENT_UNIT is
--
--Declare task entries
--
  entry ENTRY1 (. . .);
  entry ENTRY2 (. . .);
  entry ENTRY3 (. . .);
--
--Other
--
  . . .
end CONCURRENT_UNIT;
```

(a) Specification

```
task body CONCURRENT_UNIT is
begin
--
--sequence of statements for processing
--
  . . .
--
--establish an entry point
--
  accept ENTRY1 (. . .) do
  . . .
  end ENTRY1;
  . . .
  end CONCURRENT_UNIT;
```

(b) Body

FIGURE 4-1. Syntactic structure of an Ada task

### 4.2.3 Design Considerations for Concurrency

In an Ada design, the designer can specify that Ada tasks are to be declared within the independent packages to establish logical concurrency among the packages. For an example of using Ada tasks in this way, let us return to the interface control unit (ICU) problem, where messages may arrive at essentially the same time the system operator is requesting the display of previously received messages. Logically, the ICU's design could specify concurrent execution of program units that process arriving messages with program units that process display requests. This concurrency is illustrated in Figure 4-2, where parallelograms represent Ada tasks. The use of parallelograms to represent a task is used by Grady Booch in his book *Software Engineering with Ada* (1983). Processing in the body of one task can monitor the arrival of messages, while processing in the body of a second task can respond to operator requests. A design for the ICU program to be implemented in Ada could require a MESSAGE_PROCESSOR task in the COMMUNICATION_LINES package and an OPERATOR_INTERFACE task in the OPERATOR_CONSOLE package. An example of Ada source statements for such a design is shown in Figure 4-3.

A design can specify the use of Ada tasks at the high levels for concurrency among independent packages, or at lower levels within the logic of operations to be performed by a package. For example, in an independent package for an aircraft autopilot, the package might continuously monitor different sensors (e.g., airspeed and angle of attack) while at the same time controlling several devices (e.g., control surfaces and throttles).

Some designers have proposed introducing extensive tasking in a design at both high and low levels to serve different purposes. For example, *receiver tasks* can be included in a design to receive information from a calling task and perform a designated action. *Sender tasks* can be included in a design to exclusively send information to other tasks, receiving nothing in return. Tasks also can be introduced in a design to act as schedulers, buffers, secretaries, agents, transporters, managers, and so forth.

When preparing a design, extensive use of Ada tasks may not be prudent, since this approach can lead to problems. The temporal aspects of task rendezvous make testing complicated. In addition, with complex sets of task calls, timing problems can occur. Certain tasks may have to wait longer than is acceptable for their entry points to be called, or a called entry point may not become available to complete rendezvous in a timely manner. Therefore, a design should

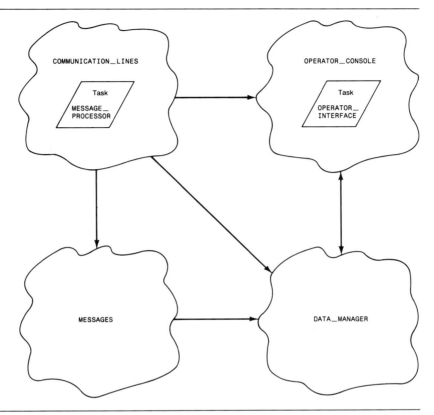

COMMUNICATION_LINES

Task
MESSAGE_
PROCESSOR

OPERATOR_CONSOLE

Task
OPERATOR_
INTERFACE

MESSAGES

DATA_MANAGER

*FIGURE 4-2.* Logical concurrency among independent packages

specify the use of Ada tasks to facilitate concurrency among independent packages, and to accomplish concurrency within a package only where logically essential to a good design.

## 4.3   Design for Interaction among Independent Packages

As already noted, a design for a large computer program will include interaction between independent packages. For example, as shown in Figure 4-4, the design for the ICU software might specify that the COMMUNICATION_LINES package is to forward messages to the DATA_MANAGER package, which then is to enter the messages into a historical database. The COMMUNICATION_LINES package also is to forward a received message to the MESSAGES package, which is to determine the destination of the message as a function of its source,

```
---------------------------------------
--
package DATA_MANAGER is
      . . .
end DATA_MANAGER;
--
package body DATA_MANAGER is
      . . .
end DATA_MANAGER;
--
---------------------------------------
--
with DATA_MANAGER;
package MESSAGES is
      . . .
end MESSAGES;
--
package body MESSAGES is
      . . .
end MESSAGES;
--
---------------------------------------
with DATA_MANAGER;
package OPERATOR_CONSOLE is
      . . .
            task OPERATOR_INTERFACE is
                  . . .
            end OPERATOR_INTERFACE;
      . . .
end OPERATOR_CONSOLE;
--
package body OPERATOR_CONSOLE is
      . . .
            task body OPERATOR_INTERFACE is
                  . . .
            end OPERATOR_INTERFACE;
      . . .
end OPERATOR_CONSOLE;
```

*FIGURE 4-3.* Example of Ada source statements for tasks within packages

establish output messages in an appropriate format, and return the messages to the COMMUNICATION_LINES package. The COMMUNICATION_LINES package, in turn, is to forward the output message to the OPERATOR_CONSOLE package for display prior to its distribution.

```
-------------------------------------
--
with DATA_MANAGER, MESSAGES, OPERATOR_CONSOLE;
package COMMUNICATION_LINES is
      . . .
            task MESSAGE_PROCESSOR is
                  . . .
            end MESSAGE_PROCESSOR;
      . . .
end COMMUNICATION_LINES;
--
package body COMMUNICATION_LINES is
      . . .
            task body MESSAGE_PROCESSOR is
                  . . .
            end MESSAGE_PROCESSOR;
      . . .
end COMMUNICATION_LINES;
```

FIGURE 4-3.   (continued)


## 4.3.1   Ada Task Rendezvous

To accomplish the passage of a message between the COMMUNICATION
_LINES and OPERATOR_CONSOLE packages, the MESSAGE_PROCESSOR
task of the COMMUNICATION_LINES package should forward an output
message ready for distribution to the OPERATOR_INTERFACE task of
the OPERATOR_CONSOLE package. To implement this message passage in Ada, the MESSAGE_PROCESSOR task can call an entry point in
the OPERATOR_INTERFACE task. The word "rendezvous" is used to
describe such calls and the interaction that follows.

During rendezvous, a task call to an entry point in another task
signals that the caller is ready to communicate. Before information is
passed, however, the caller may have to wait for the called task to
accept (i.e., the logical execution of the called task has to have
reached the called entry point to be ready to complete rendezvous
with the caller). The wait may be for an extended period of time.
(Correspondingly, if an acceptor task is ready for a call before it is
made, the acceptor task will have to wait for a call to its entry point.)
Upon acceptance, information is passed from the caller task to the
called task and/or from the called task to the caller. Upon completion
of rendezvous, tasks resume their logically concurrent states of
operation.

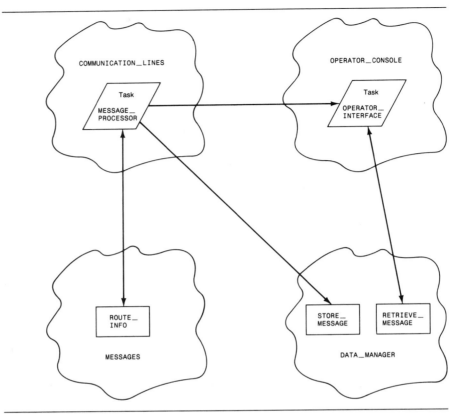

*FIGURE 4-4.* Example of Ada procedures within packages

## 4.3.2 Ada Subprograms

To accomplish the forwarding of a message from the COMMUNICATION_
LINES package to the DATA_MANAGER package and the passage of a
message from the COMMUNICATION_LINES package to the MESSAGES
package, program units visible in the COMMUNICATION_LINES package
have to call program units visible in the DATA_MANAGER and MESSAGES
packages. Ada makes such calls possible through its subprograms.

Like the other Ada program units, an Ada subprogram consists of
a specification and a body. The specification is a single Ada source
statement that establishes the name of the subprogram and the
characteristics of its parameter passing. The body can declare data
to be used and implements operations to be performed upon execution. It consists of multiple Ada source statements that are clearly
distinguishable from the specification.

There are two kinds of Ada subprograms: procedures and functions. The main program in Ada is an Ada procedure invoked upon activation of the Ada computer program. Procedures also can be declared in program units and called. When a procedure is called, information passes between the caller and the called procedure. Thus, they can be declared in the specification of packages and used to pass information between the packages. Whereas a procedure is a callable program unit that can return multiple parameters, a function call is part of an expression and returns only a single parameter. Figure 4-5 shows the syntax for the body of a procedure, and Figure 4-6 shows the syntax for the body of a function.[2]

### 4.3.3 Design Considerations for Package Interaction

In the design for the ICU based on the diagram shown in Figure 4-4, the Ada procedure ROUTE_INFO can be declared in the specification of the MESSAGES package, and STORE_MESSAGE and RETRIEVE procedures can be declared in the specification of the DATA_MANAGER package. The MESSAGE_PROCESSOR task can call the ROUTE_INFO procedure to forward a received message and receive in return a properly formatted output message. The MESSAGE_PROCESSOR task can also call the STORE_MESSAGE procedure to

---

[2]Ada keywords are used to write the body of a procedure. As shown by the example in Figure 4-5, these keywords are procedure, is, begin, and end. In the first line, the keyword procedure is followed by the name of the procedure, a specification of the parameter passing to and from the procedure in parentheses, and the keyword is. (When a procedure is acting as the main program, parameter passing is not applicable and does not have to be accounted for in the specification.) The lines that follow are used to declare data, and provide statements that delineate the processing to be performed by the procedure. The later statements are encapsulated by the keywords begin and end. A semicolon after the keyword end terminates the procedure, with the name of the procedure optionally inserted between end and the semicolon.

The keywords used to write the body of an Ada function are function, in, return, and is. As shown in Figure 4-6, in the first line the keyword function is followed by the name of the function, the declaration of the input parameters enclosed in parentheses, the keyword return, the type of the output parameter to be returned by the function, and the keyword is. The declaration of the input parameter in parentheses includes the name of the input parameter followed by a colon, the keyword in to indicate a parameter to be received from the caller, and the parameter's type. The function's body provides statements for processing to be performed between the keywords begin and end.

```
procedure NAME (. . .) is
- -
- -declarations
- -
begin
- -
- -operations
- -
.   .   .   .
end  NAME;
```

FIGURE 4-5.   Syntactic structure for the body of an Ada procedure

```
function NAME (X: in Type_For_X);
              (Y: in Type_For_Y) return NAMES is
begin
- -
- -sequence of statements
- -
- -end  NAME;
```

FIGURE 4-6.   Syntactic structure for the body of an Ada function

forward a received message for entrance into a historical database of message transactions. Also, the OPERATOR_INTERFACE task of the OPERATOR_CONSOLE package can call the RETRIEVE_MESSAGE procedure to fetch a set of messages needed to generate an operator-requested display of message transactions.

### Coupling of Independent Packages

When independent packages interact through the passage of data entities, they become coupled. This coupling is caused by task rendezvous and procedure calls. By organizing data and operations into coherent independent packages, a design can minimize coupling on a macro scale. In practice, the best coupling between independent packages is no coupling at all. In a design, several independent packages may not interact in any way; therefore, they are not coupled. Where coupling must exist, it should be constrained to the passing of data entities that are the quantitative results of services performed within the independent package. Coupling should not include passing of (or global access to) variables, types, and flags used in the formulation of the services produced by the interacting packages. If this rule is adhered to, packages remain essentially independent even though they are coupled by data passing.

If a variable or flag used in formulating services of an independent package must be passed, its type should be declared private or limited private in the visible part of the package's specification. This Ada capacity restricts the use of the data entity. For example, if a data entity is declared private, only operations defined within the package specification can be applied to it, along with assignments and tests for equality. If a state variable is declared limited private, assignment and tests for equality are no longer automatically available. (Refer to a programming book on Ada for a detailed explanation of private and limited private types.)

### 4.3.4 Ada Considerations in the Use of Subprograms and Tasks

**Ada Procedures**

The Ada source statements shown in Figure 4-7 exemplify parameter passing to and from an Ada procedure. A procedure call consists of the name of the procedure to be called, followed in parentheses by a list of variable names for the data entities to be passed between the caller and the called procedure (see Fig. 4-7a). These variables are also delineated in the specification of the called procedure, in conjunction with a mode of parameter passing and type for each variable (see Fig 4-7b). (A type designates, for example, whether passed parameters are to be integer or floating point.) The parameter-passing modes are *in* for parameters to be received by the called program unit from the caller, *out* for parameters to be established by the called program unit and returned to the caller, and *in out* for parameters to be received by the called program unit from the caller, modified by the called program unit, and returned to the caller.[3]

**Ada Tasks**

The Ada source statements shown in Figure 4-8a exemplify a call to a task entry. As indicated, the source statement for an entry call includes the name of the applicable task, a dot, and the name of the entry followed by a list of variable names enclosed in parentheses (for the data entities to be passed). A semicolon follows the parenthesis, completing the source statement. As shown in Figure 4-8b, the variables are also delineated in the specification and in the body of the called task, in conjunction with a mode of parameter passing

---

[3]Ada keywords are used to indicate the mode of parameter passing—namely, as we might expect, in for the *in* mode, out for the *out* mode, and in out for the *in out* mode.

```
ESTABLISH_OUTPUT_MESSAGES (INPUT_MESSAGE, SOURCE, OUTPUT_MESSAGE);
```

(a) Ada source statement used to call the ESTABLISH_OUTPUT_MESSAGES procedure

```
ESTABLISH_OUTPUT_MESSAGES (INPUT_MESSAGE  : in INPUT_MESSAGE_TYPE;
                           SOURCE         : in SOURCE_TYPE;
                           OUTPUT_MESSAGE: out OUTPUT_MESSAGE_
                                                         TYPE);
```

(b) Ada source statement for the specification of the ESTABLISH_OUTPUT_MESSAGES
    procedure

FIGURE 4-7.  Example of Ada source statements for passing parameters to and
from an Ada procedure

and the type for each variable.[4] As for a procedure, the parameter
passing modes are in, out, and in out.

### Ada Functions

In contrast with a procedure that is a callable entity, a function call
is part of an expression and returns a single value upon execution of
the expression. As such, a function is useful in performing calculations (e.g., trigonometric functions) that may have to be made
several times. For example, a function used to calculate the cosine of
an angle supplied in units of degrees with the following specification

```
function COS(ANGLE: in DEGREES) return FLOAT is
```

could be part of the expression

```
DISTANCE := LENGTH*COS(30.0)
```

---

[4]For each entry declared in the specification of a task, the keyword entry is
followed by the name of the entry and enclosed in parentheses for each
parameter to be passed: the variable name, a colon, the mode of parameter
passing, and the variable type. The closing parenthesis is immediately
followed by a semicolon.

In the body of the called tasks, each entry takes the same form as the
specification, except the keyword accept is used in place of the keyword
entry and, after the parenthesis enclosing the list of variables for parameters to be passed, the keyword do appears. The lines of source statements
immediately following are used to perform processing unique to the accept
statement and are followed by the keyword end and a semicolon, with the
name of the entry between them.

```
OPERATOR_INTERFACE.EXPORT (OUTPUT_MESSAGE, DESTINATION);
```

(a) Ada source statements used to call the EXPORT entry in the OPERATOR_INTERFACE task

```
task OPERATOR_INTERFACE is
    . . .
    entry EXPORT (OUTPUT_MESSAGE: out OUTPUT_MESSAGE_TYPE;
                  DESTINATION: out DESTINATION_TYPE);
    . . .
end OPERATOR_INTERFACE;
task body OPERATOR_INTERFACE is
    . . .
    accept EXPORT (OUTPUT_MESSAGE: out OUTPUT_MESSAGE_TYPE;
                   DESTINATION: out DESTINATION_TYPE) do
    . . .
    end EXPORT;
end OPERATOR_INTERFACE;
```

(b) Ada source statements for the structure of the OPERATOR_INTERFACE task

*FIGURE 4-8.* Example of Ada source statements for passing parameters to an Ada task

In this expression, : = indicates that the product of the value assigned to the variable LENGTH times the cosine of 30 degrees will be assigned to the variable DISTANCE. Upon execution of this expression, the function is invoked.

### Design Constraints
In practice, a design for subprograms and tasks should be constrained to easily understood processing, which can be formulated with five to seven variables and implemented with fewer than 200 Ada source statements. Lower-level detail can be deferred to functions or called procedures. It is also good practice to keep the number of parameters passed to and from a called procedure or task entry (e.g., to facilitate package interaction) to a minimum, passing only the data necessary and sufficient to establish the levels of processing needed to implement a design effectively.

## 4.4   Key Concepts

- In a large computer program, it is possible that two or more demands for different processing may be initiated at the same time. For such cases, designs should establish concurrency to service the demands. Concurrency can be introduced at high levels among two or more independent packages or deep within the operations of a package.

- Most high-order languages do not provide for concurrency. A programmer has to implement concurrency using an operating system or through multitasking assembly language routines. In Ada, an Ada task can be used to implement concurrency directly with Ada source statements.

- In a large computer program, some of the independent packages making up that program will interact. Interaction can be accomplished via a rendezvous between Ada tasks visible in the interacting packages or by calls to visible Ada procedures.

- When independent packages interact, they become coupled. By organizing data and operations into coherent independent packages, a design can minimize coupling on a macro scale.

- In practice, minimal coupling between independent packages is preferred. In a design, several of the independent packages may not interact in any way; therefore, they are not coupled. When coupling must exist, it should be constrained to the passing of data entities that are the qualitative results of package services. Coupling should not include the passing of (or global access to) variables, flags, and types used in the formulation of the services.

- Extensive use of tasks can lead to problems in the testing of the temporal aspects of task rendezvous and result in timing problems. Because of these problems, tasks should be limited to facilitating concurrency among independent packages and within the internal design of a package to reduce complexity and increase understandability.

- In practice, a design for subprograms and tasks should be constrained to easily understood processing, which can be formulated with five to seven variables and implemented with fewer than 200 Ada source statements. Parameter passing to and from a called procedure, or task entry point, should be kept to a minimum.

## 4.5 Exercises

1. How can we establish logical concurrency with Ada?
2. What state can an Ada task be in?
3. How can messages be passed between Ada packages? Provide examples.
4. In a large processing system, independent packages are needed to monitor system resources, perform general processing functions, and facilitate user-machine interface. What names might be given to these independent packages? What kinds of Ada program units might be visible in these packages and what purpose would they play in an Ada design?
5. In the analysis of real-world requirements for a large computer program, a designer decides that 10 real-world entities are to be modeled by independent packages in an Ada software design. Three of the packages include operations that may have to be performed at the same time. Five of the packages interact. Draw a diagram that shows a possible design for this large computer program. Include all the independent packages, their concurrency, and their interactions. To what extent are the packages coupled?
6. In the design for a large computer program, two interacting independent packages pass between them variables used in the formulation of package operations. Thus, the packages are not only coupled, they are dependent on each other. How should the designer respond to this dependency?

# CHAPTER 5

# Design of a Data Structure Internal to an Independent Package

The importance of data in software design has grown through the years. In the early years, software design often focused on operations to be performed. During the 1970s, the importance of data in design began to become recognized. New high-order languages like PASCAL introduced a variety of ways to organize and characterize data in data structures. Today, it is recognized that as a model of real-world entities, design for independent packages should focus on data entities as well as operations. In fact, some designers argue that design should be developed on a data-first basis.

## 5.1 Introduction

This chapter examines the design of an independent package's data structure in the context of Ada and provides an overview of how the capabilities offered by Ada determine how such a design can be formulated. Readers familiar with the data structure aspects of Ada need not read this chapter. Others should view this chapter as introductory, presenting basic concepts and Ada capabilities for designing a data structure. (Refer to a book on programming with Ada for a more detailed discussion of implementing data structures in Ada.)

## 5.2 Data Structures and Ada

### 5.2.1 Basic Concepts

A computer program can contain different kinds of data. For example, data can be a number (e.g., integers, decimals, and binary numbers) or a word written in English text. In a computer program, data is organized, saved, stored, changed, and accessed in single and multi-valued variables.

A single-valued variable can be thought of as a small box in which a single scalar item can be kept. The variable can be given a name, say X. Algorithms typically utilize many variables with different names and for different purposes.

A multi-valued variable can be used to store a list of data values in a vector. In practice, we can point to an element in the list or refer to the next element or the previous one, and so on. If a single-valued variable is considered analogous to a room in a hotel, a vector is analogous to a hotel corridor. In this analogy, rooms are individual variables, accessible by their index. The 15th room along a corridor on the fourth floor would be 415. In mathematical notation, the name of the vector is separated from its index by parentheses. For example, we write $R(6)$ for the sixth element of vector $R$, and similarly $X(n)$ for vector $X$ whose index is the current value of $n$. Accordingly, $X(n + 1)$ refers to the element following $X(n)$ in the list. Vectors have numerous applications, including telephone books, personnel files, and dictionaries.

In many cases data must be arranged in a two-dimensional array or matrix. For example, a multiplication table is a $10 \times 10$ array, in which the data item at each point is the product of the row and column indices. An element of a matrix can be referred to using two indices, one for the row and one for the column. For example, we write $B(6,4)$ for the element located at row 6 and column 4. If a variable is like a hotel room and a vector is like a hotel corridor, a two-dimensional array is like a cross-section of the hotel. Its rows are a corridor on all the floors, and its columns are a location along the corridor on a specific floor.

Another basic entity for storing data is a linked list, an organization of variables and pointers in which the pointers indicate the storage address of the next variable in the list. Linked lists are useful when an unknown amount of data is to be collected. Figure 5-1 illustrates a linked list and some other basic data entities.

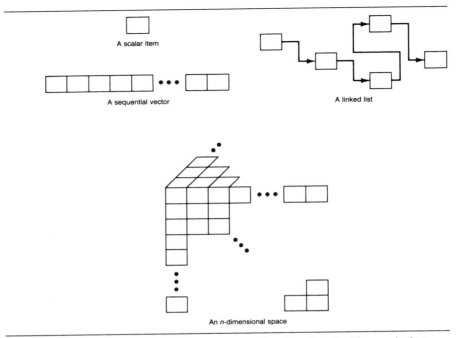

A scalar item

A sequential vector

A linked list

An *n*-dimensional space

*FIGURE 5-1.* Basic data structure entities. Reprinted with permission from Roger S. Pressman, *Software Engineering: A Practitioner's Approach.* New York: McGraw-Hill, 1977

In Ada, the concept of *type* is used to organize, order, and constrain data as scalars, vectors, linked lists, and other entities. Ada is said to be a strongly typed language, by which we mean the following:

- Every variable has a unique type.
- The definition of a type specifies the values applied to it.
- In the assignment of a value to a variable, the type of the value and the type of the variable must be the same.
- Every operator applied to a variable must belong to the set of operations defined by the variable type.

A data structure might be thought of as identifying and characterizing variables, including their range of permissible values and their type (e.g., scalar or vector).

An Ada package as an implementation of an independent package includes a visible data structure declared in its specification and a hidden data structure declared in its body. The visible data structure characterizes data entities to be passed to other independent packages through task rendezvous and procedure calls. The hidden data structure characterizes (and may define initial values for) variables and flags used in the formulation of internal operations.

In Ada, a variable or other data entity in a data structure is characterized through association with a type. Scalar types are defined and used to declare scalar variables that can be assigned one value at a time. Composite types are defined and used to declare composite variables that can be assigned two or more values at one time. The following paragraphs discuss some basic features of Ada typing that can be used in implementing design of a data structure. (Basic syntactical examples of Ada scalar and Ada composite types are provided in footnotes. For a more detailed discussion of Ada syntax applicable to Ada typing, refer to programming books.)

### Ada Scalar Types

Ada scalar types include integer, real, and enumeration types. An *integer type* is used to define a set of consecutive exact integers that can be assigned to a scalar variable, where an integer is established exactly in a computer with no error.[1] A *real type* is used to define a set of real numbers that can be assigned to a variable. These numbers are composed with a decimal point and may not be exact numbers.[2]

---

[1]Syntactically, a variable can be declared an integer in either of the following ways:

```
LOOP_COUNT_1 : INTEGER ;
LOOP_COUNT_2 : LOOP_INDEX ;
```

In the first instance, the range permissible for the variable LOOP_COUNT_1 is constrained by the predefined type INTEGER. In the second instance, LOOP_COUNT_2 is constrained by the defined type LOOP_INDEX. In the first case, the exact range permitted is a function of the machine being used. For example, on a 16-bit machine, the possible range is $-32,768$ to $32,767$. However, it is usually better practice to constrain an integer to a smaller explicit range of values. This can be done using the defined type, which is declared with the reserved words is range followed by the lower and upper limit of the range. For example, in the second case where we declare the variable LOOP_COUNT_2 to be of the type LOOP_INDEX, that type can be defined as follows:

```
type LOOP_INDEX is range 1..50;
```

[2]Syntactically, a variable can be declared real in the following ways:

```
LENGTH_1 : FLOAT ;
LENGTH_2 : DISTANCE ;
```

In the first instance, the real number LENGTH_1 is established on the basis of a predefined real type. In the second instance LENGTH_2 is constrained by the defined type DISTANCE. In the first case, the accuracy of numbers assigned to LENGTH_1 may vary from machine to machine. In a machine that uses a 32-bit

An *enumeration type* is used to define an ordered list of textual characters that can be assigned to a variable. This contrasts with languages like FORTRAN, where variables can be assigned only numeric values. For example, the values assigned to the variable SWITCH can be constrained to ON or OFF, and the values assigned to the variable WEEK_DAYS can be constrained to MONDAY, TUESDAY, WEDNESDAY, THURSDAY, and FRIDAY. Provided with textual meaning, an Ada representation can be easier to read than a representation with other languages like FORTRAN, where the variable SWITCH would have to be assigned a number to represent ON (e.g., 1) and a second number to represent OFF (e.g., 0).[3]

---

word with a 24-bit fractional part, the real number would have an accuracy of approximately seven decimal digits. In contrast, a 64-bit representation of the real number would have an accuracy of approximately 16 digits. In many situations, it is better to define explicit bounds for a real number using a defined real type, as shown in the second case. With Ada, this can be syntactically accomplished with the reserved words is digits followed by an exact integer that defines the number of decimal digits of significance. For example, the defined type DISTANCE for the variable LENGTH_2 could be established by

```
type DISTANCE is digits 5;
```

to impose an accuracy of five decimal places on the real values assigned to the scalar variable LENGTH_2. In addition, a range constraint can be established along with the accuracy constraint, as follows:

```
type DISTANCE is digits 5 range 1.0 .. 99.0;
```

where values assigned to LENGTH_2 cannot be less than 1.0 or greater than 99.0.

With Ada, we can also establish the coarseness of values assigned to a variable. For example, we might want to measure a distance accurate to one-tenth of a meter. To meet this end, syntactically we use the Ada reserved words is delta followed by a real number that defines the increment of coarseness to establish a type definition. For example, a defined type distance for the variable LENGTH_2 could be established by

```
type DISTANCE is delta 0.1 range 1.0 .. 99.0.;
```

With this type definition, the set of possible assignments to LENGTH_2 is

```
1.0, 1.1, 1.2, . . . , 98.8, 98.9, 99.0
```

[3]For example, textual character constraints for the variables SWITCH and WEEK_DAY can be written in a type definition by following the reserved word is by the set of permissible textual values enclosed in parentheses, as shown by the following examples:

```
type SWITCH_VALUES is (ON, OFF);
type WEEK_DAY_VALUES is (MONDAY, TUESDAY, WEDNESDAY,
     THURSDAY, FRIDAY);
```

### Composite Data Types

An Ada data structure may contain composite variables that can be assigned two or more values at one time, in addition to the scalar variables, which can be assigned only one value at a time. For example, the data entity ADDRESS might have the components STREET_NUMBER, STREET_NAME, STATE_NAME, and ZIP_CODE. A composite variable is declared through association with a composite data type. Ada provides two different kinds of composite types—array types and record types.

An *array type* is used to define a data entity with a set of components of the same data type. The resulting data entity can be one-dimensional (a vector), two-dimensional (a matrix), or even multidimensional (i.e., Ada places no limit on the dimensionality of an array).[4] For example, a multidimensional data entity can be used to store the values of a table with uniform components, as follows:

---

With these constraints, the variable SWITCH could not be assigned the value OPEN or CLOSED, and the variable WEEK_DAY could not be assigned the value SATURDAY or SUNDAY.

[4]As an example of a *one-dimensional array*, we could establish a vector X as follows:

```
X : VECTOR;
```

where the defined type VECTOR can be syntactically defined to be an array type using the reserved words is array, as follows:

```
type COMPONENT_TYPES is digits 2 range 1.0..99.0;
type VECTOR is array(1..5) of COMPONENT_TYPES;
```

In this example, we have defined the entity X to consist of five components with indices 1 to 5, where each component is a real number with two decimal places lying between 1.0 and 99.0. Mathematically, we have established the following:

$X = x(1), x(2), x(3), x(4), x(5)$

In Ada, the components might be assigned the following values:

$X(1) = 55.44$
$X(2) = 77.62$
$X(3) = 23.48$
$X(4) = 12.51$
$X(5) = 88.92$

As an example of a *two-dimensional array*, we could establish a matrix Y as follows:

```
Y : MATRIX
```

where the defined type MATRIX could be given by

```
type ENTRY_TYPES is digits 3 range 1.0 ..50.0;
type MATRIX is array (1..5, 1, 5) of ENTRY_TYPES;
```

| Week Day | Hours Worked |
|---|---|
| Monday | 8 |
| Tuesday | 10 |
| Wednesday | 8 |
| Thursday | 12 |
| Friday | 8 |

A *record type* can be used to define a data entity with a set of components with nonuniform data types.[5] For example, a multidimensional data entity associated with a record type can be used to store the values of a table with nonuniform components, for example,

---

In this example, we have defined a matrix Y with five rows and five columns, where each entry of the matrix is to be a real number with three decimal places lying between 1.0 and 50.0. Mathematically, we have established the following:

$$Y = \begin{matrix} y(11) & y(21) & y(31) & y(41) & y(51) \\ y(12) & y(22) & y(32) & y(42) & y(52) \\ y(13) & y(23) & y(33) & y(43) & y(53) \\ y(14) & y(24) & y(34) & y(44) & y(54) \\ y(15) & y(25) & y(35) & y(45) & y(55) \end{matrix}$$

In Ada, the components can be assigned numeric values with three decimal places, as illustrated by the following values:

$Y(1,1) = 25.333$
$Y(1,2) = 14.154$

. . .

$Y(4,5) = 43.627$
$Y(5,5) = 32.138$

[5]Syntactically, we can declare the entity DATE to be of type DAY_OF_THE_YEAR, as follows:

```
DATE : DAY_OF_THE_YEAR ;
```

where the defined type DAY_OF_THE_YEAR can be defined to be a record type using the reserved words record and end record, as follows:

```
type MONTH_NAME is (JANUARY, FEBRUARY, MARCH, APRIL, MAY,
                    JUNE, JULY, AUGUST, SEPTEMBER, OCTOBER,
                    NOVEMBER, DECEMBER);

type DAY_OF_THE_YEAR
  record
    DAY   : INTEGER range 1..31 ;
    MONTH : MONTH_NAME ;
    YEAR  : INTEGER range 1..2000 ;
  end record;
```

| Date  | Value |
|-------|-------|
| Day   | 20    |
| Month | June  |
| Year  | 1940  |

## 5.2.2 Specifying Requirements for a Data Structure

When the design for a data structure to be implemented in Ada is being specified, descriptors can be used to characterize variables and their types to specify requirements for the data structure. For example, a design might specify an entity of an Ada data structure with the following descriptors:

- the name of the data entity
- the name of the independent package in which the data element is to be declared
- whether the data entity is to be visible or hidden
- the name of the type for the data entity
- the category of the type (e.g., scalar or composite)
- a concise and crisp description of the data entity, including the following information, as appropriate:
  —purpose and use
  —units of measure
  —format
  —the source of the data element (i.e., where it is generated)
  —the user of the data element
  —where the data element is stored (e.g., in the state variable part of an independent package's data structure, in a database, or in a data file)
  —the frequency at which the data entity is calculated, received, or exported

A sample standard template for this information is shown in Figure 5-2.

The data types named in this abstraction also have to be defined. For example, a design might use the following descriptors to define the Ada data types:

- the name of the data type
- the name of the independent package in which the type is to be declared

```
Name of Data Entity: _____
Name of Encapsulating Package: _____
Accessible to Other Independent Packages (Yes or No): _____
Name of Data Entity's Type: _____
Category of Type (Scalar, Composite, Private): _____
Description: _____
            _____
            _____
            _____
            _____
            _____
            _____
            _____
            _____
            _____
            _____
            _____
```

*FIGURE 5-2.* Standard template of descriptors for a data structure

- the category of the type (e.g., scalar or composite)
- if the type is scalar, whether the type is to be integer, real, or enumeration
  —for an integer type, the upper and lower limits on the range of permissible values (inclusive)
  —for a real type, the number of decimal places to be maintained, the upper and lower limits on the range of permissible values (inclusive), and, if applicable, the increment of coarseness in the real values (i.e., readings with a coarseness of 0.01 might be 1.01, 1.02, and so forth)
  —for an enumeration type, the set of permissible textual characters
- if the type is composite, whether the type is to be an array type or a record type
  —for an array type, the dimension of the array, the number of indices for each dimension, and the name of the type for the array's components
  —for a record type, the name of the components of the record and the name of the type for each component

A sample standard template for this information is shown in Figure 5-3.

### Example

During preparation of a design, a table of descriptor values can be used to specify data structures. As an example of this approach, let us address the data structure for the package ICU_MESSAGES in the ICU problem. This package is to account for the data and operations shown in Figure 5-4.

The design of this package is to specify a visible data structure accounting for messages to be received and to be routed to other packages. A possible specification for this data structure is shown in Table 5-1. Specifically, the Variables section of this table provides descriptors that define messages received from the radar station in format X and from the communications channels in format Z, as well as messages to be distributed to the operations centers in format Y. The Record Types section provides descriptors for record data types applicable to these formats. The Array Types section provides descriptors for an array type. The Scalar Types section provides descriptors for scalar data types applicable to components of the record and array types.

```
Name of Data Type: _____
Name of Encapsulating Package: _____
Category (Integer, Real or Enumeration): _____
  Permissible Values: _____
         _____
         _____
         _____

For a Real Type
  Number of Decimal Places: _____
  Increment of Coarseness: _____

For an Array Type
  Dimension: _____
  Number of Indices for each Dimension: _____

  Name of the Type of the Array's Components: _____

For a Record Type
  Name of each Component: _____
         _____
         _____
         _____
         _____

  Name of the Type for each Component: _____
         _____
         _____
         _____
         _____
         _____
```

FIGURE 5-3.   Standard template of descriptors for a data type

TABLE 5-1. Visible data structure in package ICU_ROUTER

| Name of Data Entity | Type | | Comments |
| --- | --- | --- | --- |
| | Name | Category | |
| | | **Variables** | |
| INPUT_MESSAGE | FORMAT_X | Composite | A message to be formatted as follows: |
| | | | • Byte 1 is a frame-start flag. |
| | | | • Byte 2 is the X coordinate of an aircraft's position. |
| | | | • Byte 3 is the Y coordinate of an aircraft's position. |
| | | | • Byte 4 is the Z coordinate of an aircraft's position. |
| | | | • Byte 5 is the velocity of the aircraft. |
| | | | • Byte 6 is an aircraft identifier. |
| | | | • Byte 7 is a flight path identifier. |
| | | | • Byte 8 is a frame-end flag. |
| SOURCE | TYPE_FOR_PLACE | Scalar | The data entities SOURCE, DESTINATION and |
| DESTINATION | TYPE_FOR_PLACE | Scalar | SOURCE_OR_DESTINATION are variables used to signify |
| SOURCE_OR_DESTINATION | TYPE_FOR_PLACE | Scalar | the source or destination of a message, as appropriate. |
| DATE | TYPE_FOR_DATE | Composite | |
| TIME | TYPE_FOR_TIME | Composite | |
| OUTPUT_MESSAGE | FORMAT_Y | Composite | A message to be formatted as follows: |
| | | | • Byte 1 is a frame-start flag. |
| | | | • Byte 2 is the aircraft identifier. |
| | | | • Byte 3 is the flight path identifier. |
| | | | • Byte 4 is an X coordinate. |
| | | | • Byte 5 is a Y coordinate. |
| | | | • Byte 6 is a Z coordinate. |
| | | | • Byte 7 is velocity. |
| | | | • Byte 8 is an end-frame flag. |

TABLE 5-1. (continued)

| Name of Data Type | Name of Each Component | Record Types Name of Type for Each Component | Comments |
|---|---|---|---|
| FORMAT_X | START_FRAME_FLAG | TYPE_FOR_FRAME_FLAGS | |
| | X_COORDINATE | TYPE_FOR_POSITION_COORDINATES | |
| | Y_COORDINATE | | |
| | Z_COORDINATE | | |
| | VELOCITY | TYPE_FOR_VELOCITY | |
| | AIRCRAFT_IDENTIFIER | TYPE_FOR_IDENTIFIERS | |
| | FLIGHT_PATH_IDENTIFIER | | |
| | END_FRAME_FLAG | TYPE_FOR_FRAME_FLAGS | |
| FORMAT_Z | START_FRAME_FLAG | TYPE_FOR_FRAME_FLAGS | |
| | FLIGHT_PATH_IDENTIFIER | TYPE_FOR_IDENTIFIERS | |
| | AIRCRAFT_IDENTIFIER | | |
| | VELOCITY | TYPE_FOR_VELOCITY | |
| | X_COORDINATE | TYPE_FOR_POSITION_COORDINATE | |
| | Y_COORDINATE | | |
| | Z_COORDINATE | | |
| | END_FRAME_FLAG | TYPE_FOR_FRAME_FLAGS | |
| FORMAT_Y | START_FRAME_FLAG | TYPE_FOR_FRAME_FLAGS | |
| | AIRCRAFT_IDENTIFIER | TYPE_FOR_IDENTIFIERS | |
| | FLIGHT_PATH_IDENTIFIER | | |
| | X_COORDINATE | TYPE_FOR_POSITION_COORDINATES | |
| | Y_COORDINATE | | |
| | Z_COORDINATE | | |
| | VELOCITY | TYPE_FOR_VELOCITY | |
| | END_FRAME_FLAG | TYPE_FOR_FRAME_FLAGS | |

TABLE 5-1. (continued)

**Record Types (continued)**

| Name of Data Type | Name of Each Component | Name of Type for Each Component | Comments |
|---|---|---|---|
| TYPE_FOR_DATE | DAY<br>MONTH | TYPE_FOR_DAY<br>TYPE_FOR_MONTH | |

**Array Types**

| Name of Data Type | Dimension | Indices for Dimension | Components Type | Comments |
|---|---|---|---|---|
| TYPE_FOR_TIME | One | 3 | TYPE_FOR_TIME_COMPONENT | |

**Scalar Types**

| Name of Data Type | Category | Permissible Values | Decimal Places/ Increment of Coarseness |
|---|---|---|---|
| TYPE_FOR_DESTINATIONS | Enumeration | CONSOLE_A, CONSOLE_B, both | |
| TYPE_FOR_FRAME_FLAGS | Integer | 1 to 10 | |
| TYPE_FOR_POSITION_COORDINATES | Real | 1.0 to 100,000.0 | One decimal place |
| TYPE_FOR_VELOCITY | Real | 1.0 to 1,000.0 | One decimal place |
| TYPE_FOR_IDENTIFIERS | Integer | 1 to 20 | |
| TYPE_FOR_REQUESTS | Enumeration | CONSOLE_A_REQUEST, CONSOLE_B_REQUEST | |
| TYPE_FOR_TIME_COMPONENT | Integer | 1 to 60 | |
| TYPE_FOR_DAY | Enumeration | MONDAY, TUESDAY, WEDNESDAY, THURSDAY, FRIDAY, SATURDAY, SUNDAY | |
| TYPE_FOR_MONTH | Enumeration | JANUARY, FEBRUARY, MARCH, APRIL, MAY, JUNE, JULY, AUGUST, SEPTEMBER, OCTOBER, NOVEMBER, DECEMBER | |
| TYPE_FOR_YEAR | Integer | 1989 to 1999 | |

| ICU_MESSAGES | |
|---|---|
| *Data* | *Operations* |
| Messages (format X) | Input received messages |
| Messages (format Z) | Determine destinations |
| Destination table | Prepare output messages |
| Destination of a message | Return output messages |
| Source of a message | |
| Messages (format Y) | |
| Flags | |
|    Destination of a message | |
|    Source of a message | |
|    Message kind (i.e., input or output) | |
|    Source or destination | |
| Variables | |
|    Time | |
|    Date | |
|      Day | |
|      Month | |
|      Year | |

*FIGURE 5-4.* Data and operations for package ICU_MESSAGES

The design for package ICU_MESSAGES also is to include a specification for the hidden data structure, accounting for the variables, constants, and types used in the formulation of operations internal to the package. A possible specification for this data structure is shown in Table 5-2. Specifically, the Variables section of this table provides descriptors that define variables; the Constants section provides descriptors defining constants; and the Scalar Types, Array Types, and Record Types sections provide descriptors that define scalar, array, and record types, respectively.

## 5.2.3 Additional Design Considerations

When designing a data structure for an independent package, various factors and additional Ada considerations can influence the design. This section addresses data structure design as a function of such factors, and the related Ada considerations. Specifically, it addresses reflecting in the design of a data structure the use of pointers to arrays and records of a database, the dynamic use of memory, restrictions on the passage of variables used in the formulating of a package's operations, and restrictions on the use of variable values in the internal design of an independent package.

TABLE 5-2. Hidden data structure in package ICU_Router

**Variables**

| Name of Data Entity | Type | | Comments |
| --- | --- | --- | --- |
| | Name | Category | |
| POSITION | TYPE_FOR_POSITION | Composite | The position of an aircraft in the X, Y, Z coordinates in meters |
| VELOCITY | TYPE_FOR_VELOCITY | Scalar | The velocity of an aircraft in meters per hour |
| OUTPUT_COMPONENT | TYPE_FOR_OUTPUT_COMPONENT | Composite | A formatted message with the following components:<br>• X coordinate<br>• Y coordinate<br>• Z coordinate<br>• velocity |

**Constants**

| Name of Constant | Value | Comments |
| --- | --- | --- |
| CALIBRATION_FACTOR_Z | 139.0 | Factor used to calibrate the information field of a message received in format Z from a communications channel |
| METERS_TO_FEET | 0.305 | Factor used to convert a coordinate reading in meters to feet |
| KILOMETER/HOUR_TO_MILES/HOUR | 0.620 | Factor used to convert a velocity value in kilometers per hour to miles per hour |

**Scalar Types**

| Name of Data Type | Category | Permissible Values | Comments<br>Decimal Places/Increment of Coarseness |
| --- | --- | --- | --- |
| TYPE_FOR_COORDINATE | Real | -1000.00 to 1000.00 | Two decimal places/0.1 increment of coarseness |
| TYPE_FOR_VELOCITY | Integer | 50 to 350 | |

TABLE 5-2. (continued)

**Array Types**

| Name of Data Type | Dimension | Indices per Dimension | Component Type | Comments |
|---|---|---|---|---|
| TYPE_FOR_POSITION | One | 3 | TYPE_FOR_COORDINATE | |

**Record Types**

| Name of Data Type | Name of Each Component | Name of Type for Each Component | Comments |
|---|---|---|---|
| TYPE_FOR_OUTPUT_COMPONENT | X_COORDINATE<br>Y_COORDINATE<br>Z_COORDINATE | TYPE_FOR_COORDINATE | |

### Pointers to Arrays and Records

The design of a data structure may have to reflect the use of pointers to arrays and records. In a design, it may be necessary to `pool` a large amount of data as a series of arrays and records (e.g., to maintain personnel data for a company, or reservations and flight information for an airline). For example, a designer may specify the retrieval of arrays and records of information from a database that is to be maintained by one independent package for subsequent processing by a second independent package. To meet this end, the designer could specify the use of procedure calls or task rendezvous. Data could then be moved from the database maintained by the first package to a buffer associated with the second package. This approach is clear and understandable, but the execution of its implementation may be unnecessarily time consuming.

As an alternative, a design could specify the use of pointers to the location in memory of the arrays and records. Then, rather than requiring the movement of all the data in the arrays and records, the design could specify moving only pointers. This approach would lead to a more efficient execution of the design implementation, since it will be less time consuming to move a pointer than a large amount of data.

Ada provides a mechanism for implementing pointers through its access type.[6] Access types are so called because variables declared to be an access type can take on values that refer to, and thus point to or provide access to, variables, including multicomponent variables as arrays and records.

---

[6]An access type declaration is written in Ada with the reserved word `access`. For example, in the following, `TYPE_FOR_POINTER` is the access type, and `POINTER` is the pointer or access variable.

```
type TYPE_FOR_LIST is
  record
    ITEM_A : INTEGER range 2..20;
    ITEM_B : INTEGER range 10..100;
    ITEM_C : INTEGER range 3..30;
    ITEM_D : INTEGER range 5..50;
  end record;
type TYPE_FOR_POINTER is access TYPE_FOR_LIST;
POINTER : TYPE_FOR_POINTER;
```

Initially `POINTER` is set to the value null (indicating that it points to nothing, i.e., Ada defines an implicit default value). A reference value can be assigned to `POINTER` through the reserved word new as follows:

```
POINTER := new TYPE_FOR_LIST;
```

As an example, consider a design for collecting together a set of experiment readings into a data sample. The design is to require the data sample to consist of a fixed number of experiment readings to be stored as an array. The contents of the sample are to be collected together and saved by a DATABASE_MANAGER package, and operated by a second package named STATISTICS. A pointer is to be assigned to the data sample in a variable SAMPLE_POINTER. To meet this end, the design specifies an access type as follows:

| Name of Data Entity | Type | |
| --- | --- | --- |
| | Name | Category |
| SAMPLE_POINTER | TYPE_FOR_SAMPLE_POINTER | Access |

Then, a procedure visible in the second package STATISTICS can call a procedure in the package DATABASE_MANAGER and receive (in the out mode) the pointer value in SAMPLE_POINTER.

### Dynamic Allocation of Data

The design of a data structure can reflect the use of pointers in dynamically assigning variable values to memory. In an independent package, the design for the data structure is easy to understand when it is static in nature (i.e., of known content and specific size). If memory restrictions exist, however, such a design can result in an unsatisfactory waste of storage. Also, such a design could lead to problems if, in practice, data amounts exceed those expected due to growth beyond allocated bounds. In such cases, data could be lost during program execution. Because of these factors, it might be better to formulate a design that calls for the dynamic use of available storage space. The Ada access type can be used to implement such a design, as a linked list with no specific restriction as to the size of the list. Specifically, the list can contain the values of each variable in the list and a pointer to each of the variable values. The list can grow as necessary by establishing a pointer for each variable value added to the list.

### Private Types and Limited Private Types

The design of data structures can reflect restrictions on the use of variable values exported from one independent package to another. As discussed in Chapter 4, data entities passed from one independent package to another should not, to the extent possible, include the values of variables, types, or flags used in the formulation of services of the independent package, referred to as its state variables. If such a variable or flag has to be exported, its type should be declared private or limited private in the visible part of the package's specifications to restrict its use.[7] If a data entity is declared private, only operations defined within the package specification can be applied to it, along with assignments and tests for equality. If a state variable is declared limited private, then assignments and tests for equality are no longer automatically available. By restricting accessibility of a data entity using a private or limited private type, we can enforce the privacy of data entities encapsulated in the implementation of an independent package. Private and limited private types therefore provide capabilities for control over the operations available on a state variable exported from one package implementation to another.

### Ada Typing and the Detailed Design of an Independent Package

The detailed design of an independent package can lead to detailed refinements of its data structure. When specifying the detailed internal operations of an independent package, Ada provides capabilities to constrain the use of a data type. For example, in the application of a specific type, a design could specify that a variable is to be constrained to a subset of the values permitted for a specific type. As a simple example, a variable WEEK_DAY could be of a type DAYS_OF_THE_WEEK but constrained to MONDAY through FRIDAY. When this is the case, an Ada subtype can be used.[8]

---

[7]Syntactically, a type can be declared private using the Ada keywords is private, as follows:

```
type STATE_ENTITY_A_CONSTRAINT is private;
```

The full declaration provided in a private part of a package specification using the Ada keyword private is shown in the following example:

```
package OBJECT_I_IMPLEMENTATION is
   type STATE_ENTITY_A_CONSTRAINT is private;
   . . .
private
   type STATE_ENTITY_A_CONSTRAINT is INTEGER range 0..15;
end OBJECT_I_IMPLEMENTATION;
```

[8]Syntactically, a subtype can be declared using the Ada keyword subtype as follows:

```
subtype WEEK_DAY is DAYS_OF_THE_WEEK range MONDAY. .FRIDAY
```

As another detailed design consideration, a design may result in two or more variables that are similar in structure but are to be treated separately. When this is the case, an Ada derived type can be used.[9]

Such low-level design considerations may well not appear in the specification of the design for a large and complex computer program. Upon implementation of a design by a programmer, however, such detailed design judgements may be made and documented by the programmer (e.g., through comments in the source statement listing).

### Check if the Data Structure is Comprehensible

The design for a data structure should be clear, crisp, and easy to comprehend. If in the judgement of a design review team this is not the case for a specific independent package, changes to that design should be considered. As one approach, requirements for the problematic package can be thought of as defining a separate problem. A design for this problem can then be undertaken, specifying two or more new independent packages with their own new data structures. These data structures should be clear and comprehensible. Applying this process, a large and cumbersome data structure can be eliminated, and replaced by new structures for each of the new independent packages introduced into the design. This is very important from an engineering point of view, since clear and understandable data structures are fundamental to cost-effective computer program implementation and maintenance.

## 5.3   Key Concepts

- Data entities internal to the implementation of an independent package may include constants, single-valued scalar variables, and composite variables that are assigned two or more values at one time (e.g., vectors, matrices, and other multivalued entities). These data entities can be organized, ordered, and constrained in the design for a data structure of an independent package.
- In Ada, the concept of *type* is used to organize, order, and constrain data entities as a data structure. Ada is said to be a strongly typed language. By that, we mean the following:

---

[9]Syntactically, a derived type can be declared using the Ada key words `is new` as follows:

```
type MERCEDES is new TYPE_FOR_CAR;
type FORD is new TYPE_FOR_CAR;
```

- Every variable has a unique type.
- The definition of a type specifies values permissible for a variable.
- In the assignment of a value to a variable, the type of the value and the type of the variable must be the same.
- Every operator applied to a variable must belong to the set of operations defined by the variable type.

■ The Ada type associated with a scalar variable can constrain that scalar variable to one value from a set of integers, real numbers, or ordered lists of textual characters (e.g., the variable COLOR might be constrained to the values RED, WHITE, and BLUE). Types constraining variables to real numbers can also constrain the number of decimal places to be maintained and their increment of coarseness (e.g., variable values with a coarseness of 0.01 might be 1.01, 1.02, and so forth).

■ Ada types available to constrain a multivalued composite data entity include array types and record types. For an array type, a design can use descriptors to indicate the dimension of the array, the number of indices for each dimension, and the name of the type that constrains the array components. For a record type, a design can use descriptors to indicate the name of each component of the record and the name of the type unique to each component of the record.

■ Some data entities collected or operated on by program units within an independent package may not be predetermined or of known bounds. A designer could apply static data types to establish the maximum bounds on such data. However, when such a bound results in the unsatisfactory waste of storage or other problems, a designer should utilize dynamic means of using available storage space. To meet this end, Ada provides a mechanism for allocating data entities dynamically with its access type.

■ Parameters passed from one independent package to another should not include the values of variables, types, and flags used in the formulation of operations within an independent package. If for some reason such data entities have to be exported, they should be declared private or limited private in the visible part of the object's package specification. This restricts the use of such state variables.

## 5.4    Exercises

1. How does Ada establish a data structure?
2. What constraints can be put on real numbers using Ada typing?
3. What constraints can be put on multilevel composite data entities using Ada typing?
4. Give an example of a data structure design for variables unique to an independent package. Specify the requirements for the data structure in a table, where the variables are to include a counter with positive integer values not to exceed 100, a variable with one decimal place not to exceed 1000, a variable with two decimal places not to exceed 500 and with a .01 increment of coarseness, a variable that can take the values ORANGE and GREEN, and a three-dimensional vector.
5. Specify in a table the requirements for a data structure record that contains two variables and the date the variables are received, where each variable is to be a real number with one decimal place and is not to exceed 10.

# CHAPTER 6

# Design of Operations Internal to an Independent Package

The software design for an independent package as a model of a real-world entity specifies operations to be performed by program units in the package, as well as a data structure. Depending on the scope of requirements needed to characterize the real-world entity, in some cases the operations may be concise and straightforward, perhaps exclusively accounted for in program units to be visible in the package. In other cases, the operations may be extensive and complex, perhaps accounted for in a set of program units both visible and internal to the package.

## 6.1 Introduction

This chapter examines the design of operations unique to an independent package. A design specifies a set of program units used to segment processing operations into easily understood and cohesive parts, and specific operations that are to be undertaken by each of the program units. Capabilities offered by Ada determine how such operations can be formulated; this chapter provides an overview of such basic Ada capabilities. Readers familiar with these features of Ada need not read this chapter. Other readers should view this chapter as an introduction to the basic Ada capabilities. (Refer to a book on programming with Ada for a detailed discussion on Ada source statements available to implement operations.)

## 6.2 Operations and Ada

### 6.2.1 Basic Concepts

Requirements for an independent package include attributes and services. As a model of a real-world entity, the design for an independent package models attributes in a data structure and services in operations. The operations account for *actions* to be taken, including data movement, the transformation of data from one form to another, and the storage and retrieval of data. For example, a basic action would be to model a queue in which elements are added to the end of the queue and removed from the front of the queue. Another basic action would be to model a stack like those used in a restaurant for storing plates; elements are added and removed only at the top of the queue.

In a design for operations, the sequence in which actions are to be taken must be specified clearly and unambiguously. The design therefore should specify *control logic* that determines the specific sequence of actions to be taken by the program. A basic example of control logic is conditional branching of the form "if $Q$ then do $A$ otherwise do $B$" (or just "if $Q$ then do $A$"), where $Q$ is some condition. Another basic example is direct sequencing of the form "do $A$ followed by $B$" (or "do $A$ and then $B$").

These operations can be specified by introducing iteration and looping into a design. A basic example is bounded iteration of the form "do $A$ exactly $N$ times" (where $N$ is a number). Another example is conditional iteration of the form "do $A$ until $Q$" (or "while $Q$ do $A$"), where $Q$ is a condition.

A design for relatively complex operations may require the use of control-flow in nontrivial combinations. Sequencing, branching, and iteration can be interleaved and nested within each other. For example, a design can specify nested iterations (referred to as nested loops) of the form "do $A$ exactly $N$ times," where $A$ itself is of the form "do $B$ until $Q$." When a program that implements such logic is executed, each time the outer loop is traversed, the inner loop is traversed repeatedly until $Q$ becomes true. Of course, the $A$ part of the outer loop could contain many other subparts, each of which can in turn employ sequencing, branching, and iteration.

### 6.2.2 Establishing Logic with Ada

To implement control logic specified in a design, Ada provides if statements, case statements, and loop statements. An if statement specifies an alternative action to be taken depending on a condition.[1] A case statement makes multiple tests of a variable. Since only one alternative is selected, the alternatives must be mutually exclusive.[2] A loop statement is used to repeat execution of a sequence of statements.[3]

---

[1]In Ada, the reserved words if, then, else, and end if establish if statements. For example, a variable X can be tested as follows:

```
if X > 0 then
     Y := 1;
else
     Y := -1;
end if;
```

In this example, the statement between then and else is executed when the condition X > 0 is true. Otherwise, the statement between else and end if is executed. If the latter were not required, it could be omitted to yield the following:

```
if X > 0 then
     Y:=1;
end if;
```

For multiple tests of a variable, multiple responses can be established using elsif, as follows:

```
if X = 1 then
     Y := 2;
elsif X = 2 then
     Y := 3;
else
     Y := 4;
end if;
```

[2]An example of an Ada case statement is

```
case X is
  when 1 => Y := 2;
  when 2 => Y := 3;
  when 3 => Y := 4;
  when others => null;
end case;
```

[3]The number of repetitions of a loop can be set with a for iteration clause, for example:

```
FACTORIAL := 1;
for I in 2 .. N loop
  FACTORIAL := FACTORIAL*I;
end loop;
```

In this example, the index I successively takes on the values 2, 3, ... N. When the loop is completed, the factorial N! has been calculated and assigned to the variable FACTORIAL, while the index I ceases to exist. If not specifically defined, the type of the loop parameter is inferred from the type of the range bound (i.e., in this example, the index I is the same type as N).

## 6.2.3  Actions

In the design for an independent package, the package's unique operations are specified by action to be taken in conjunction with control logic. For example, the value of one variable may have to be assigned to another variable, components of tables may have to be accessed, vector and matrix components may have to be accessed, and various mathematical algorithms may have to be performed. Therefore, the preparation of a design for operations to be implemented in Ada requires knowledge of Ada features relevant to using scalar variables, arrays, and records, all in the context of Ada typing rules.

### *Using Scalar Variables*

As part of the design for an independent package, it may be necessary to assign a value computed in an arithmetic expression to a scalar variable.[4] In Ada, for an assignment of a value to a scalar variable, the type of the value and the type of the scalar variable must be the same. This means, for example, that a scalar variable of type `INTEGER` cannot be assigned an ASCII character.

When preparing a design, the designer can take advantage of Ada typing rules to control how values are assigned to different variables.

---

In contrast with a loop of predefined size in a `for` iteration, the Ada `while` iteration can be used to loop until a specified condition is no longer true. For example,

```
A := 0;
B := 1;
while A < N loop
   B := B + 1;
   A := A + B*B;
end loop;
```

As an alternative, the keyword `exit` could be used to establish an unconditional exit from the loop, as follows:

```
A := 0;
B := 1;
loop
   B := B + 1;
   A := A + B*B;
   exit when A < N;
end loop;
```

[4]Syntactically, the assignment is accomplished by use of the symbol `:=` between the variable and the expression. For example, we can cause $z$ to take the value of the sum of $x$ and $y$ in Ada as follows:

```
Z := X + Y;
```

where Z, X, and Y must be declared of the same type.

As an example, consider a package implementation that reads in the names and ages of several people. Ada typing rules mandate that ages not be assigned to variables of enumeration types (for names) and names not be assigned to variables of integer types (for ages). Furthermore, in the design for such a package, variables for age numbers may not be the only variables to which integers can be assigned. For example, data received for different people could include the number of years of employment at their latest employer and the number of years they have lived at their current address. In this case, the variables AGE_OF_PERSON, YEARS_OF_EMPLOYMENT, and YEARS_AT_CURRENT_ADDRESS are all declared of the type INTEGER. We do not want a person's age assigned to YEARS_OF_EMPLOYMENT, the years at a current address assigned to AGE_OF_PERSON, or other inappropriate assignments. With Ada, we can avoid such inappropriate assignments by defining separate distinct types for AGE_OF_PERSON, YEARS_OF_EMPLOYMENT, and YEARS_AT_CURRENT_ADDRESS.[5]

### Using Arrays

As part of the design for an independent package, it may be necessary to move data encompassed by one array to a second array. As a basic Ada feature, such whole array assignments require arrays of equal size. For example, if

```
ARRAY_A : VECTOR_A(0..9);
ARRAY_B : VECTOR_B(0..9);
```

then

```
ARRAY_A := ARRAY_B;
```

---

[5]Syntactically, derived types are implemented with the Ada reserved words is new, as follows:

```
type TYPE_FOR_AGE_OF_PERSON is new INTEGER range 0 . . 120;
type TYPE_FOR_YEARS_OF_EMPLOYMENT is new INTEGER range
                                               0 . . 50;
type TYPE_FOR_YEARS_AT_CURRENT_ADDRESS is new INTEGER range
                                               0 . . 70;
```

These types all have properties of an INTEGER type; nevertheless, they can be used to make AGE_OF_PERSON, YEARS_OF_EMPLOYMENT, and YEARS_AT_CURRENT_ADDRESS distinct. Accordingly, AGE_OF_PERSON := YEARS_OF_EMPLOYMENT; is not legal. AGE_OF_PERSON := 150; is also illegal because 150 is greater than the declared bound in the type TYPE_FOR_AGE_OF_PERSON.

can be used to assign all the components of ARRAY_B to ARRAY_A. If the size of ARRAY_A is not equal to the size of ARRAY_B, the assignment is not legal.

To satisfy software requirements in a design, it may be necessary to access and utilize components of an array. This is accomplished syntactically by indexing an array's name, as shown in the following example for a one-dimensional array:

```
ARRAY_A(1) := ARRAY_B(4);
```

or as shown in the following example for a two-dimensional array named MATRIX[6]:

```
MATRIX(1,1) := 0;
MATRIX(1,2) := 5;
MATRIX(2,1) := 10;
      .
      .
      .
MATRIX(10,10) := 100;
```

Not only can we refer to a single component, we can also name a set of consecutive components in a one-dimensional array, called a slice. Slices are useful if large blocks of data have to be moved from one array to another. For example,

```
DATA_SUBSET(1..20) := DATA_RECORD(31..50);
```

### Using Records

To satisfy software requirements in a design, it may be necessary to access components of a record. This is accomplished syntactically by writing the name of the record, a period, and the name of the component, as illustrated by the following example:

```
RECORD_NAME.COMPONENT_A := RED;
```

where we have assigned the word RED to COMPONENT_A of record RECORD_NAME. The component of the record may be a scalar variable, an array, or even another record, in each case subject to the Ada typing rules.

---

[6]In addition to the assignment operation, the comparison operations = and /= can be applied to any two arrays of the same type and size. For a one-dimensional array, additional operations are applicable (e.g., <, <=, >, and >=).

## 6.2.4 Exception Handling

Ada provides an explicit mechanism for responding to anomalies that may occur in the execution of code that implements an independent package. The anomalies could be associated with, for example, erroneous overflow conditions, violations of typing constraints, dividing by zero, or the assignment of unacceptable values to a variable. The exception handling mechanism can check for specific anomalies at critical points, suspend execution upon detection of an anomaly, and transfer control to an exception handler. The exception handler then makes an appropriate programmed response to the anomaly. Upon completion of processing in the exception handler, control transfers out of the enclosing program unit or block body.

This feature of Ada allows continued execution of an independent package even when problems occur. In an exception handler, different courses of action are possible. The exception handler can again try the operation that led to the error, initiate an alternative course of action, print out an error message and abort the attempted processing, or attempt to determine the reason for the error and introduce corrective action.[7]

## 6.2.5 Segmenting Operations among Modules

### Basic Concepts

A design for operations unique to an independent package should specify a set of modules to be used to segment the operations into

---

[7]For a simple example of Ada syntax for exception handling, consider a scalar variable X that is supposed to be positive at all times in the execution of a program unit. A design for the program unit can specify that X is to be checked at strategic points in the sequential and logical flow of actions to be performed, and an exception raised if it is not positive. Syntactically, this could be accomplished as follows:

```
    . . .
SIGN_ERROR : exception;
    . . .
if X < 0 then
  raise SIGN_ERROR;
end if;
    . . .
exception
  when SIGN ERROR=>
  --sequence of statements dictating
  --a response to the error X < 0
end;
```

easily understood and cohesive parts and the Ada program units to be used to implement each module. For simple operations, the design might segment processing operations among visible Ada program units declared in the specification of the Ada package, as illustrated in Figure 6-1(a).

For complex and extensive operations, the design might segment processing operations among program units visible in a package, and program units to be called by the visible program units. The called program units are to be hidden in the body of an Ada package, as illustrated in Figure 6-1(b).

The selection and organization of the program units in a design for an independent package are determined by the designer. In most cases, there is no optimum way to select and organize the program units. Because of this, different designers could produce different organizations of program units for the same independent package, as illustrated in Figure 6-2. Regardless of the pattern of program units specified, designs should segment processing internal to an independent package among a set of relatively small program units that are easy to understand and implement. The design for each program unit should be constrained to seven or fewer variables, and typically should be implementable with 200 or fewer Ada source statements.

### Design Example

As an example, let us address a design for operations unique to the ICU_MESSAGES package of the ICU. A designer could specify segmenting operations among a set of program units organized as shown in Figure 6-3(a), with data flow between the program units as shown in Figure 6-3(b). In this design, the ROUTE_INFO procedure is presumed to have received an input message and an indication of its source. ROUTE_INFO forwards the input message in INPUT_MESSAGE and the source in SOURCE to the ESTABLISH_OUTPUT_MESSAGE procedure, which coordinates the construction of output messages for subsequent routing. The ESTABLISH_OUTPUT_MESSAGE procedure forwards the input message to the STRIP_FORMAT_X (or Z) procedure. This procedure could, for example, strip off control fields to isolate the data embedded in the information field of the message, which indicate the position of an aircraft and its velocity. The position is inserted into a vector POSITION and the velocity into a scalar VELOCITY. The vector and scalar are forwarded to the CALIBRATE procedure for proper calibration as a function of the message source (i.e., communications channel or radar). The calibrated vector POSITION and the calibrated scalar VELOCITY are returned to the

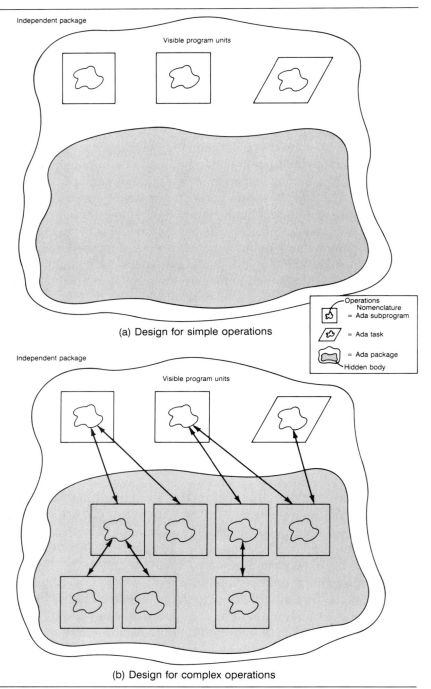

Independent package

Visible program units

Operations
Nomenclature
= Ada subprogram

= Ada task

= Ada package
Hidden body

(a) Design for simple operations

Independent package

Visible program units

(b) Design for complex operations

FIGURE 6-1.   Design for an independent package

**114**   BASIC DESIGN CONSIDERATIONS

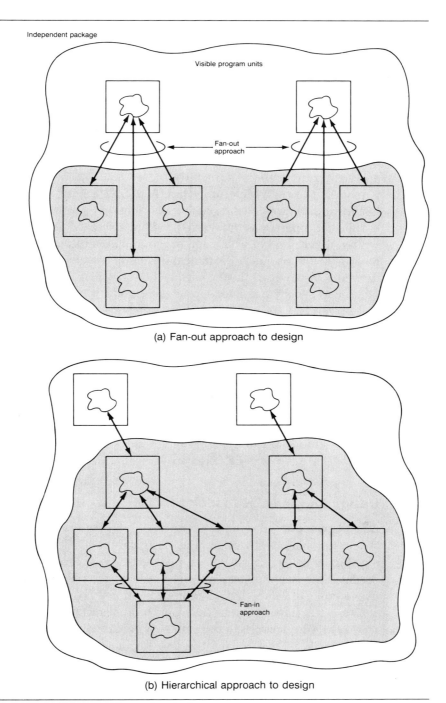

Independent package

Visible program units

Fan-out
approach

(a) Fan-out approach to design

Fan-in
approach

(b) Hierarchical approach to design

*FIGURE 6-2.* Alternative designs

STRIP_FORMAT procedure, which in turn returns them to the ESTABLISH_OUTPUT_MESSAGES procedure. They are then forwarded to the BUILD_FORMAT procedure. This procedure calls the SET_UNITS procedure to convert position and velocity components to the proper units. The BUILD_FORMAT procedure then establishes OUTPUT_COMPONENTS, which consists of the position vector, velocity scalar, and message start and end flags. The BUILD_FORMAT procedure forwards OUTPUT_COMPONENTS to the ESTABLISH_OUTPUT_ MESSAGE procedure, which adds the aircraft identification number and flight path number to form OUTPUT_MESSAGE. OUTPUT_MESSAGE is exported to the visible procedure ROUTE_INFO for storage in a historical database and subsequent distribution.

Specific operations for each program unit can be listed in a written description of what each program unit is to do, or they can be specified in pseudocode, indicating actions, decision points, and iterations. As an example, the pseudocode shown in Figure 6-4 could be used to specify operations to be undertaken by the ROUTE_INFO and ESTABLISH_OUTPUT_MESSAGES procedures. These procedures are to transform a received input message into an output message. The pseudocode uses Ada if statements to specify conditional branching, with the Ada keywords if, then, elsif, else, and end if. Specifically, in the pseudocode for the ESTABLISH_OUTPUT_ MESSAGE procedure, the source flag is checked to determine the format of the received message. In the pseudocode for the ROUTE _INFO procedure, the source flag is checked depending on its value, used to set a destination flag. Program unit calls are also specified, and specific actions to be taken are indicated by English text.

### 6.2.6  Design for Reusable Modules

#### Basic Concepts

When formulating a design, the designer may consider reusing existing modules that have been cataloged for easy reference, standardized for easy application, and validated for reliable operation over a range of values and operating conditions. To be able to notice software design requirements that could be implemented by an existing module, the designer has to be completely familiar with the catalog. For each module in the catalog, the designer must know exactly what operations it encompasses and other design considerations such as what input the module is to receive and in what form, how it outputs information, and how it has been validated. A designer who is sufficiently familiar with a set of existing modules can recognize specific

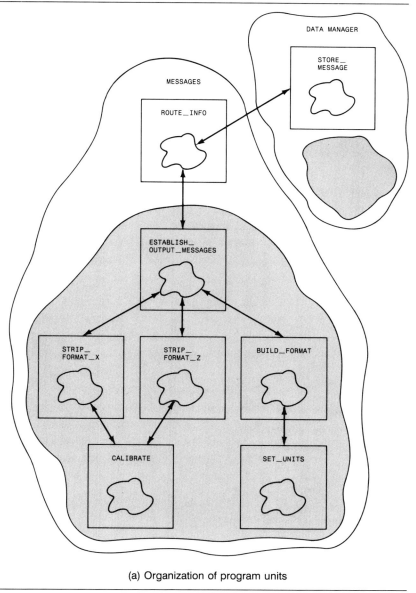

(a) Organization of program units

*FIGURE 6-3.* Internal design of ICU MESSAGES package

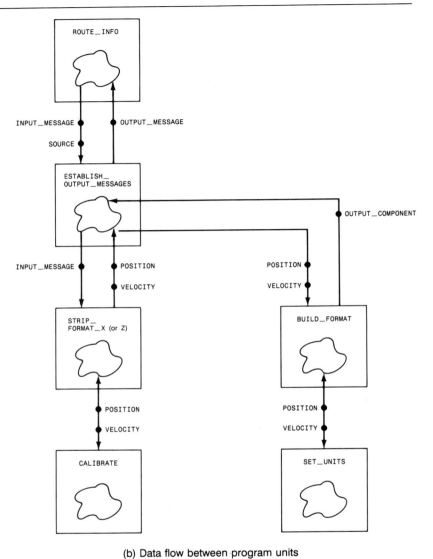

(b) Data flow between program units

*FIGURE 6-3.* (*continued*)

Begin Procedure ROUTE_INFO

Receive an input message in INPUT_MESSAGE and its source in SOURCE

Call Procedure ESTABLISH_OUTPUT_MESSAGES
to establish an output message in OUTPUT_MESSAGE

Receive OUTPUT_MESSAGE from Procedure ESTABLISH_OUTPUT_MESSAGE

Determine the destination of OUTPUT_MESSAGE as follows:
If SOURCE indicates the radar station then
    set DESTINATION to A_and_B (to signify both operations centers)
elsif SOURCE indicates Communication Channel a then
    set DESTINATION to A (to signify Operations Center A)
elsif SOURCE indicates Communication Channel b then
    set DESTINATION to B (to signify Operations Center B)
elsif SOURCE indicates Communication Channel c or d then
    set DESTINATION to A_and_B
else set OUTPUT_MESSAGE and DESTINATION to zero (to signify incorrect
            value found in SOURCE)
end if
Forward OUTPUT_MESSAGE and DESTINATION to caller
End Procedure ROUTE_INFO


Begin Procedure ESTABLISH_OUTPUT_MESSAGE

Receive input message in INPUT_MESSAGE and its source in SOURCE

If SOURCE is RADAR_STATION then
    Call Procedure STRIP_FORMAT_X
        to obtain the calibrated position vector in POSITION and velocity in VELOCITY

Elsif SOURCE is COMM_A, COMM_B, COMM_C or COMM_D then
    Call Procedure STRIP_FORMAT_Z
        to obtain the calibrated position vector in POSITION and velocity in VELOCITY

End if

Call Procedure BUILD_FORMAT
    to establish output message components in proper units

Construct OUTPUT_MESSAGE
    consisting of the frame start flag, x position, y position, z position, velocity, and
    frame end flag

Return OUTPUT_COMPONENTS to caller
End Procedure ESTABLISH_OUTPUT_MESSAGE

FIGURE 6-4.   Pseudocode for ESTABLISH_OUTPUT_MESSAGES procedure

design requirements that can be implemented using one or more of the existing modules. A catalog of reusable modules might include, for example, Ada functions for trigonometric functions and Ada procedures for stacks, queues, and trees.

### Generic Ada Subprograms

To increase the possibility of its being reused, an existing Ada subprogram can be made generic. (An Ada package can also be made generic, but an Ada task cannot.) A generic subprogram can be thought of as a nonexecutable template with incomplete type defintions that can be tailored to satisfy different needs. The incomplete type definitions are completed to establish different instances or versions of the sub-program. In essence, a generic subprogram is a shell or pattern that is not executable. Rather, it is a completed version of the generic subprogram (as a specific instance of the shell) that is executed.

Syntactically, a generic subprogram has a generic formal part that declares any generic formal parameters.[8] The generic part can contain incomplete type defintions.[9] The incomplete type definitions are completed (to establish specific constraints on data entities) at instantiation, where a specific name is assigned to the instance of the subprogram.[10] This generality in type definitions helps support wider

---

[8]An example of a generic procedure is
```
generic
  . . .
procedure EX_PATTERN is
  . . .
end EX_PATTERN;
```

[9]An example of a dummy type for a generic procedure is
```
generic
  type GENERAL is (<>);
  . . .
procedure EX_PATTERN is
begin
  . . .
end EX_PATTERN;
```
where the box symbol <> denotes any discrete type.

[10]An example of an instantiation of a generic procedure is
```
type SPECIFIC_PARTS is (SCREW,BOLT,NUT);
procedure BIKE_ASSEMBLY is new EX_PATTERN(GENERAL =>
SPECIFIC_PARTS);
```

*TABLE 6-1.* Examples of generic type definitions

| Kind of incomplete type | Example |
|---|---|
| Enumeration | `type ENUMERATION is (<>);` |
| Integer | `type INTEGER_ELEMENT is range <>;` |
| Fixed point | `type FIXED_ELEMENT is delta <>;` |
| Floating point | `type FLOAT_ELEMENT is digits <>;` |
| Array | `type ARRAY_ELEMENT is array (SOME_TYPE range <>) of SOME_ELEMENT;` |

reuse of a subprogram. Table 6-1 lists various generic type parameters. As subprograms, both procedures and functions can be generic.[11]

## Design Considerations

A design can specify the reuse of an existing module when planned operations match the functionality of the existing module, and the existing module has been validated to operate in a reliable manner over the range of values and conditions inherent in the problem. Such validation of a module is obtained through extensive testing.

In general, reusable modules should be firm and fixed in nature and not subject to change. In addition, they should have been tested extensively in both nominal and stress situations and for extended periods of time. Better yet, they should have been proved mature and reliable through widespread use.

If a design includes a module with requirements close to the capabilities of an existing module but not exactly matching functionality or range of operations (or both), then the existing module has to be modified. Such modification requires extensive retesting, changes to user manuals, changes to design documentation and test procedures, and so forth. Some industry observers feel that reuse of a module subject to modification is not necessarily reliable or cost effective.

---

[11]An example of a generic function is
```
generic
   type DISCRETE is (<>);
function EX_SHELL (X: in DISCRETE) return DISCRETE;
```
which can be instantiated in different ways, such as the following:
```
function SPECIFIC_A is new EX_SHELL(INTEGER);
function SPECIFIC_B is new EX_SHELL(BOOLEAN);
```

## 6.3    Key Concepts

- When designing the operations for an independent package to be implemented in Ada, the designer should specify actions, logic, and exceptions unique to that package.
- With respect to decisions to be made and loops to be established, Ada provides various if statements (e.g., if-then, if-then-else, and if-then-elsif), case statements (i.e., multiple tests of a variable), and loop statements (e.g., loop-while).
- For actions to be performed, values can be assigned to scalar variables, arrays, and records. All assignments have to be made in the context of Ada typing rules.
- For exceptions, Ada provides an explicit mechanism for responding to an anomaly that may occur in the execution of code that implements an operation (e.g., erroneous overflow conditions, dividing by zero, and the assignment of unacceptable values to a variable).
- In the design for an independent package, operations are segmented among visible and hidden program units.
- A designer can specify that an existing Ada module be reused. An existing module can be implemented as a generic Ada subprogram. A generic subprogram can be thought of as a nonexecutable template with incomplete type definitions that can be tailored to satisfy different needs. In essence, a generic subprogram is a shell or pattern that is not to be executed. Completed versions establish specific instances of the shell that are executable.

## 6.4    Exercises

1. Give examples of Ada logic that can be used to specify conditional branching, bounded iteration, conditional iteration, and nested iteration in design for operations.
2. Present design requirements for operations in an Ada subprogram that is to calculate the area of a square, a rectangle, or a circle, upon request by a user.
3. How does a design specify the use of an Ada exception? Give an example.
4. Present design requirements for an exception in an Ada subprogram, where the exception is initiated when values assigned to a variable are outside permissible bounds. If the value is too large, set the variable to its largest permissible value. If the value is too small, set the variable to its lowest permissible value.

# CHAPTER 7

# Design for Classes of Data and Concurrent Operations

In a real-world problem, a set of real-world entities may receive, filter, organize, and store a large amount of data. For such problems, two or more of the real-world entities may be characterized by similar attributes and services. When this is the case, it may be possible to organize common attributes and services into a class and develop a design that recognizes commonality in data and operations that model the class.

## 7.1    Introduction

As a basic approach, an Ada package can be used to model a class. Common data and operations of the class can be reapplied (reused) several times by other packages, which are often referred to as members of the class. This leads to the general subject of reusing Ada packages, increasing the scope of reusable packages through Ada generics, and designing a class as a generic Ada package. Correspondingly, a design can account for multiple concurrent services that are similar in nature through the application of an Ada task type. (Basic examples of syntax for Ada generic packages and task types are given. For a more detailed discussion on Ada generics and task types, refer to programming books on Ada.)

## 7.2 Analyzing Requirements for Computer Programs with Complex Data Structures

### 7.2.1 Class-Member Relationship

Similar to object-oriented analysis, a class of requirements could be thought of as encompassing attributes and services common to a group of two or more independent packages. Attributes and services unique to each individual package in the group are said to define members of the class. The relationship of a class to its members is represented graphically in Figure 7-1. As shown, the class and the members of the class are represented by rectangles with rounded corners, each of which is divided into three parts. The upper part denotes the name of the class or member, the middle part lists the names of applicable attributes, and the lower part lists the names of applicable services. In the terminology of object-oriented design, attributes of a class are said to be "inherited" by its members.

To organize requirements for a program in this way, we

- identify and define attributes and services for each package to be used to model the problem
- identify the subset of the attributes and services common to two or more of the packages

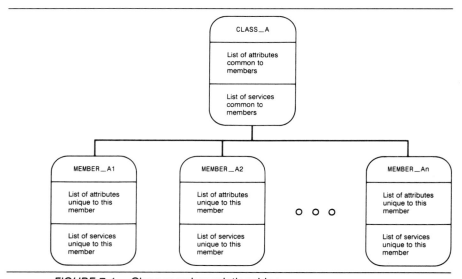

FIGURE 7-1. Class-member relationships

- group the common attributes and services together to define a class

For example, consider attributes and services that have been assigned to the following set of independent packages:

- Independent package CAR
    - Id, Name, Base, Passenger Capacity, License Number, Vehicle Identification Number
    - Passenger Movement, Local Delivery
- Independent package AIRCRAFT
    - Id, Name, Base, Passenger Capacity, Number of Engines, Missiles
    - Passenger Movement, Air Mail Delivery
- Independent package SHIP
    - Id, Name, Base, Passenger Capacity, Tonnage, Missiles
    - Passenger Movement, Fishing Trips

These attributes and services can be distributed into the class-member structure shown in Figure 7-2. In the list of attributes, the attributes Id, Name, Base and Passenger Capacity are common to the set of members and thus are assigned to the class. The attributes License Number and Vehicle Identification Number are unique to the member named CAR, the attributes Number of Engines and Missiles are unique to the member named AIRCRAFT, and the attributes Tonnage and Missiles are unique to the member SHIP. Correspondingly, the service Passenger Movement is common to the set of members and is assigned to the class. The service Local Delivery is unique to the member CAR, the service Air Mail Delivery is unique to the member AIRCRAFT, and the service Fishing Trips is unique to the member SHIP.

In object-oriented analysis, relationships between members (if any) can also be determined and shown graphically in a class-member structure by drawing lines between the members that interact. However, lines should never connect class icons, since classes are passive entities that do not execute. As shown in Figure 7-3(a), an arrowhead can point to the package that is to receive data or services. As shown in Figure 7-3(b), an arrow can point to both of the connected packages if both packages are to supply data or services to each other.

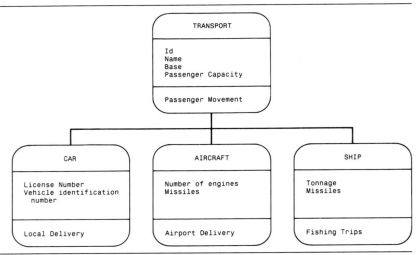

FIGURE 7-2.   Sample representation of class names, attributes, services, and inherited attributes and services

As shown in Figure 7-3(c), a tilde near the appropriate end of the connecting line indicates any constraints or conditionality associated with the relationship. As this item also shows, attributes that are directly involved in the relationship between packages are shown adjacent to the connecting line.

## 7.2.2  Attributes and Services

As discussed in earlier chapters, Ada packages can be used to model real-world entities in software designs. In such designs, attributes found in the requirements are modeled by data entities declared in the packages. *Attributes* characterize separate and distinct aspects of a real-world entity. For example, the attributes of a sensor might include the sensor's identification number, location, priority, state, threshold, and tolerances. The attributes of a vehicle might include its identification number, year, make, model, capacity, color, and net cost. Each attribute can be defined by such things as units of measure, precision, and permissible range of values. For example, the attribute color could be defined to be red, white, and blue. When defining a name for such a data structure entity as a model of an attribute, we might include the name of the real-world entity that the attribute is characterizing in conjunction with the scope of the attribute (i.e., Data Structure Entity Name = Real-World Entity

Name_Attribute Scope). For example, the names of data structure entities in the model of a sensor could be named `Sensor_ Location`, `Sensor_State`, and so forth.

*Services* provided by a real-world entity are modeled by operations to be performed by the package that models the entity. For example, a service might involve transforming received data into a different form. The name of the service can be defined by a verb plus a descriptor. In the case of a database management package, the record retrieval service could be called `RETRIEVE_RECORD`.

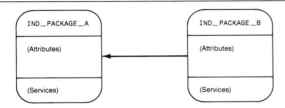

(a) Representation of a relationship between
    independent packages

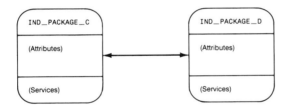

(b) Representation of a relationship between
    objects that both provide services

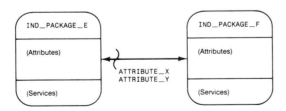

(c) Representation of a conditional relationship
    between objects

*FIGURE 7-3.* Graphical representation of relationships between independent packages

In a specification of requirements for a large computer program, an attribute or a service may be defined or characterized in some way. Definitions should be presented from a behavioral point of view and should be kept focused and concise. This can be accomplished by making extensive use of bullets or perhaps by providing information in a standard template, such as those shown in Figure 7-4. The attribute definition could include a brief description of the real-world object to which the attribute applies (or a reference to such a description) and a description of the scope of the attribute. It also might include such things as units of measure, range of values, and

---

Name of Attribute: _____

Traceability to Software Requirements Specification: _____

_____

Applicable Packages: _____

Description: _____

_____

_____

_____

Units of Measure: _____

Range of Values: _____

_____

Precision: _____

(a) Template for Defining an Attribute

---

Name of Service: _____

Traceability to Computer Program Requirements Documentation: _____

_____

Applicable Packages: _____

Control Considerations:

   System States (Modes): _____

   External Events: _____

   Constraints: _____

Interface with Other Systems:

   Inputs: _____

   Outputs: _____

Description: _____

_____

_____

_____

_____

(b) Template for Defining a Service

---

FIGURE 7-4.   Templates for defining an attribute and a service

precision. The service description could include such phrases as the following:

- For the ... system mode, ...
- Upon receipt of ...
- At time ...

The service description could also be presented in the context of if-then clauses.

## 7.3    Design for Class-Member Relationships

We can introduce class-member relationships into a design for a large and complex computer program. This section suggests alternative approaches in the context of Ada packages, Ada generic packages, and task types.

### 7.3.1    Basic Approach to Class-Member Design

Upon assessing real-world requirements, an analyst may recognize attributes and services that are common and present these requirements in a software requirements specification as a class-member relationship. When this is the case, a software design can be prepared as a model of the class-member relationship. As such, the software design can specify common data entities that model common attributes and common operations that model common services.

In a basic and straightforward approach to modeling a class-member relationship, a design can specify the use of an Ada package to model the class. Specifically, the design could establish a package to encapsulate data entities modeling common attributes and operations modeling common services. In turn, the design could require that attributes and services unique to specific members be accounted for in specific Ada packages to be declared for each member, each of which is to have access to the class package through the Ada with clause.

An example of this approach is provided in Figure 7-5. As shown, a package named CLASS_TRANSPORT is used to establish a class of data entities for attributes and operations for services. Specifically, class attributes are accounted for in the specification of this package through type definitions for ID, NAME, BASE, and PASSENGER_ CAPACITY, which are called ID_TYPE, NAME_TYPE, BASE_TYPE, and CAPACITY_TYPE. A class service is provided in the procedure PASSENGER_MOVEMENT. Packages named MEMBER_CAR, MEMBER_

AIRCRAFT, and MEMBER_SHIP are used to establish a set of members. Attributes are accounted for in the specification of the MEMBER_CAR package through type definitions for LICENSE_NUMBER and VEHICLE _ID (i.e., in LICENSE_NUMBER_TYPE and VEHICLE_ID_TYPE), and a service is provided in the LOCAL_DELIVERY procedure. Attributes are accounted for in the specification of the MEMBER_ AIRCRAFT package through type definitions for NUMBER_ENGINES and MISSILES (i.e., in NUMBER_ENGINES_TYPE and MISSILES_ TYPE) and a service is provided in the AIRCRAFT_DELIVERY procedure. Attributes are accounted for in the specification of the MEMBER _SHIP package through type definitions for TONNAGE and MISSILES (i.e., in TONNAGE_TYPE and MISSILES_TYPE) and a service is provided in the FISHING_TRIPS procedure. The member packages gain access to the class package through use of the Ada with clause.

## 7.3.2   Reusable Generic Packages

### Basic Concepts

A class package can be designed as an independent package that can be reapplied as often as necessary. The concept of multiple application of an Ada package as a model of a class leads to the general subject of reusability of existing independent packages.

A key rationale for the design of the Ada language was the concept of software reusability. Many industry observers believe that reusable software will include catalogs of independent packages as *software ICs*. Reusable packages might facilitate processing for classes of data entities and such things as I/O device drivers, network protocols, special-purpose processing algorithms, database management systems, and mathematical algorithms, as well as collections of reusable subprograms (e.g., for stacks, queues, and trees).

When a design calls for partitioning a software system into a set of independent packages, reusable Ada packages that are also independent and self-sufficient can be added to a system without disturbing other processing in the system. To be independent and self-sufficient, a reusable Ada package has to be constructed with its own unique local data structure and operations. As such, it will not have to use variables and flags in other parts of the software system and will not permit other parts of the software system to access its internal formulation. Because of this, changes made to other parts of the software system will not affect the reusable independent package or its performance.

```
package CLASS_TRANSPORT is
--
  type ID_TYPE is range 1 . . 1000;
  type NAME_TYPE is (CAR, AIRCRAFT, SHIP);
  type BASE_TYPE is (AIR, GROUND, WATER);
  type CAPACITY_TYPE is range 5 . . 800;
-- Data entities for class attributes
  ID : ID_TYPE;
  NAME : NAME_TYPE;
  BASE : BASE_TYPE;
  CAPACITY : CAPACITY_TYPE;
--Procedure for class service
  procedure PASSENGER_MOVEMENT (ID : in ID_TYPE;
                                NAME : in NAME_TYPE;
                                BASE : in BASE_TYPE;
                 PASSENGER_CAPACITY : out CAPACITY_TYPE);
    . . .
  end CLASS_TRANSPORT;
  package body CLASS_TRANSPORT is
    . . .
  begin
    . . .
  end CLASS_TRANSPORT;
```

(a) Modeling a Class

```
with CLASS_TRANSPORT;
package MEMBER_CAR is
--
  type LICENSE_NUMBER_TYPE is . . .
  type VEHICLE_ID_TYPE is . . .
--Data entities for member attributes
  LICENSE_NUMBER : LICENSE_NUMBER_TYPE;
      VEHICLE_ID : VEHICLE_ID_TYPE;
--Procedure for member service
  procedure LOCAL_DELIVERY (. . .);


    . . .
  end MEMBER_CAR;
  package body MEMBER_CAR is
    . . .
  begin
    . . .
  end MEMBER_CAR;
```

(b) Modeling member MEMBER_CAR

FIGURE 7-5.   Example of a basic Ada implementation of a class-member relationship

```
with CLASS_TRANSPORT;
package MEMBER_AIRCRAFT is
--
  type NUMBER_ENGINES_TYPE is . . .
  type MISSILES_TYPE is . . .
--Data entities for member attributes
  NUMBER_ENGINES : NUMBER_ENGINES_TYPE;
        MISSILES : MISSILES_TYPE;
--Procedure for member service
  procedure AIRPORT_DELIVERY (. . .);
    . . .
end MEMBER_AIRCRAFT;
package body MEMBER_AIRCRAFT is
    . . .
begin
    . . .
end MEMBER_AIRCRAFT;
```

(c) Modeling member MEMBER_AIRCRAFT

```
with CLASS_TRANSPORT;
package MEMBER_SHIP is
--
  type TONNAGE_TYPE is . . .
  type MISSILES_TYPE is . . .
--Data entities for member attributes
   TONNAGE : TONNAGE_TYPE;
   MISSILES : MISSILES_TYPE;
--Procedure for member service
  procedure FISHING_TRIPS (. . .);
    . . .
end MEMBER_SHIP;
package body MEMBER_SHIP is
    . . .
begin
    . . .
end MEMBER_SHIP;
```

(d) Modeling member MEMBER_SHIP

FIGURE 7-5.   (continued)

A designer may be familiar with and have access to a set of reusable packages that have been cataloged for easy reference, standarized for easy application, and validated for reliable operation over a range of values and operating conditions. To reapply existing packages, a designer has to be completely familiar with the catalog and know exactly how each package in the catalog has been constructed, how it performs, and how it has been validated. With this familiarity, a designer can readily recognize in a design's requirements where an existing package can be applied.

In practice, it is important to note that reuse of an existing package is not without risk and cost. To reuse a package, a designer needs to know exactly what the package does, what information it expects and in what form, how it outputs information, and so on. Therefore, a designer needs to have access to extensive and very readable documentation, which he or she must study carefully. The designer also must be sure that the software will work reliably for all extremes of its possible reapplication—a difficult problem in itself. To meet this end, the reused package may have to be tested extensively in both nominal and stress situations, over the full range of conditions called for by the problem, and for extended periods of time.

### Generic Ada Package

To widen the scope of reapplication of a package, the package can be made generic, so that data variable names, type definitions, subprogram names, and so forth, can be generalized. Instances of the reusable generic package can then be applied for specific applications. Like a generic subprogram, a generic Ada package can be thought of as a nonexecutable template that can be tailored to satisfy different needs. As a nonexecutable template, type definitions, variables values, and the name of the generic package are incomplete, to be supplied prior to reapplication to establish different instances (versions) of the package. Thus, like a generic subprogram, a generic package is written only once, but it can be reapplied several times through instantiation.

Again like a generic subprogram, a generic Ada package has a generic part and a "regular" package part.[1] The generic part

---

[1]Syntactically, to make an Ada package generic, we precede it with the keyword generic, followed by source code for entities of the package that are incomplete or defined with default values. The missing parameters are established as part of the instantiation of the generic package, or default parameters are replaced as part of instantiation. For example, consider a two-dimensional matrix that is defined in a generic Ada package as follows:

```
generic
      ROWS : in INTEGER := 20;
   COLUMNS : in INTEGER := 30;
   package MATRIX is
      . . .
```

contains the shells of data entities, generalizing constraints applicable to them. The basic idea is that dummy type constraints are to be replaced by specific constraints at instantiation.[2] The generic part can also include subprograms accessible through the Ada with clause, which can be used to establish operations related to member services.[3] Instances of the generic package can then be used to establish specific data entities and operations.[4] The "regular" pack-

---

Because this package is generic, we can create several instances of it. Syntactically, instantiation is accomplished by using Ada source statements that include the Ada keywords is new. For example, two different instances might be as follows:

```
a. package MATRIX is new SQUARE_MATRIX (ROWS => 10;
                                        COLUMNS => 10);
b. package MATRIX is new RECTANGULAR_MATRIX (ROWS => 10;
                                             COLUMNS => 20);
```

Therefore, as indicated, the name of the member and the number of rows and columns can be changed from default values to new values in each instantiation of the generic matrix.

[2]An example of generic type parameters is
```
generic
  type LIST_ELEMENT is (<>);
  type ATRIBUTE_LIST is array (INTEGER range <>) of
                                        LIST_ELEMENT;
```
where the box symbol <> denotes a dummy to be supplied at instantiation.

[3]An example of introducing subprograms in the generic part is
```
generic
    ROWS : in INTEGER := 20;
  COLUMNS : in INTEGER := 30;
  with procedure RECEIVE(VALUE  : in CHARACTER);
  with procedure RETRIEVE(VALUE : out CHARACTER);
package DATA_MANAGER is

    . . .
```

[4]An example of instantiation is
```
  procedure ICU_RECEIVE_MESSAGE (VALUE: in CHARACTER) is
  procedure ICU_RETRIEVE        (VALUE: out CHARACTER) is
  package ICU_DATA_MANAGER is new DATA_MANAGER(ROWS => 30,
                                  COLUMNS => 40,
                    RECEIVE => ICU_RECEIVE_MESSAGE,
                    RETRIEVE => ICU_RETRIEVE);
```
where the name of procedures made available to the package are changed from default values to values appropriate for a specific instance as part of the instantiation.

age part contains various complete operations and declarations of data entities.

## 7.3.3 Modeling a Class-Member Relationship with an Ada Generic Package

A generic package is not itself directly executable (just as a class is not executable in object-oriented programming), but instances of it formed at compile time are executable (just as members of a class are executable in object-oriented programming). This suggests the possibility of modeling a class-member relationship directly with a single generic Ada package.

An example of this approach is shown in Figure 7-6 for the class-member relationship shown in Figure 7-2. As shown, a shell for member attributes is in the generic part in ATTRIBUTE_A and ATTRIBUTE_B. Member services are provided in Ada procedures LOCAL_DELIVERY, AIR_MAIL_DELIVERY, and FISHING_TRIPS, which are available to the generic package in the generic part through the use of the Ada with clause. The class attributes are accounted for in the specification of the generic package through type definitions for ID, NAME, BASE, and PASSENGER_CAPACITY, which are called ID_TYPE, NAME_TYPE, BASE_TYPE, and CAPACITY_TYPE. The class services are provided in the procedure PASSENGER_MOVEMENT. When called, this procedure receives specific values for ID, NAME, BASE, and PASSENGER_CAPACITY. In the body of this procedure, NAME is checked to determine which member service is applicable. When NAME is CAR, then the LOCAL_DELIVERY procedure is called. When NAME is AIRCRAFT, the AIR_MAIL_DELIVERY procedure is called. When NAME is SHIP, the FISHING_TRIPS procedure is called.

Introducing a class-member relationship into a design in the context of a single generic Ada package is limited to cases where the fit is right with respect to both attributes and services. With respect to attributes, this design approach is appropriate if the number of attributes of a class far exceeds the number of attributes unique to each member, and member attributes are similar in form (e.g., accounting for the same number of variables to which values have to be assigned). If the number of attributes of each member is greater than the number of common attributes of a class, then the use of a single generic Ada package to directly model the class-member

```
generic
--member attributes
  ATTRIBUTE_A: INTEGER;
  ATTRIBUTE_B: INTEGER;
--member services
  with procedure LOCAL_DELIVERY (. . .);
  with procedure AIR_MAIL_DELIVERY (. . .);
  with procedure FISHING_TRIPS (. . .);
--
package TRANSPORT is
--class attributes
  type ID_TYPE is range 1 . . 1000;
  type NAME_TYPE is (CAR, AIRCRAFT, SHIP);
  type BASE_TYPE is (AIR, GROUND, WATER);
  type CAPACITY_TYPE is range 5 . .800;
--class service
  procedure PASSENGER_MOVEMENT (ID   : in ID_TYPE;
                                NAME : in NAME_TYPE;
                                BASE : in BASE_TYPE;
        PASSENGER_CAPACITY: out CAPACITY_TYPE);
     . . .
end TRANSPORT;
package body TRANSPORT is
     . . .
  procedure PASSENGER_MOVEMENT (ID   : in ID_TYPE;
                                NAME : in NAME_TYPE;
                                BASE : in BASE_TYPE;
        PASSENGER_CAPACITY: out CAPACITY_TYPE) is
begin
     . . .
  case NAME is
    when CAR ⇒ LOCAL_DELIVERY (. . .);
    when AIRCRAFT ⇒ AIR_MAIL_DELIVERY (. . .);
    when SHIP ⇒ FISHING_TRIPS (. . .);
     . . .
end PASSENGER_MOVEMENT;
     . . .
end TRANSPORT;
```

*FIGURE 7-6.* Example of implementing a class-member relationship with a single generic Ada package

relationship should probably not be introduced into a design, since little is to be gained. In that case, a small amount of redundancy in the data structures of individual packages may well be less complex than the introduction of a design that contains a class with only a few attributes and services. With respect to services, this design approach is appropriate if member services do not require "withing" too many subprograms. When member services do require "withing" several subprograms, the logic in the body of the generic package (e.g., to decide which subprograms apply to a specific member) may become complex. Therefore, the practical use of an Ada generic package to model a class-member relationship is limited to special cases where the fit is right with respect to both attributes and services.

Independent packages chosen in the early stages of design may determine the extent to which a class-member relationship is practical in the context of an individual Ada generic package. For example, extensive attributes and services for the members CAR, AIRCRAFT, and SHIP in our previous example might result in a large number of data entities and operations unique to members, but not necessarily similar in nature. In such cases, upon analysis of the requirements, a designer might consider the members CAR, AIRCRAFT, and SHIP as subclasses of the class TRANSPORT. Then, for example, in the subclass CAR, members might be Cadillac, Mercedes, Nissan, Toyota, and BMW, resulting in several common attributes. In general, choosing members with similar characteristics increases the chances that an individual Ada generic package as a model of the class-member relationship will be practical, especially with respect to modeling attributes with data entities.

### 7.3.4 Design Approach with Task Types

Another feature of Ada that may be useful in a design for common services that may have to operate concurrently is the task type. In this situation, if a design results in the use of multiple Ada tasks with the same bodies and corresponding entry points, the designer might consider applying an Ada task type. A task type can be thought of as a template that can be used to create several task objects as instances of the task type. A task type is a limited private data type, which may not be assigned or tested for equality (but it can be used as input parameters to a subprogram or task entry). An example of applying a task type would be a design for the ICU problem that opts to read input messages from communications channels a, b, c, and d in a logically concurrent manner using four tasks. When the protocol for receiving data over each channel is the same, a task type could be used to define a template that can be used to create four task objects as instances of the task type.[5]

---

[5]Syntactically, a task type is defined as follows:

Certain problems might result in designs that call for arrays of tasks.[6] Also, since a task type is a limited private data type, certain problems might result in a task type as part of a data record declaration.[7] Furthermore, instances of task types may be created dynamically by one of the following:

- declaring instances of task types in a dynamic context (e.g., locally in a procedure)
- defining access variables (pointers) to task types and creating instances of these types using a "new" statement

(Refer to a book on programming with Ada for a detailed discussion of using task types in these ways.)

---

```
task type MULTIPLE_INPUT_TYPE is
  entry MESSAGE_RECEIVE;
    . . .
  end MULTIPLE_INPUT_TYPE;
```
Several instances of such a task type can introduce the needed task objects:
```
CHANNEL_A_INPUT: MULTIPLE_INPUT_TYPE;
CHANNEL_B_INPUT: MULTIPLE_INPUT_TYPE;
CHANNEL_C_INPUT: MULTIPLE_INPUT_TYPE;
CHANNEL_D_INPUT: MULTIPLE_INPUT_TYPE;
```
We may refer to entries of specific objects as follows:
```
CHANNEL_A_INPUT.MESSAGE_RECEIVE;
CHANNEL_B_INPUT.MESSAGE_RECEIVE;
CHANNEL_C_INPUT.MESSAGE_RECEIVE;
CHANNEL_D_INPUT.MESSAGE_RECEIVE;
```

[6]In the ICU problem, the following array might be defined:
```
CHANNEL_INPUT : array (A,B,C,D) of MULTIPLE_INPUT_TYPE;
```
We can refer to entries of specific objects as follows:
```
CHANNEL_INPUT(A).MESSAGE_RECEIVE;
CHANNEL_INPUT(B).MESSAGE_RECEIVE;
CHANNEL_INPUT(C).MESSAGE_RECEIVE;
CHANNEL_INPUT(D).MESSAGE_RECEIVE;
```

[7]For example,
```
type DATA is
  record
    INPUT : INTEGER;
    READ_INPUT : MULTIPLE_INPUT_TYPE;
  end record;
ICU_DATA : DATA;
```
where with the elaboration of ICU_DATA, the READ_INPUT task object is activated.

## 7.3.5 Ada Considerations for the Design of Class-Member Relationships

An individual Ada generic package to facilitate data-driven class-member relationships and an Ada task type to facilitate services with similar properties might be used in a design to reduce complexity (when the specialized situation exists to make these approaches appropriate). But from an engineering point of view, care must be taken *not* to produce the exact opposite effect. When applying Ada generics and task types, the designer should consider the pros and cons of the design approach. On the positive side, designs calling for the use of an individual Ada generic package or task types can reduce the amount of code necessary to implement the design. Less code may be easier to develop and maintain. On the negative side, the use of an Ada generic package and task types to account for common attributes and/or services may be difficult for an implementer and maintainer to understand and may add run-time overhead, which can lead to timing problems. This combination can lead to debugging and testing nightmares. When you are considering the use of Ada generics and task types in a design, remember that the basic strategy is to reduce overall complexity so a design can be comprehended readily by average programmers responsible for software system implementation and maintenance. The more basic approach to modeling a class as a package and each member as a separate package might be a better approach in most applications. Such an approach, although not as close to object-oriented programming as the use of an Ada generic package to model members, has wider application and may be easier for implementing programmers and programmers responsible for maintenance to understand.

## 7.4 Key Concepts

- In a class-member relationship of requirements for a computer program, a class encompasses attributes and services found in the requirements that are common to the members of the class. Each member encompasses attributes and services in the requirements that are unique to it, which are not to be shared with the other members.

- During analysis of requirements of a program with a complex data structure, it may (or may not) be possible to organize requirements into a class-member relationship. Where possible, the class-member approach saves the repetition of definitions for member attributes and services in a data structure.

- In a basic and straightforward approach to modeling a class-member relationship, a design can specify the use of an Ada package to model the class and a set of different packages to model the members. The member packages gain access to the class package through use of the Ada with clause.

- The concept of the multiple application of an Ada package as a model of a class leads to the general subject of reusing existing independent packages. If a reusable package is independent and self-sufficient, it can be added to a software system without disturbing other processing in the system. To recognize the use of an existing package in a design, a designer must be familiar with and have access to the package, and have assurance that the package will perform correctly over the full range of values and conditions specified in the software requirements.

- To widen the scope of reapplication of a package, it can be made generic, so that data variable names, type definitions, and subprogram names can be generalized. Instances of the reusable generic package can then be reapplied for specific applications.

- In some cases, an Ada generic package can be used to model a class-member relationship. The internals for such a package can be used to implement class attributes and services. Instances of the package can then be used to establish a set of specific members, each sharing class attributes and services internal to the generic package. A generic package is not itself directly executable (just as a class is not executable). Rather, instances of the generic package formed at compile time are executable (just as members of a class are executable).

- When software requirements include common services that may have to operate concurrently, a design can specify applying an Ada task type. A task type can be thought of as a template that can be used to create several task objects as instances of the task type.

- When considering the use of Ada generics and task types in a design, we should consider the advantages and disadvantages of the resulting design. Remember our basic objective is to reduce complexity in the overall design, and not produce the exact opposite effect.

## 7.5    Exercises

1. When requirements are organized into a class-member relationship, what is the role of a class? What is the role of a member? Why would an analyst attempt to organize requirements into a class-member relationship?

2. Describe two different approaches to preparing a design for requirements that have been organized into a class-member relationship. To what extent can each approach be applied in practice?

3. What must a designer do to introduce reusable Ada packages into a design?

4. Describe a design for a problem that contains five different real-world entities, two of which have common data and services.

5. In requirements for a problem, two real-world entities have several common attributes and services, while two other real-world entities have only a few common attributes and services. Describe possible approaches to a software design for such a problem.

# PART III

# Design Steps for Programs and Software Systems

*The third part of this book delineates a set of specific engineering steps to design a large computer program and a software system as a set of computer programs. These steps are referred to as "engineering steps" because they are based upon experience and a pragmatic approach to design that lays the foundation for economical software development and maintenance.*

*Chapter 8 addresses using graphics, pseudocode, and program design language to represent a design concisely and crisply in a series of different views. To be able to specify design for computer programs to be implemented in Ada, we need a notation to represent the results of each design step, directly reflecting Ada in an abstracted manner.*

*Chapter 9 presents steps for designing a computer program, and Chapter 10 presents steps for designing a software system as a set of computer programs. A design example in Chapter 9 exemplifies the use of the steps for designing a large computer program, and an example, in Chapter 10, exemplifies the steps for designing a software system. These examples are relatively large and complicated and are meant to demonstrate problems in bulk and the steps taken to systematically resolve those problems. Even though the examples are lengthy, the reader must realize they are just examples—real-world problems are much larger and more difficult.*

# Representing Design Requirements

Various fields of engineering use specific notations to represent design. Blueprints are used to represent the design of civil engineering systems, mechanical drawings are used to represent mechanical systems, and schematic and wiring diagrams are used to represent electrical systems. These design views and the analyses necessary to produce them are developed over a significant period of time. They can be read by the various members of the project team, including project managers and engineering personnel.

Software engineers also need to prepare abstracted views of a design for a computer program. However, there is a tendency in software engineering not to put sufficient time and effort into the design process, but rather to jump to programming too quickly. Perhaps this tendency exists because the project staff includes programmers who are engrossed in the game-like process of coding. Worse yet, it may be because *lines of code* are often used to measure the progress of a project—both management personnel and customers tend to correlate progress with the amount of code that has been written. The result is that design and a "good" representation of a design may not be prepared, which can lead to the disaster phase of a software project described in Chapter 1. For a software project to be successful, it is critical that project managers, system engineers, and software engineers recognize the need for a software design and a clear understandable representation of that design.

# 8.1 Introduction

This chapter discusses the representation of design requirements for a computer program. A notation is introduced to help handle the bulk and multidimensions inherent in a design for a large and complex computer program. This design notation directly reflects Ada in an abstracted manner; as such, it can be readily translated into Ada source statements.

# 8.2 Program Design Language (PDL)

A design for a large and complex computer program can be presented with a program design language, or PDL. PDL is meant to establish an abstracted representation of a large computer program. Because the representation is abstracted, certain details about the program are not specified. The information included in a design and the details excluded depend on the designer, his or her comprehension of the program, and what the designer feels is especially important.

The Ada language itself has been used as a PDL as well as a programming language. This usage is appropriate in the sense that Ada can be used to represent a computer program in an abstracted manner, with certain implementation details left unspecified. Such PDL can be read by programmers and others familiar with the syntax of Ada, but not by those unfamiliar with Ada syntax, typically project managers, system engineers, and configuration management personnel.

In practice, the use of Ada as a PDL has meant different things to different people. For example, Ada PDL has been used to represent the architecture of a computer program and data flow between architectural components. Such PDL can be checked with an Ada compiler to ensure the accuracy and completeness of data flow between the architectural components. In addition, Ada PDL has been used to represent data structures and operations in program units.

With Ada PDL, the distinction between design and the ultimate Ada computer program may become blurred. Some software engineers view this as a major problem: the software development team may develop final implementation code directly, in the absence of an abstracted design. Others view it as an advantage because an abstracted design representation with Ada can be systematically expanded and refined, eventually evolving into the implementing code.

When a PDL is used to represent the design of a large computer program, the bulk and complexity of a comprehensive PDL may become an issue. For example, in a large program that consists of thousands of program units, it could take a large number of pages of textual PDL (perhaps 600 or more) to represent just the architectural structure of a design and a great number of additional pages (perhaps several thousand) to represent the complete design. Such bulk can be cumbersome. For example, a reader would have to wade through all these pages just to realize and piece together the architectural structure of a program.

A more concise representation of design information for a large program would make its design more comprehensible. Graphics, for instance, can present architectural and data flow information in a concise and abstracted manner. The following sections introduce a notation for such graphics in the context of Ada, referred to as *schematic multiview abstracted representation techniques* for Ada, or SMART Ada. SMART Ada presents design information in a concise and crisp manner in different design views that correspond to the views used in civil, mechanical, and electrical engineering. In addition, pseudocode is introduced to represent operations and descriptors are introduced to represent the contents of data structures. SMART Ada is used in conjunction with the pseudocode and descriptors to represent the results of steps in design examples presented in Chapters 9 and 10.

## 8.3 SMART Geometric Figures for Ada Program Units

As a basis for the graphical aspects of SMART Ada, let's use geometric figures to represent Ada program units. Specifically, as shown in Figure 8-1, a square represents an Ada procedure, a circle an Ada function, a parallelogram an Ada task, and a rectangle an Ada package. In each case, the geometric figure is divided into a narrow part, which represents the program unit's specification, and a wide part, which represents the body. For the task geometric figure, small parallelograms that overlap the task's specification and body represent entries, as shown in Figure 8-2. As indicated by arrows pointing to the small parallelograms, the entries can be called to initiate task rendezvous. For the package geometric figure, subprograms and tasks internal to a package are represented by their geometric figures inside the package geometric figure. As shown in Figure 8-3, the

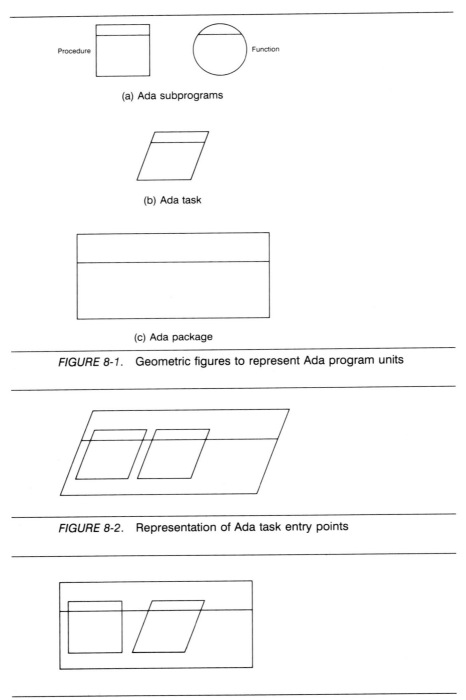

Procedure

Function

(a) Ada subprograms

(b) Ada task

(c) Ada package

FIGURE 8-1. Geometric figures to represent Ada program units

FIGURE 8-2. Representation of Ada task entry points

FIGURE 8-3. Representation of visible program units in an Ada package

geometric representation of the specifications for visible program units are inside the geometric representation of the package's specification, and the geometric representation of the bodies of these program units are inside the geometric representation of the body of the package.

As shown in Figure 8-4(a), a data structure in a package is represented by a rectangle with dashed lines for its sides. This geometric figure for a data structure can also overlap the specification and the body of the package specification to indicate that some of the data entities are to be declared in the specification of the package (e.g., parameters to be passed to other packages) while others are to be declared in the body of the package. Alternatively, a visible data structure can be represented by the geometric figure for a data structure in the specification of the package, while a hidden data structure can be represented by the geometric figure for a data structure in the body of the package, as shown in Figure 8-4(b).

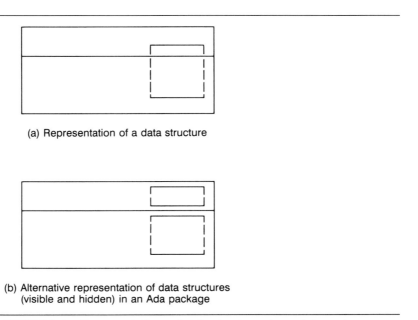

(a) Representation of a data structure

(b) Alternative representation of data structures (visible and hidden) in an Ada package

FIGURE 8-4. Representations of data structures in an Ada package

## 8.4    SMART Views of a Design

To represent the design of a large computer program, we need a notation that reduces and consolidates the large amount of information necessary to present a design. It is not possible to consolidate all the details of a design into one or two views, so we use a series of SMART views.

### 8.4.1    Views of Independent Packages

A SMART view can represent Ada packages for a set of independent packages selected in the design of a computer program, as shown in Figure 8-5. Ada code for this design information is shown in Figure 8-6. As indicated, packages can gain access to visible entities within other packages through the Ada with clause.

The with clause is represented in SMART Ada by a small rectangle that contains the names of the packages to be accessed. For example, access to package P2 by entities in P1 is designated by a line drawn from the with geometric figure that contains P2 to the specification of P1 (i.e., to represent the Ada source statement with P2;). Correspondingly, access to package P3 by entities in package P2 is designated by a line drawn from the geometric figure that contains P3 to the specification of P2 (i.e., to represent the Ada source statement with P3;). Access to packages P4 and P5 by entities in package P3 is designated by a line drawn from the geometric figure that contains P4 and P5 to the specification of P3 (i.e., to represent the Ada source statement with P4, P5;).

In Figure 8-5, the geometric figures for packages contain other geometric figures that represent visible procedures. The body of a visible procedure is inside the body of a package. Package interaction between a visible procedure in one package and a visible procedure in a second package is shown graphically by an arrow from the body part of the calling procedure to the specification part of the called procedure. For example, in Figure 8-5, the design specifies that procedure PU_P1 in package P1 is to access package P2 through calls to procedures PU_P2a and PU_P2b; procedure PU_P2a is to access package P3 through calls to procedure PU_P3; and so forth. The program units declared within the bodies of the visible procedures are not shown in this view, since they are hidden in the bodies of packages. With SMART Ada, these program units can be shown in a separate view for the internal structure of a package.

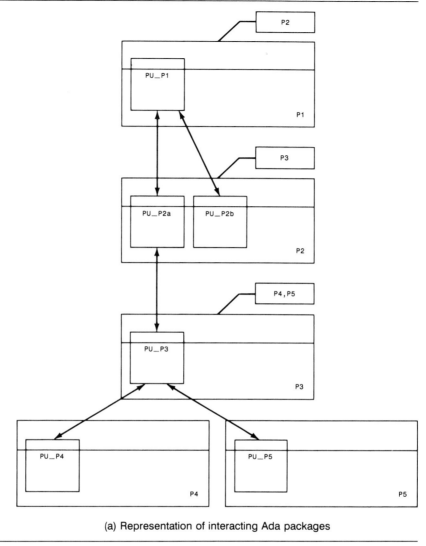

(a) Representation of interacting Ada packages

*FIGURE 8-5.* SMART view of interacting Ada packages

## 8.4.2 Views of Subprograms

### *Representing Program Unit Declarations*

A SMART view can represent program unit declarations that a design may require for segmenting lengthy operations. If the design specifies a hierarchy of program units, a program unit can be assigned to

```
----------------------------------------
--Independent Packages P4 and P5
----------------------------------------
  Package P4 is
    procedure PU_P4 (. . .);
    . . .
  end P4;
  Package body P4 is
    procedure PU_P4 (. . .) is
    . . .
    begin
    . . .
    end PU_P4;
    . . .
  end P4;
  Package P5 is
    procedure PU_P5 (. . .);
    . . .
  end P5;
  Package body P5 is
    procedure PU_P5 (. . .) is
    . . .
    begin
    . . .
    end PU_P5;
    . . .
  end P5;
----------------------------
--Independent Package P3
----------------------------
  with P4, P5;
  package P3 is
    procedure PU_P3 (. . .);
    . . .
  end P3;
  package body P3 is
    procedure PU_P3 (. . .) is
    . . .
    begin
    . . .
    end PU_P3;
    . . .
  end P3;
```

FIGURE 8-6. Source statements for the Ada packages shown in
Figure 8-5

one level, with program units declared within it assigned to a lower
level (i.e., a program unit declared within a program unit at level $n$
is to be assigned to level $n + 1$), as shown in Figure 8-7. In this
figure, lines running horizontally and vertically interconnect geometric figures for the bodies of program units at level $n$ to geometric

```
------------------------
--Independent Package P2
------------------------
  with P3;
  package P2 is
    procedure PU_P2a (. . .);
    procedure PU_P2b (. . .);
      . . .
  end P2;
  package body P2 is
    procedure PU_P2a (. . .) is
      . . .
    begin
      . . .
    end PU_P2a;
    procedure PU_P2b (. . .) is
      . . .
    begin
      . . .
    end PU_P2b;
      . . .
  end P2;
------------------------
--Independent Package P1
------------------------
  with P2;
  package P1 is
    procedure PU_P1 (. . .);
      . . .
  end P1;
  package body P1 is
    procedure PU_P1 (. . .) is
      . . .
    begin
      . . .
    end PU_P1;
      . . .
  end P1;
```

FIGURE 8-6. (continued)

figures for the specification of declared program units at level $n + 1$. Corresponding Ada source statements are given in Figure 8-8. The Ada keywords is separate separate the bodies of procedures from their specifications. Note that the graphic in Figure 8-7 is far more concise than the "skeleton" code shown in Figure 8-8.

The name of each program unit can be in the program unit's geometric figure or adjacent to it. In Figure 8-8, each program unit is named using the letters PU (for Program Unit) followed by an underscore and an identifier. The identifier consists of the program

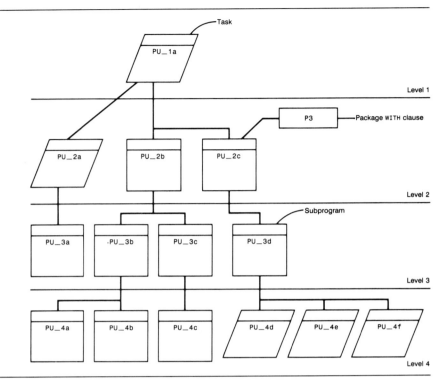

*FIGURE 8-7.* SMART view of program unit declarations

unit's level number and unit letter (e.g., PU_3b indicates unit b in level 3). In practice, we could replace PU with a name representative of the object or function implemented by the program unit (e.g., RADAR_TRACKER_2d). In Figure 8-7, task PU_2a and procedures PU_2b and PU_2c are declared in specification of task PU_1a. Procedure PU_3a is declared in the specification of task PU_2a, procedures PU_3b and PU_3c are declared in the body of procedure PU_2b, and so forth.

### Representing Sequences of Program Unit Calls

A SMART view can also represent a sequence of program unit calls in a hierarchy of program units. Figure 8-9 represents a chain of program unit calls; the corresponding Ada source statements are shown in Figure 8-10. As shown in Figure 8-9, a line with an arrowhead at both ends connects the geometric figure for a calling program unit to the geometric figure for the called program unit. The

```
-------------------------
--Level 1, Unit a
-------------------------
Task PU_1a is
   . . .
end PU_1a;
task body PU_1a is
begin
  task PU_2a is
   . . .
  end PU_2a;
  task body PU_2a is separate;
  procedure PU_2b is separate;
  procedure PU_2c is separate;
end PU_1a;
-------------------------
--Level 2, Unit a
-------------------------
separate (PU_1a)
task body PU_2a is
begin
  procedure PU_3a is separate;
   . . .
end PU_2a;
-------------------------
--Level 2, Unit b
-------------------------
separate (PU_1a)
procedure PU_2b (. . .) is
  procedure PU_3b is separate;
  procedure PU_3c is separate;
begin
   . . .
end PU_2b;
-------------------------
--Level 2, Unit c
-------------------------
with P3;
separate (PU_1a)
procedure PU_2c (. . .) is
  procedure PU_3d is separate;
begin
   . . .
end PU_2c;
```

FIGURE 8-8.   Ada source statements for the hierarchy of program units shown in Figure 8-7

```
--------------------------
--Level 3, Unit a
--------------------------
separate (PU_1a. PU_2a)
procedure PU_3a (. . .) is
   . . .
begin
   . . .
end PU_3a;
--------------------------
--Level 3, Unit b
--------------------------
separate (PU_1a. PU_2b)
procedure PU_3b (. . .) is
   . . .
   procedure PU_4a is separate;
   procedure PU-4b is separate;
   . . .
begin
   . . .
end PU_3b;
--------------------------
--Level 3, Unit c
--------------------------
separate (PU_1a. PU_2b)
procedure PU_3c (. . .) is
   . . .
   procedure PU_4a is separate;
   . . .
begin
   . . .
end PU_3c;
--------------------------
--Level 3, Unit d
--------------------------
separate (PU_1a. PU_2c)
procedure PU_3d (. . .) is
   . . .
   task PU_4d is
   . . .
   end PU_4d;
   task body PU_4d is separate;
   task PU_4e is
   . . .
   end PU_4e;
   task body PU_4e is separate;
   task PU_4f is
   . . .
   end PU_4f;
   task body PU_4f is separate;
   . . .
   end PU_3d;
```

FIGURE 8-8.   (continued)

```
------------------------
--Level 4, Unit a
------------------------
separate (PU1a.PU_2b.PU_3b)
procedure PU_4a (. . .) is

    . . .
end PU_4a;
------------------------
--Level 4, Unit b
------------------------
separate (PU_1a.PU_2b.PU_3b)
procedure PU_4b (. . .) is

    . . .
end PU_4b;
------------------------
--Level 4, Unit c
------------------------
separate (PU_1a.PU_2b.PU_3c)
procedure PU_4c is

    . . .
end PU_4c;
------------------------
--Level 4, Unit d
------------------------
separate (PU_1a.PU_2c.PU_3d)
task body PU_4d is

    . . .
end PU_4d;
------------------------
--Level 4, Unit e
------------------------
separate (PU_1a.PU_2c.PU_3d)
task body PU_4e is

    . . .
end PU_4e;
------------------------
--Level 4, Unit f
------------------------
separate (PU_1a.PU_2c.PU_3d)
task body PU_4f is

    . . .
end PU_4f;
```

FIGURE 8-8.   (continued)

arrowhead at each end signifies a call and a return from the call. A conditional call (a call that takes place only if certain conditions are met) is indicated by a tilde placed on the two-headed arrow. For example, Figure 8-9 indicates that procedure PU_2b is to call procedure PU_3b if certain conditions are met or, alternatively, procedure PU_3c if other conditions are met. Again, notice that the graphic in Figure 8-9 is more concise than the corresponding skeleton Ada code in Figure 8-10.

In a SMART view for a sequence of program unit calls, task rendezvous is represented by a curved arrow from the body of the calling task to the specification of the acceptor task. The declaration of a task in a procedure is represented by a straight arrow from the geometric figure for the procedure's body to the geometric figure for the task. For example, in Figure 8-9, tasks PU_4d, PU_4e, and PU_4f are declared in the body of procedure PU_3d. Task PU_4d calls an entry point in PU_4e, and task PU_4f calls another entry point in PU_4e.

A SMART view can be used to represent a sequence of program unit calls for program units internal to a package. In that case, a called program unit defined in a package other than the subject

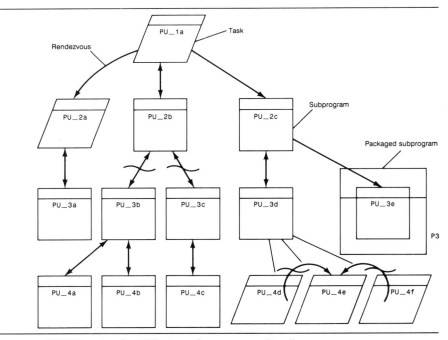

*FIGURE 8-9.* SMART view of program unit calls

```
------------------------
--Level 1, Unit a
------------------------
Task PU_1a is

  . . .

end PU_1a;
task body PU_1a is
begin
  task PU_2a is

    . . .

  end PU_2a;
  task body PU_2a is separate;
  procedure PU_2b is separate;
  procedure PU_2c is separate;

    . . .

  PU_2a (. . .);

    . . .

  PU_2b (. . .);

    . . .

  PU_2c (. . .);

    . . .

end PU_1a;
------------------------
Level 2, Unit a
------------------------
separate (PU_1a)
task body PU_2a is

    . . .

begin

    . . .

  procedure PU_3a is separate;

    . . .

  accept . . . (. . .);

    . . .

  PU_3a (. . .);

    . . .

end PU_2a;
```

FIGURE 8-10. Ada source statements for the program unit calls shown
in Figure 8-9 (Figure 8-10 continues on pages 160–162)

package is in a geometric figure for that foreign package, as shown
in Figure 8-9. The name of the foreign package is adjacent to the
package geometric figure.

In a SMART view of program unit invocation, a program unit
calling itself recursively is represented by a semicircular arrow,
beginning at the bottom of the geometric figure that represents the
program unit and ending on its side, as shown in Figure 8-11(a). Two
program units that call each other recursively are flagged by asterisks placed adjacent to the two-headed arrow, as shown in Figure

```
--------------------------
--Level 2, Unit b
--------------------------
separate (PU_1a)
procedure PU_2b (. . .) is
  procedure PU_3b is separate;
  procedure PU_3c is separate;
   . . .
begin
   . . .
  if . . . then
    PU_3b (. . .);
  else
    PU_3c (. . .);
  end if;
   . . .
end PU_2b;
--------------------------
--Level 2, Unit c
--------------------------
with P3;
separate (PU_1a)
procedure PU_2c (. . .) is
  procedure PU_3d is separate;
   . . .
begin
   . . .
PU_3d (. . .);
   . . .
P3.PU_3e (. . .);
   . . .
end PU_2c;
--------------------------
--Level 3, Unit a
--------------------------
separate (PU_1a. PU_2a)
procedure PU_3a (. . .) is
   . . .
begin
   . . .
end PU_3a;
```

FIGURE 8-10.  (continued)

8-11(b). More than two program units involved in a recursive process are flagged by asterisks adjacent to a "feedback loop," as shown in Figure 8-11(c).

### Representing Data Flow between Program Units

A SMART view can also represent the passage of data from one procedure to another. When a program unit calls a procedure, the

```
--------------------------
--Level 3, Unit b
--------------------------
separate (PU_1a.PU_2b)
procedure PU_3b (. . .) is
  procedure PU_4a is separate;
  procedure PU_4b is separate;

  . . .
begin

  . . .
  PU_4a (. . .);

  . . .
  PU_4b (. . .);

  . . .
end PU_3b;
--------------------------
--Level 3, Unit c
--------------------------
separate (PU_1a.PU_2b)
procedure PU_3c (. . .) is
  procedure PU_4c is separate;

  . . .
begin

  . . .
PU_4c (. . .);

  . . .
end PU_3c;
--------------------------
--Level 3, Unit d
--------------------------
separate (PU_1a.PU_2c)
procedure PU_3d (. . .) is
  task PU_4d is

  . . .
  end PU_4d;
  task body PU_4d is separate;
  task PU_4e is

  . . .
  end PU_4e;
  task body PU_4e is separate;
  task PU_4f is

  . . .
  end PU_4f;
  task body PU_4f is separate;

  . . .
  end PU_3d;
```

FIGURE 8-10.   (continued)

```
-------------------------
--Level 4, Unit a
-------------------------
with P5;
separate (PU_1a.PU_2b.PU_3b)
procedure PU_4a (. . .) is
   . . .
begin
   . . .
end PU_4a;
-------------------------
--Level 4, Unit b
-------------------------
separate (PU_1a.PU_2b.PU_3b)
procedure PU_4b (. . .) is
   . . .
begin
   . . .
end PU_4b;
-------------------------
--Level 4, Unit c
-------------------------
separate (PU_1a.PU_2b.PU_3c)
procedure PU_4c is
   . . .
begin
   . . .
end PU_4c;
-------------------------
--Level 4, Unit d
-------------------------
separate (PU_1a.PU_2c.PU_3d)
task body PU_4d is
begin
   . . .
end PU_4d;
-------------------------
--Level 4, Unit e
-------------------------
separate (PU_1a.PU_2c.PU_3d)
task body PU_4e is
begin
   . . .
end PU_4e;
-------------------------
--Level 4, Unit f
-------------------------
separate (PU_1a.PU_2c.PU_3d)
task body PU_4f is
begin
   . . .
end PU_4f;
```

FIGURE 8-10.   (continued)

(a) Representation of a single recursive program unit

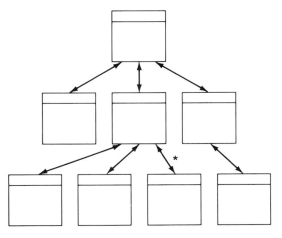

(b) Representation of two recursive program units

FIGURE 8-11.   SMART views for recursive subprogram calls

design may specify that data are to flow between the caller and the called procedure. In Ada, the specification of the called procedure indicates the mode of parameter passing, which is one of the following:

- in (i.e., a parameter is to be passed from a caller to a called program unit and not modified)
- out (i.e., a parameter is created by the called program unit and returned to the caller)
- in out (i.e., a parameter is received by the called program unit, modified, and returned to the caller).

To represent data flow between program units, the SMART geometric figure for a calling program unit is shown above the SMART geometric figure for the called program unit, as shown in Figure 8-12(a). This diagram represents the Ada source statement for a calling program unit, as shown in Figure 8-12(b), and the Ada source

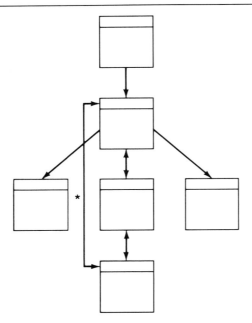

(c) Representation of recursive program unit calls
with more than two subprograms

*FIGURE 8-11.  (continued)*

statements for a called program unit, as shown in Figure 8-12(c).
Parameters received by the called program unit (i.e., the in mode)
are shown as shaded circles on an arrow that points from the
geometric figure for the body of the calling program unit to the
geometric figure for the specification of the called program unit.
Parameters to be returned by the called program unit (i.e., the out
mode) are shown as shaded circles on an arrow that points from the
geometric figure for the specification of the called program unit to
the geometric figure for the body of the caller. Parameters received,
modified, and exported (i.e., the in out mode) are shown as shaded
circles on an arrow that points to both the calling program unit and
the called procedure. A subprogram call that does not require all
parameter-passing modes can be represented by only one or two
arrows, as appropriate.

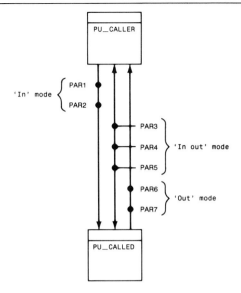

(a) Representation of data flow between
Ada procedures

```
PU_CALLED (PAR1, PAR2, PAR3, PAR4, PAR5, PAR6, PAR7);
```

(b) Ada statement used to call procedure PU_CALLED

```
procedure PU_CALLED (PAR1 : in INTEGER;
                     PAR2 : in FLOAT;
                     PAR3 : in out FLOAT;
                     PAR4 : in out FLOAT;
                     PAR5 : in out INTEGER;
                     PAR6 : out FLOAT;
                     PAR7 : out INTEGER) is
begin
  . . .
end PU_CALLED;
```

(c) Ada statements for procedure PU_CALLED

FIGURE 8-12.   SMART view of data flow between subprograms

### Representing Library Units External to a Main Subprogram

We can also use the notation for SMART to represent library units external to a main Ada subprogram. Specifically, Figure 8-13(a) shows SMART notation to specify library units to be external to a main procedure, accessible to it through the use of the Ada with clause. As also shown, SMART notation can specify packages to be declared within the body of the main Ada procedure. As shown in Figure 8-13(b), a SMART view can specify a sequence of calls to the procedures visible in declared packages and packages external to the main Ada procedure.

## 8.4.3   Views of Task Rendezvous

A SMART view can represent the passage of data from one task to another during rendezvous, which is initiated by one task calling an entry in a second task. As is the case for a procedure, data to be passed can be of the in, out, or in out modes. Design requirements for such data passage are represented as shown in Figure 8-14(a). (Ada source statements for the acceptor task named FACTOR_ CORRECT are shown in Figure 8-14(b).) As Figure 8-14(a) shows, design requirements for parameter passing between two tasks at rendezvous is represented by arrows drawn diagonally between the calling task and an entry in the acceptor task. An arrow is provided for each possible mode of passage, with circles on the arrow representing the data entities to be transferred. A task entry not requiring all parameter-passing modes can be represented by one or two arrows. For example, a task entry with only the in and out modes is shown in Figure 8-15(a). (Ada source statements for the acceptor task named ALARM are shown in Figure 8-15(b).)

In addition to representing unconditional entry calls, where caller tasks wait indefinitely for a rendezvous, the SMART view just described can represent conditional entry calls. A conditional entry call occurs when the calling task can take an alternative action upon not receiving immediate response from the acceptor task. In a SMART view for task rendezvous, a conditional task entry call is represented by a tilde on the arrows that connect the calling tasks and the acceptor tasks, as shown in Figure 8-16(a). (Ada source statements for the calling task are shown in Figure 8-16(b).) A conditional task entry call may also be time-conditional. In that case, the caller task takes alternative action if its call is not accepted within $T$ units of time. A time-conditional call is represented by a $T$ adjacent to the

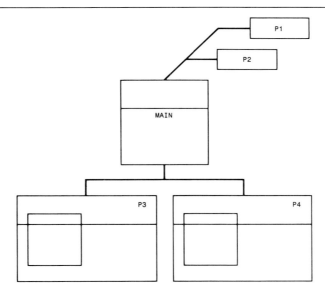

(a) Library units internal and external to the main
    Ada subprogram

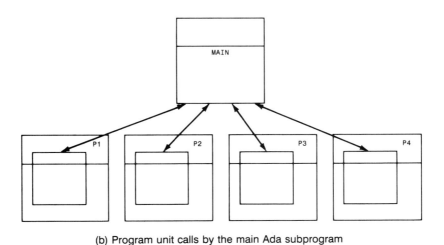

(b) Program unit calls by the main Ada subprogram

FIGURE 8-13.   SMART view of the main Ada subprogram

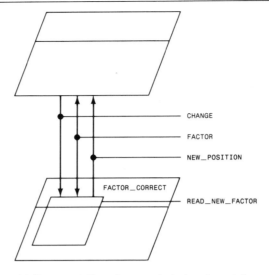

(a) Representation of access to task entry points
(all modes)

```
task FACTOR_CORRECT is
  entry READ_NEW_FACTOR (CHANGE      : in FACTOR_TYPE;
                         FACTOR      : in out FACTOR_TYPE;
                         NEW_FACTOR : out FACTOR_TYPE);
end FACTOR_CORRECT;

task body FACTOR_CORRECT is
  . . .
  accept READ_NEW_FACTOR (CHANGE        : in FACTOR_TYPE;
                          FACTOR        : in out FACTOR_TYPE;
                          NEW_POSITION : out FACTOR_TYPE) do

  . . .
  end READ_NEW_FACTOR;
end FACTOR_CORRECT;
```

(b) Ada source statements for task FACTOR_CORRECT

FIGURE 8-14.   SMART view of task rendezvous with parameter passing
in the in, in out, and out modes

tilde, as illustrated in Figure 8-17(a). (Ada source statements for the calling task are shown in Figure 8-17(b).)

Like the caller task, the acceptor task may have conditions associated with its acceptance of an entry call. When that is the case, a tilde is placed inside the acceptor task's entry representation, as shown in Figure 8-18(a). (Ada source statements for the body of the acceptor task are shown in Figure 8-18(b).) Also like the caller task, the acceptor task may be time-conditional. When that is the case, a

T is placed inside the entry representation, as shown in Figure 8-19(a). (Ada source statements for the body of the acceptor task are shown in Figure 8-19(b).)

In addition to the preceding two cases, acceptance of entry calls may be in a specified fixed order or in time order (on a first-come, first-served basis). Entries accepted in fixed order are represented by numbers within the affected entry points: 1 indicates first in order, as illustrated in Figure 8-20(a). (Ada source statements for the body of the acceptor task are shown in Figure 8-20(b).) Acceptance on a first-arrival basis is assumed unless fixed order is directly specified.

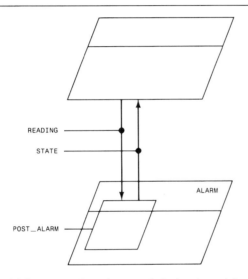

(a) Representation of access to task entry point

```
task ALARM is
  entry POST_ALARM (READING : in READING_TYPE;
                    STATE   : out STATUS_TYPE);
end ALARM;

task body ALARM is
  . . .
  accept POST_ALARM (READING : in READING_TYPE;
                     STATE   : out STATE_TYPE do
  . . .
  end POST_ALARM;
end ALARM;
```

(b) Ada source statements for task ALARM

FIGURE 8-15. SMART view for task rendezvous with parameter passing in the in and out modes

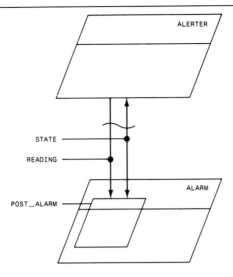

(a) Representation of a conditional task entry call

```
task ALERTER is
   . . .
end ALERTER;
task body ALERTER is
   . . .
   select
     ALARM.POST_ALARM (READING, STATE);
   else
     . . . -- some alternative action
   end select;
   . . .
end ALERTER;
```

(b) Ada source statements for the task entry call

*FIGURE 8-16.*   SMART view of a conditional task entry call

## 8.4.4  Views of Ada Generics

SMART views can represent generic procedures and packages, as described next.

### *Representing a Generic Procedure*

A generic procedure is represented by a dashed version of the geometric figure for a procedure, as shown in Figure 8-21. In a SMART view that represents parameter passing to and from a generic Ada procedure, passed data entities with generic type information are represented by unshaded circles, as shown in Figure 8-22(a). Ada permits the range of values permissible in a type definition for the passed data entity to be generic for the in and in out modes of data passing. (The out mode cannot be used with a generic parameter. Ada source statements for the generic procedure in Figure 8-22(a) are shown in Figure 8-22(b).) Values of missing parameters in the incomplete type definitions can be supplied as part of generic instantiations, as needed at different points in a large computer program. Pseudocode can be used to represent a generic instantiation, as shown in Figure 8-22(c). Missing type information can be supplied in a table, as shown in Figure 8-23. (Ada source statements for this instantiation are shown in Figure 8-24.) Note that in Figure 8-22(c),

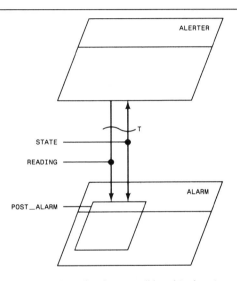

(a) Representation of a time-conditional task entry call

```
task ALERTER is
   . . .
end ALERTER;
task body ALERTER is

   . . .
 select
   ALARM.POST_ALARM (READING,STATE);
 or
   delay T;
 end select;
   . . .
end ALERTER;
```

(b) Ada source statements for the task entry calls

*FIGURE 8-17.* SMART view of a time-conditional task entry call

pseudocode for an instantiation of a generic procedure is indicated by dashed lines; in Figure 8-23, values for incomplete parameters in generic type definitions are provided.

### Representing Generic Packages

A generic package is represented by a dashed version of the geometric figure for the package with a dashed generic part drawn above it, as shown in Figure 8-25(a). The predefined packages SEQUENTIAL _IO and DIRECT_IO are examples of generic Ada packages. These

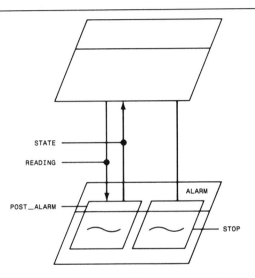

STATE

READING

POST_ALARM

ALARM

STOP

(a) Representation of conditional task acceptance

```
. . .
task body ALARM is
  . . .
  select
    when X = ? =>
      accept POST_ALARM (READING : in READING_TYPE;
                         STATE   : out STATE_TYPE) do
        . . .
      end POST_ALARM;
  or
    when Y = ? =>
      accept STOP do
        . . .
      end STOP;
  end select;
  . . .
end ALARM;
```

(b) Ada source statements for the task acceptance

*FIGURE 8-18.* SMART view of conditional task acceptance

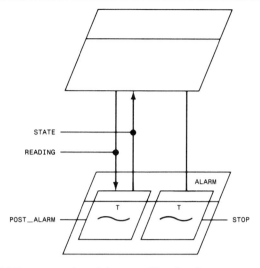

(a) Representation of time conditional task acceptance

```
        . . .
    task body ALARM is
        . . .
      select
        accept POST_ALARM (READING : in READING_TYPE;
                           STATE   : out STATE_TYPE) do
          . . .
        end POST_ALARM;
      or
        accept STOP do
          . . .
        end STOP;
      or
        delay T;      -- timeout
      end select;
        . . .
    end ALARM;
```

(b) Ada source statements for the entry call
    acceptance

FIGURE 8-19.   SMART view of time-conditional task entry call
acceptance

packages are used for data written and read by a computer (e.g., to store data on disc or magnetic tape). Their access is represented by dashed versions of the geometric figure for an Ada with clause, as shown in Figure 8-25(b).

Another predefined Ada package named TEXT_IO is used for input and output of data readable by users. Unlike SEQUENTIAL_IO and DIRECT_IO, TEXT_IO is not generic but an ordinary Ada

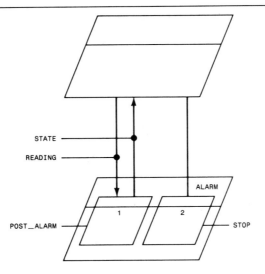

(a) Representation acceptance on a fixed order basis

```
. . .
task body ALARM is
. . .
   accept POST_ALARM (READING : in READING_TYPE;
                      STATE   : out STATE_TYPE) do
. . .
   accept STOP;
. . .
end ALARM;
```

(b) Ada source statements for the entry call
    acceptance

FIGURE 8-20.   SMART view of fixed order task entry call acceptance

FIGURE 8-21.   Geometric figure for a generic procedure

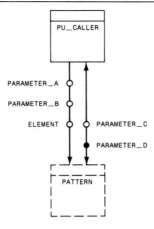

(a) Representation of data passage to and from a
generic procedure

```
generic
  type PARAMETER_A_TYPE is (<>);
  type PARAMETER_B_TYPE is digits <> range <>;
  type ELEMENT_TYPE is (<>);
  type PARAMETER_C_TYPE is array (INTEGER range <>) of
    ELEMENT_TYPE;

procedure PATTERN (PARAMETER_A : in PARAMETER_A_TYPE;
                   PARAMETER_B : in PARAMETER_B_TYPE;
                   ELEMENT     : in ELEMENT_TYPE;
                   PARAMETER_C : in out PARAMETER_C_TYPE;
                   PARAMETER_D : in out PARAMETER_D_TYPE);
begin

  . . .

end PATTERN;
```

(b) Ada source statements for generic procedure
PATTERN

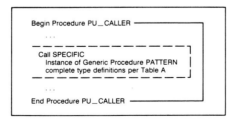

(c) Pseudocode for an instance of generic procedure
PATTERN

FIGURE 8-22. Representation of a generic procedure

| Scalar Types | | | |
|---|---|---|---|
| Name of Data Type | Category | Permissible Values | Increment of Coarseness/ Decimal Places |
| PARAMETER_A_TYPE | Enumeration | A, B, C, D | |
| PARAMETER_B_TYPE | Real | 1.0 to 99.0 | 2 decimal places |
| ELEMENT_TYPE | Integer | | |

| Array Type | | | |
|---|---|---|---|
| Name of Data Type | Dimension | Indices per Dimension | Component Type |
| PARAMETER_C_TYPE | 3 | 1 | ELEMENT_TYPE |

FIGURE 8-23. Completion of type definitions for instance SPECIFIC of generic procedure PATTERN

```
    . . .
type INSTANCE_A_TYPE is (A, B, C, D);
type INSTANCE_B_TYPE is digits 2 range 1.0 . . 99.0;
type INSTANCE_ELEMENT_TYPE is INTEGER;
type INSTANCE_C_TYPE is array (1 . . 3) of ELEMENT_TYPE;
procedure SPECIFIC is new PATTERN
                (PARAMETER_A_TYPE ⇒ INSTANCE_A_TYPE,
                 PARAMETER_B_TYPE ⇒ INSTANCE_B_TYPE,
                    ELEMENT_TYPE ⇒ INSTANCE_ELEMENT_TYPE,
                 PARAMETER_C_TYPE ⇒ INSTANCE_C_TYPE);
```

FIGURE 8-24. Ada source statements for instance SPECIFIC of generic procedure PATTERN

package. Accordingly, a SMART geometric figure for an Ada package can be used to represent TEXT_IO, and its access can be represented by the standard geometric figure for an Ada with clause.

### Representing Instances of Ada Generic Packages
A SMART view can represent instances of generic Ada packages. Specifically, zigzag lines are drawn from a geometric figure for an Ada generic package to boldface representations of two or more Ada packages, one for each instance of the generic, as shown in Figure 8-26. Corresponding Ada source statements are shown in Figure 8-27.

(a) Representation of a generic Ada package

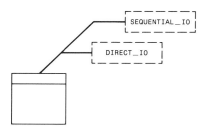

(b) Representation of with clause access to generic
Ada packages

*FIGURE 8-25.* SMART views for generic packages

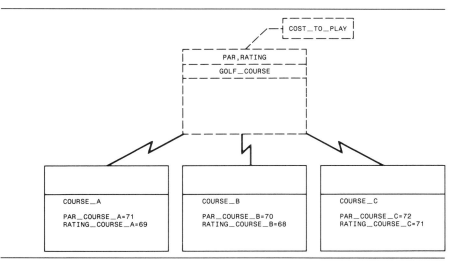

*FIGURE 8-26.* SMART view of instances of a generic package

```
 generic package
 generic
   PAR     : in INTEGER := 72;
   RATING  : in INTEGER := 72;
 with procedure COST_TO_PLAY (MONTH : in MONTH_TYPE;
                          TIME_OF_DAY : in TIME_OF_DAY_TYPE);
   package GOLF_COURSE is
   . . .
```

```
 INSTANCE A
 procedure COST_COURSE_A (MONTH : in MONTH_TYPE;
                       TIME_OF_DAY : in TIME_OF_DAY_TYPE) is . . .
 package COURSE_A is new GOLF_COURSE (PAR_COURSE_A ⇒ 71;
                                   RATING_COURSE_A ⇒ 69);
```

```
 INSTANCE B
 procedure COST_COURSE_B (MONTH : in MONTH_TYPE;
                       TIME_OF_DAY : in TIME_OF_DAY_TYPE) is . . .
 package COURSE_B is new GOLF_COURSE (PAR_COURSE_B ⇒ 70;
                                   RATING_COURSE_B ⇒ 68);
```

```
 INSTANCE C
 procedure COST_COURSE_C (MONTH : in MONTH_TYPE;
                       TIME_OF_DAY : in TIME_OF_DAY_TYPE) is . . .
 package COURSE_C is new GOLF_COURSE (PAR_COURSE_C ⇒ 72;
                                   RATING_COURSE_C ⇒ 71);
```

*FIGURE 8-27.* Ada source statements for the Ada generic package and instances of it shown in Figure 8-26

## 8.4.5  Views of Task Types

SMART views can represent task types and instances of task types. The SMART representation of a task type is a dashed version of the geometric figure for a task. To represent instances of the task type, zigzag lines connect the geometric figure for a task type with bold-face geometric figures for a task, one for each instance of the task type, as shown in Figure 8-28. Corresponding Ada source statements are shown in Figure 8-29.

## 8.4.6  Representing the Design of Data Structures and Operations

Different points of view exist on how to represent data structures and operations internal to an independent package. Some software engineers feel the Ada language itself can be used to represent such design requirements. In fact, certain advanced features of Ada might best be represented by Ada source statements. In this context, some

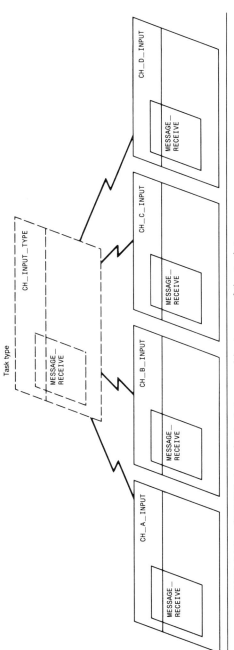

*FIGURE 8-28.* SMART view of a task type and instances of the task type

```
┌─────────────────────────┐
│ task type declaration   │
└─────────────────────────┘
task type CH_INPUT_TYPE is
  entry MESSAGE_RECEIVE;

   . . .

end CH_INPUT_TYPE;
┌───────────────────────────┐
│ Instances of the Task Type │
└───────────────────────────┘
  CH_A_INPUT : CH_INPUT_TYPE;
  CH_B_INPUT : CH_INPUT_TYPE;
  CH_C_INPUT : CH_INPUT_TYPE;
  CH_D_INPUT : CH_INPUT_TYPE;
```

*FIGURE 8-29.* Ada source statements for the task type and instances of it shown in Figure 8-28

software engineers feel a subset of Ada syntax should be used, others feel the complete Ada language should be used, and still others feel a superset of Ada should be used. And there are some software engineers who feel this view of a design is best specified by descriptors for data elements and pseudocode for operations. The approach depends on the nature of the program to be designed, the background of the program development team, and the contractual requirements. Designers must keep in mind that the program under development eventually will be maintained by personnel who are not part of the development team. Therefore, a straightforward approach to specifying design requirements is important.

### Representing Design for Data Structures

For the design examples in this book, the designs for a data structure are represented by descriptors in tables. For example, descriptors suggested in Chapter 5 could be provided in the tabular format shown in Table 8-1, where part (a) specifies requirements for constants, part (b) specifies variables, part (c) specifies scalar types, part (d) specifies array types, and part (e) specifies record types. This representation of a data structure should be readable by all project members, including project managers and system engineers as well as software engineers and programmers.

### Representing Design for Operations

For the design examples in this book, the design for operations of a program unit is represented by pseudocode. In pseudocode, Ada `if`, `case`, and `loop` statements are used to specify logic and decisions to be made in the body of a program unit, as illustrated in Figure 8-30.

TABLE 8-1.   Tabular formats for data structure descriptors

| Name of Constant | Value | Comments |
|---|---|---|
| . | . | . |
| . | . | . |
| . | . | . |

(a) Constants

| Name of Data Entity | Type | | Comments |
|---|---|---|---|
| | Name | Category | |
| . | . | . | . |
| . | . | . | . |
| . | . | . | . |

(b) Variables

| Name of Data Type | Category | Permissible Values | Increment of Coarseness Decimal Places |
|---|---|---|---|
| . | . | . | . |
| . | . | . | . |
| . | . | . | . |

(c) Scalar types

| Name of Data Type | Dimension | Indices per Dimension | Component Type | Comments |
|---|---|---|---|---|
| . | . | . | . | . |
| . | . | . | . | . |
| . | . | . | . | . |

(d) Array types

| Name of Data Type | Name of Each Component | Name of Type for Each Component | Comments |
|---|---|---|---|
| . | . | . | . |
| . | . | . | . |
| . | . | . | . |

(e) Record types

The if statement selects a course of action, depending on the truth value of one or more conditions. In Ada, there are three basic forms of the if statement:

- if-then
- if-then-else
- if-then-elsif

In each case, the if statement is terminated with an end if clause.

In pseudocode, *mathematical algorithms* to be implemented in the body of a program unit are represented by notations from mathematics and physics. In pseudocode, *program unit calls* also are shown. However, for the sake of clarity and simplification, we can omit parameters passed in conjunction with each call and represent such parameter passing in a SMART view for data flow. In addition, we can use annotation to indicate that a called program unit resides in an Ada package to be accessed through an Ada with clause. Specifically, as illustrated in Figure 8-31, this can be represented by the geometric figure for the Ada with clause, which is a small rectangle enclosing the name of the package in which the called program unit resides.

Pseudocode for a specific program unit can be preceded by an abstract and can include bracketing to help sort out logic. An abstract briefly describes the purpose of the program unit and factors relevant to algorithms, action, logic, and so forth. Bracketing can help make complex logic understandable.

To make the pseudocode clear, we can use the following:

- if statements with brackets bounding the beginning and the end of the statement, as illustrated in Figure 8-30(a)
- case statements with brackets, as illustrated in Figure 8-30(b)
- loop statements as illustrated in Figure 8-30(c)
- for and while statements with brackets, as illustrated in Figure 8-30(d).

To repeat a loop a specific number of times, the basic loop can be preceded by a for iteration clause. Another form of iteration can be accomplished with the while statement, whereby a sequence of statements is repeated as long as some condition is true.

```
Begin Procedure SAMPLE_2A
    . . .
if Y > 0 then
    . . .
end if

if X > 0 then
    . . .
else
    . . .
end if

if A = B then
    . . .
elsif A = C then
    . . .
else
    . . .
end if
    . . .
End Procedure SAMPLE_A
```

(a) Use of IF statements

```
Begin Procedure SAMPLE_2B
    . . .
case TEST is
    when PASS ⇒ Call Procedure CONTINUE
    when FAIL ⇒ Call Procedure RESTART
end case
    . . .
End Procedure SAMPLE_2B
```

(b) Use of the CASE statement

```
Begin Procedure SAMPLE_2C
    . . .
loop
    . . .
end loop

loop
    . . .
    exit when B < MAX
    . . .
end loop
    . . .
End Procedure SAMPLE_2c
```

(c) Use of the LOOP statement

*FIGURE 8-30.* Pseudocode

```
Begin Procedure SAMPLE_2D ──┐
 . . .                       │
loop for (i = 1,4) ──┐       │
 . . .               │       │
end loop ────────────┘       │

while B>0 loop ──────┐       │
     .               │       │
 . . .               │       │
end loop ────────────┘       │
 . . .                       │
End Procedure SAMPLE_2D ─────┘
```

(d) Use of the FOR and WHILE statements

*FIGURE 8-30.* (*continued*)

```
Begin Procedure SAMPLE_3 ────────────────────┐
  . . .                                       │
Call Procedure EX_1                           │
Call Procedure COMMON_R1───┤ Package P1 │     │
Call Procedure EX_2                           │

  . . .                                       │

Call Entry A in Task BUFFER                   │
Call Entry B in Task BUFFER                   │

  . . .                                       │

End Procedure SAMPLE_3 ───────────────────────┘
```

*FIGURE 8-31.* Representation of program unit calls

## 8.5 Key Concepts

- Selected aspects of a design for a large and complex computer program can be presented with program design language, or PDL. PDL is meant to establish an abstracted representation of a large computer program; as such, certain detail about the program is not specified. In practice, the information included in a design and the detail excluded may depend upon the designer, his or her comprehension of the program, and what he or she feels is especially important.
- The Ada language itself is used as a PDL as well as a programming language. Such use is appropriate because Ada can be used to represent a computer program in an abstracted manner, excluding certain implementation detail.

- In practice, a comprehensive PDL for a program unit to be implemented in Ada should specify a package's data structures and operations, as well as the architecture of a large computer program as a set of packages and data flow between the packages.
- For large and complex computer programs, the bulk and complexity of design representation with PDL may become an issue. Because of this, the design representation should be concise and crisp.
- Schematic multiview abstracted representation techniques for Ada, or SMART Ada, can be used to represent certain design views for a large Ada computer program in a concise and crisp manner. Because it is not possible to consolidate all the details of a design into one or two views, SMART Ada presents design information in different views.
- SMART Ada uses geometric figures for Ada program units as the basis for its graphical views. Specifically, a square represents an Ada procedure, a circle represents an Ada function, a parallelogram represents an Ada task, and a rectangle represents an Ada package. Each of these geometric figures is divided into a narrow part, which represents the program unit's specification, and a wide part, which represents the program unit's body.
- SMART views can represent Ada packages and program units that are to be visible in the Ada packages.
- SMART views can represent subprograms and tasks used in the implementation of the body of a package, the passage of data from one procedure to another, and the passage of data between tasks during rendezvous.
- SMART views can represent generic program units and instances of the generic program units. SMART views can also represent task types and instances of task types.
- Pseudocode can be used to specify operations to be performed by program units, and tables of descriptors can be used to specify data structures.

## 8.6   Exercises

1. In what ways can Ada be used as a PDL?
2. What are the advantages of using Ada as a PDL? The disadvantages?
3. What are the geometric figures of SMART Ada?

4. What design views are provided by SMART Ada? What is the purpose of each?
5. Give an example of a SMART view for packages A, B, C, D, and E, where
   a. package B interacts with packages A, B, C, and D
   b. package C interacts with package E
6. Give an example of a SMART view for three different data entities being passed between procedure A and procedure B in the in, in out, and out modes, when procedure A calls procedure B.
7. Give an example of a SMART view for five different data entities being passed between task A and task B in the in and out modes during rendezvous, where task B is the acceptor task.
8. Say that a generic package is applied in five different ways in a large computer program. Give an example of a SMART view for the five different instances of the generic package, which includes two incomplete type definitions.
9. Say that a design identifies four tasks with the same bodies and a single corresponding entry point. Provide a SMART view of four instances of a task type that can be used in the design to replace the four tasks.
10. Specify the requirements for a data structure, that includes a counter with positive integer values not to exceed 1000, a variable with two decimal places not to exceed 10 and not to be less than $-10$, a variable with three decimal places not to exceed 2 and with an increment of coarseness of .001, and a record for time, including the hour, day, month, and year. Represent the requirements by descriptors in a table.
11. Present design requirements for operations in an Ada subprogram that is to calculate the area of a square, a rectangle, or a circle. Represent the design by pseudocode and provide an abstract of the scope of the program unit.

# CHAPTER 9

# Steps for Designing
# a Large Computer Program

Design is fundamental in the development of engineering systems. A design is developed at great expense over a significant period of time. As we discussed in Chapter 8, blueprints are developed in the design of civil engineering systems, mechanical drawings are developed in the design of mechanical systems, and schematic and wiring diagrams are developed in the design of electrical systems. Like other fields of engineering, design is fundamental to the economical development of software systems.

When preparing a design for a computer program, we make the transition from software requirements to an abstracted representation of the computer program. The design can be thought of as a representation of the program lying somewhere between the requirements and implementing code. In preparing a design, the software requirements can be assessed to identify real-world entities, independent packages can be selected to model the real-world entities, and an abstracted design can be prepared for each package. Therefore, a design specifies a set of independent packages as the basic building blocks of a large and complex computer program. These building blocks establish a much coarser level of granularity in the architectural structure of a program than levels of small program units used in the past.

## 9.1    Introduction

In this chapter, we describe steps for designing a computer program as a set of independent packages that will be independent and self-sufficient.

## 9.2    Steps for Designing a Computer Program

The following are basic engineering steps for designing a large computer program:

1. Identify and define a set of packages that partition a program into independent parts.
2. Specify logical concurrency among the independent packages.
3. Specify interfaces for the independent packages.
4. Specify the internal design of each independent package, defining data structures and operations.
5. Review and refine the design.

These steps are expanded on next.

### 9.2.1    Step 1: Identify and Define Independent Packages

To begin the design process, we assess the requirements for a large computer program to identify real-world entities that can be modeled as a set of independent packages. To meet this end, documented requirements for the program (and possibly reports or textbooks describing algorithms or events encompassed by the program) can be collected together and analyzed. When selecting the real-world entities as independent packages, designers should keep in mind the role they are to play, information they have to keep track of and store, organizations and locations they should have knowledge of, entities they are to interact with, entities and devices they are to control, and entities and devices they are to use. It is important that the requirements for the real-world entities assigned to each independent package are (a) related and consistent (e.g., requirements for database management should not be mixed with requirements for statistical processing and display), and (b) easy to understand, implement, and test.

In a software design, we bridge the gap between a system engineering view of a problem space and a software engineering view. From a systems engineering point of view, the program design can be thought of as a model of the real-world entities found in the problem.

From a software engineering point of view, the real-world entities are to be modeled as independent software entities that receive, process, and output information.

It is also important for designers to remember that requirements assigned to each independent package must be independent and self-sufficient. Each package is designed to have its own unique local data structure and operations.

When selecting a set of independent packages, the designer should review the objective of the subject computer program, for instance, as stated in the software requirements specification (which was described in Section 2.2.3 of Chapter 2), and delineate an overview of how the computer program is to meet that objective. For example, the objective in the ICU example was to (a) receive and route messages between communication channels, operator work-stations, and a radar station, (b) make a record of message transactions, and (c) respond to operator commands.

An overview of how the ICU could fulfill this role might read as follows: "The ICU is to receive messages from a radar station in format X and from the communications channels a, b, c, and d in format Z and is to route information contained in these messages to the operation centers as messages in format Y. Messages received from the radar station are to be routed to both operation centers. Messages received over communications line a are to be routed to operations center A, messages received over communications line b are to be routed to operations center B, and messages to be received over communications lines c and d are to be routed to both operations centers. The ICU is to record all messages received and all messages routed, along with the date and time the message was received or distributed and the source or destination of the message. Upon request by a system operator, the ICU is to retrieve historical records of message transactions and is to generate tabular displays of those transactions."

This overview was written in the context of data and operations on those data and does not include software terminology (e.g., program units, data types, task rendezvous). It was written more from the point of view of a system engineer, not from the point of view of programmers responsible for developing and maintaining the large computer program.

Upon assessing this overview, the designer might decide that the design for the ICU should specify that a single Ada package is to be used to encapsulate the implementation of the ICU. In that case, a visible data structure in the package would include type definitions for the various messages to be received. Unique operations might include operators for receiving messages, routing the messages, establishing a historical database of message transactions, and responding to operator requests. If all this could be accomplished with 5,000 to 10,000 source statements with clear and understandable data structures and operations, then this design might be appropriate.

However, if the messages were sufficiently complex that the data structure was not easy to understand, the designer might decide that the design for the ICU should specify that more than one independent package is to be used to model real-world entities found in requirements. Assuming this to be the case, from a system engineering point of view the design might specify the independent packages for the real-world entities *communications lines, messages, data manager,* and *operator console.*

As shown in Figure 9-1(a), from a software engineering point of view the *communications lines* independent package would encapsulate a data structure that defines messages in formats X and Z, and data entities unique to the formulation of operations needed to receive messages from communications channels a, b, c, and d and from the radar station and ultimately to forward them for distribution. The *messages* independent package (Figure 9-1(b)) would encapsulate a unique data structure for messages and data entities unique to the formulation of operations needed to prepare messages and distribute them to the operations centers. The *data manager* independent package would encapsulate a unique data structure for the data entities shown in Figure 9-1(c) and the data entities unique to the formulation of operations needed to make a historical record of received messages and their sources and of routed messages and their destinations. The *operator console* independent package would encapsulate a unique data structure for the data entities shown in Figure 9-1(d), and data entities unique to the formulation of operations and specific program units for operations needed to respond to operator demands from consoles A and B.

As shown in Figure 9-1, such a design might specify that data and operations for the *communications lines* model are to be encapsulated in an Ada package called ICU_COMMUNICATION_LINES, for the *messages* model in an Ada package called ICU_MESSAGES, for the *data manager* model in an Ada package called ICU_DATA_MANAGER, and for the *operator console* model in an Ada package called ICU_CONSOLE.

| ICU_COMMUNICATION_LINES | |
|---|---|
| *Data* | *Operations* |
| Messages (format X) | Monitor I/O board |
| Messages (format Z) | Receive messages |
| | Process messages |
| | Export for routing |
| | Export for recording |

(a) *Communications lines* independent package

| ICU_MESSAGES | |
|---|---|
| *Data* | *Operations* |
| Messages (format X) | Input received messages |
| Messages (format Z) | Determine destinations |
| Destination table | Prepare output messages |
| Destination of message | Export for recording |
| Source of message | Distribute output messages |
| Messages (format Y) | |

(b) *Messages* independent package

| ICU_DATA_MANAGER | |
|---|---|
| *Data* | *Operations* |
| Messages (format X) | Receive input messages |
| Messages (format Z) | Receive output messages |
| Messages (format Y) | Stack messages |
| Source of message | Build historical database |
| Destination of message | Retrieve data |
| Date/time | |

(c) *Data manager* independent package

| ICU_CONSOLE | |
|---|---|
| *Data* | *Operations* |
| Messages (format Y) | Receive operator requests |
| Operator requests | Receive messages |
| Error messages | Receive data |
| Data displays | Display data |
| Historical data | Print data |
| Source/destination | Display received message |
| Free text | Display text |

(d) *Operator console* independent package

*FIGURE 9-1.* Data and operations for ICU packages

## 9.2.2 Step 2: Specify Logical Concurrency among the Independent Packages

The second step in designing a large computer program in Ada is to specify logical concurrency to be introduced among the set of independent packages to account for activities that may happen at the same time. In a real-world problem, two or more independent packages may have to logically execute concurrently to satisfy real-world requirements. For example, at essentially the same time, one package could be monitoring sensors, while a second is servicing operator requests, while a third is receiving information over a communications link.

As discussed in Chapter 4, an Ada design can specify the use of Ada tasks to facilitate concurrency. For the ICU example, the design could specify that Ada tasks are to be declared within Ada packages as models of independent packages meant to operate in a logically concurrent manner. Let us again consider the concurrency that could be introduced into the ICU design. Since messages may arrive at the ICU at essentially the same time an ICU operator is making a request, the ICU's design could call for the logically concurrent execution of two of the independent packages. As shown in Figure 9-2, this could be accomplished by encapsulating the task MESSAGE_ PROCESSOR in the package ICU_COMMUNICATION_LINES and the task OPERATOR_INTERFACE in the package ICU_CONSOLE.

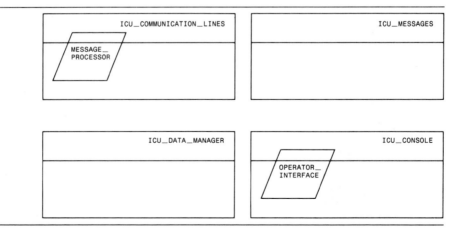

FIGURE 9-2. Design for concurrency among the independent packages in the ICU problem

## 9.2.3 Step 3: Specify Interfaces for the Independent Packages

The third step is to specify interfaces for the independent packages. These interfaces are to service multiple demands on the computer program and facilitate interaction between the packages when necessary.

### *Servicing Multiple Demands*

To service multiple demands in the ICU problem, the ICU design could specify a set of entry points for the task MESSAGE_PROCESSOR of the package ICU_COMMUNICATION_LINES and the task OPERATOR_INTERFACE of the package ICU_CONSOLE. The entry points of the task MESSAGE_PROCESSOR would facilitate receiving messages from the communications channels and the radar station. The entry points of the task OPERATOR_INTERFACE would facilitate response to requests from the operator consoles. Specifically, as shown in Figure 9-3(a), the design could specify that the task MESSAGE_PROCESSOR is to receive messages from channel A in CH_A_INPUT_MESSAGE via its entry CH_A_RECEIVE, in CH_B_INPUT_MESSAGE via its entry CH_B_RECEIVE, in CH_C_INPUT_MESSAGE via its entry CH_C_RECEIVE, and in CH_D_INPUT_MESSAGE via its entry CH_D_RECEIVE, where each message is to be in format Z. Also, through rendezvous with the radar station, the task MESSAGE_PROCESSOR could receive messages in RADAR_MESSAGE via its entry point RADAR_RECEIVE, where each message is to be in format X. As indicated in Figure 9-3, the acceptance of calls to the entry points would be conditional, that is, if a call is not pending for acceptance, then an alternative action is to be taken. We do not want the program to stop processing at an acceptance statement while it is waiting for a call to be made.

As shown in Figure 9-3(b), the design could specify that the task OPERATOR_INTERFACE is to receive requests in REQUEST_A from operations center A via its entry point OPS_A_RECEIVE and in REQUEST_B from operations center B via its entry point OPS_B_RECEIVE. The design could specify that REQUEST_A and REQUEST_B are to be enumeration types with the value FREE_TEXT or MESSAGE_TRANSACTIONS. When entry point OPS_A_RECEIVE receives FREE_TEXT in REQUEST_A, this input would be followed by textual data in the input entity FREE_TEXT_A. When it received MESSAGE_TRANSACTIONS in REQUEST_A, this input would be followed by TIME_BEGIN_A and TIME_END_A, indicating the time interval over

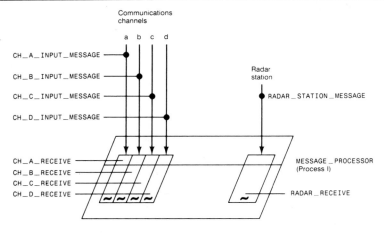

Communications channels

(a) Task MESSAGE_PROCESSOR of package
ICU_COMMUNICATION_LINES

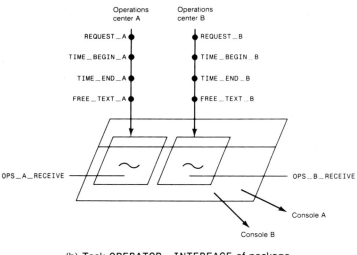

(b) Task OPERATOR_INTERFACE of package
ICU_CONSOLE

*FIGURE 9-3.* Tasks for servicing multiple demands

which a record of message transactions is wanted. As also shown in Figure 9-3(b), the design could specify that the task OPERATOR_ INTERFACE is to export messages to consoles at operation centers A and B.

### Interaction between Independent Packages

To enable interaction between packages, the ICU design could specify that the procedure ROUTE_INFO is to be declared in the package ICU_MESSAGES and that the procedures STORE_MESSAGE and RETRIEVE are to be declared in ICU_DATA_MANAGER, as shown in Figure 9-4. These procedures, along with the tasks MESSAGE_PROCESSOR and OPERATOR_INTERFACE, are to allow information passing between interacting packages. Specifically, as shown in Figure 9-5, the design could specify information is to pass between these visible program units as follows:

■ For historical record purposes, messages received by the task MESSAGE_PROCESSOR of the package ICU_COMMUNICATION_LINES can be forwarded to the procedure STORE_MESSAGE of the package ICU_DATA_MANAGER in INPUT_MESSAGE, the date of the message's reception in DATE, the time of reception in TIME, and an indication of the source of the message in SOURCE.

■ For routing purposes, the messages received by the task MESSAGE_PROCESSOR of the package ICU_COMMUNICATION_LINES can be forwarded to the procedure ROUTE_INFO of the package ICU_MESSAGES in INPUT_MESSAGE, along with its source in SOURCE. The procedure ROUTE_INFO is to establish an output message in the appropriate format and return it in OUTPUT_MESSAGE, along with its destination in DESTINATION.

■ For storage purposes, the procedure ROUTE_INFO is to forward each output message to the procedure STORE_MESSAGE of the package ICU_DATA_MANAGER in OUTPUT_MESSAGE, along with the date in DATE, the time of routing in TIME, and the destination in DESTINATION.

■ Specific routing of the messages is to be accomplished by the task MESSAGE_PROCESSOR, which is to forward the output messages to their destinations and to entry DISPLAY of the task OPERATOR_INTERFACE in the package ICU_CONSOLE for automatic display at the operations centers.

■ To satisfy operator requests for displays, the task OPERATOR_INTERFACE can retrieve data from the historical record of message transactions by calling the procedure RETRIEVE of the package ICU_DATA_MANAGER.

Thus, data would be moved between independent packages. However, variables and flags used to implement the operations unique to

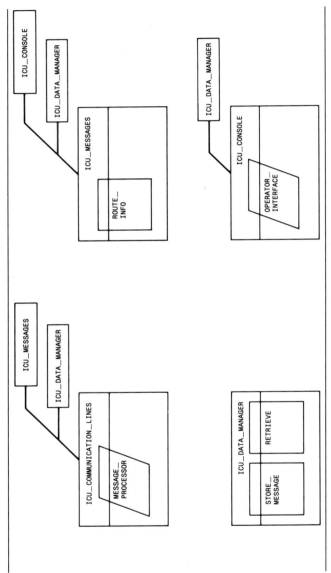

FIGURE 9-4. Procedures for interaction between independent packages

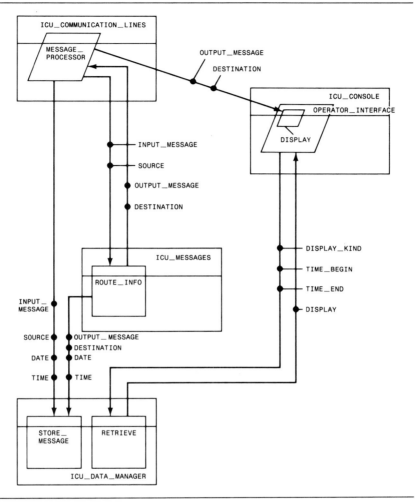

*FIGURE 9-5.* Data flow between independent packages

each package (e.g., for message storage/retrieval and message routing) would not be passed. Because of this, the design would specify packages that are essentially independent. Accordingly, changes made to the implementation of one package would not affect the implementations of the other packages. This simplifies development, testing, and maintenance.

## 9.2.4 Step 4: Specify the Internal Design of Each Independent Package

For the fourth step, we can establish the internal design of each independent package by specifying the following:

- a visible data structure (for data entities to be received and exported)
- operations
- a hidden data structure (for variables, flags, constants, and types used in the formulation of operations)

As described in Chapter 5, the design for the visible and hidden data structures can be specified by using descriptors, provided in a tabular format. The names of data structure entities should be descriptive, their definitions clear and concise, and the size of the data structure within the comprehension of the average programmer.

As noted in Chapter 6, the design for operations to be undertaken by independent packages can vary in magnitude and scope. Simple and constrained operations might be undertaken within the bodies of the visible program units. Complex and extensive operations might be segmented among visible program units and hidden program units called by the visible program units.

As an example of a design for an independent package, let's return to the ICU problem. Specifically, we will address a design for the package ICU_MESSAGES.

### *Define Descriptors for the Visible Data Structure of Package* ICU_MESSAGES

A design for the visible data structure of the package ICU_MESSAGES could be specified by the descriptor values shown in Table 9-1. Section a of this table provides descriptor values for input messages which are to be received from the radar station or the communications channels, and for messages to be distributed to the operations centers in format Y. This section also provides descriptors for data entities to be forwarded to the package ICU_DATA_MANAGER. Section b of Table 9-1 provides descriptors for record types applicable to format Y and the date. Section c provides descriptors for array types, and Section d provides descriptors for scalar types, including those applicable to components of the record types.

### *Specify Program Units Internal to Package* ICU_MESSAGES

A design should segment operations among a set of relatively small program units that are easy to understand and implement. To meet

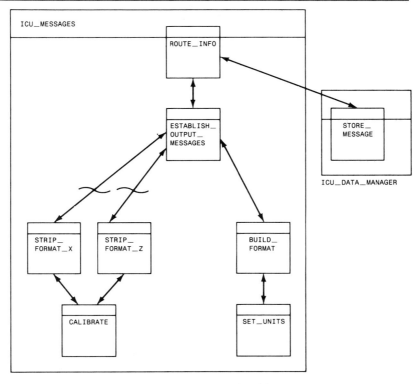

(b) Invocation of program units encapsulated in package ICU_MESSAGES

FIGURE 9-6. *(continued)*

design for operations might specify such things as decision points, repetitive action, sequences of actions, exceptions due to erroneous results, and logically concurrent events.

As an example of *design for a visible program unit*, design requirements for the procedure ROUTE_INFO could be specified as shown in Figures 9-7 and 9-8. As Figure 9-7 indicates, the procedure ROUTE_INFO is to receive an input message in INPUT_MESSAGE (and the source of the input message in SOURCE) from the task MESSAGE_PROCESSOR of the package ICU_COMMUNICATION_LINES. ROUTE_INFO then is to forward this input to the procedure ESTABLISH_OUTPUT_MESSAGES and to receive in return a properly formatted output message in OUTPUT_MESSAGE. The procedure ROUTE_INFO then is to establish the destination of the output in DESTINATION and forward the output in OUTPUT_MESSAGE (and an indication of its destination in DESTINATION) to the procedure STORE_MESSAGE of the package ICU_DATA_MANAGER (along with the date in DATE and the time of routing in TIME). Finally, ROUTE_INFO is to forward the output message in OUTPUT_MESSAGE and its destination in DESTINATION to the task MESSAGE_PROCESSOR of the package ICU_COMMUNICATION_LINES. Pseudocode for the specific processing to be performed by the procedure ROUTE_INFO is in Figure 9-8.

As an example of *design for hidden program units*, Figure 9-9 shows the data flow for program units in the body of the package ICU_MESSAGES. As this figure indicates, the procedure ESTABLISH _OUTPUT_MESSAGE is to forward the input message to the procedure

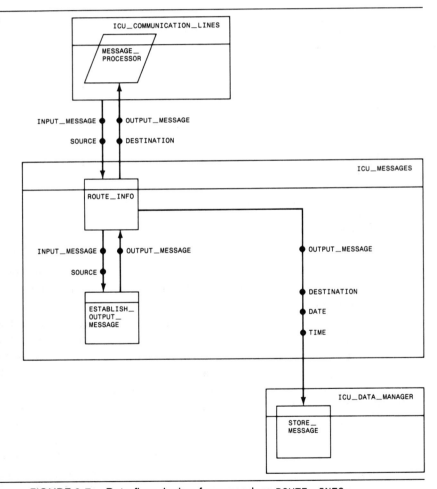

*FIGURE 9-7.* Data flow design for procedure ROUTE_INFO

```
Begin Procedure ROUTE_INFO

Receive an input message in INPUT_MESSAGE and
its source in SOURCE. All eight bytes of
input message in INPUT_MESSAGE.

Call Procedure ESTABLISH_OUTPUT_MESSAGE
to establish an output message in OUTPUT_MESSAGE

Receive OUTPUT_MESSAGE from Procedure ESTABLISH_OUTPUT_MESSAGE

Determine the destination of OUTPUT_MESSAGE as follows:
If SOURCE indicates the radar station then
    set DESTINATION to A_and_B (to signify both operations centers)
elsif SOURCE indicates Communication Channel a then
    set DESTINATION to A (to signify Operations Center A)
elsif SOURCE indicates Communication Channel b then
    set DESTINATION to B (to signify Operations Center B)
elsif SOURCE indicates Communication Channel c or d then
    set DESTINATION to A_and_B
else set OUTPUT_MESSAGE and DESTINATION to zero
    (to signify incorrect value found in SOURCE)
end if
Call Procedure STORE_MESSAGE ─── ICU_DATA_MANAGER
to store output message in historical data base
Return OUTPUT_MESSAGE and DESTINATION to caller
End Procedure ROUTE_INFO
```

FIGURE 9-8.  Pseudocode for procedure ROUTE_INFO

STRIP_FORMAT_X (or Z) to isolate the data embedded in the information field, which contains the position of an aircraft and its velocity. The position is to be inserted into the vector POSITION and the velocity into the scalar VELOCITY. The vector and the scalar are to be forwarded to the procedure CALIBRATE for proper calibration as a function of the message source (i.e., a communications channel or the radar). They are then to be forwarded to the procedure BUILD_FORMAT, which is to call the procedure SET_UNITS to convert position and velocity components to the proper units. The procedure BUILD_FORMAT then is to establish OUTPUT_COMPONENT, which is to consist of the position vector, velocity scalar, and message-start and -end flags. The procedure BUILD_FORMAT is to forward OUTPUT_COMPONENT to the procedure ESTABLISH_OUTPUT_MESSAGE, which is to add the aircraft identification number and flight path number to form OUTPUT_MESSAGE. Finally, OUTPUT_MESSAGE is to be exported to the visible procedure ROUTE_INFO for subsequent record storage and distribution.

The designer should specify the operations to be undertaken by each hidden procedure. For example, design requirements for the

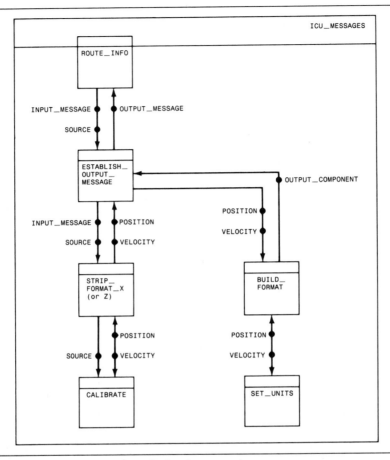

*FIGURE 9-9.* Data flow design for procedure
ESTABLISH_OUTPUT_MESSAGE

procedure ESTABLISH_OUTPUT_MESSAGE could be specified as shown in Figures 9-9 and 9-10. As the pseudocode in Figure 9-10 indicates, the procedure ESTABLISH_OUTPUT_MESSAGE is to receive an input message and its source. If the source is the radar station (format X), then the procedure STRIP_FORMAT_X is to be called to obtain the information field of the input message and to properly calibrate it. If the source is one of the communication lines (format Z), then the procedure STRIP_FORMAT_Z is to be called to obtain the information field of the input message and to properly calibrate it. In both cases, the procedure BUILD_FORMAT then is to be called to establish proper units for the output message.

```
Begin Procedure ESTABLISH_OUTPUT_MESSAGE
Receive input message in INPUT_MESSAGE and its source
in SOURCE

If SOURCE is RADAR_STATION then
    Call Procedure STRIP_FORMAT_X
        to obtain the calibrated position vector in
        POSITION and velocity in VELOCITY
Elsif SOURCE is COMM_A, COMM_B, COMM_C or COMM_D then
    Call Procedure STRIP_FORMAT_Z
        to obtain the calibrated position vector in
        POSITION and velocity in VELOCITY
End if

Call Procedure BUILD_FORMAT
    to establish output components in proper units

Construct OUTPUT_MESSAGE in format Y

Return OUTPUT_MESSAGE to caller
End Procedure ESTABLISH_OUTPUT_MESSAGE
```

*FIGURE 9-10.* Pseudocode for procedure ESTABLISH_OUTPUT_MESSAGE

Note that messages are routed from the package ICU_MESSAGES to the package ICU_COMMUNICATION_LINES. The task MESSAGE _PROCESSOR of the package ICU_COMMUNICATION_LINES forwards the output message to operations center A, operations center B, or both, as appropriate. In this way, a received message is routed to its final destination in accordance with system requirements. It also forwards the message to task OPERATOR_INTERFACE of package ICU_CONSOLE for display.

### Define Descriptors for the Hidden Data Structure
### of Package ICU_MESSAGES

The designer next would specify the requirements for the hidden data structure of the package ICU_MESSAGES. This data structure is to account for variables, constants, flags, and types used in the formulation of operations internal to the package ICU_MESSAGES. An example of an initial version of this data structure is shown in Table 9-2. Upon implementation of the package with Ada source statements, the data entities of this version would be refined, and additional data entities identified and added to the data structure. Thus, the hidden data structure can be thought of as evolving in a stepwise refinement manner. We begin with a highly abstracted

TABLE 9-2. Hidden data structure in package ICU_MESSAGES

(a) Variables

| Name of Data Entity | Type — Name | Category | Description |
|---|---|---|---|
| POSITION | TYPE_FOR_POSITION | Composite | The position of an aircraft in the X, Y, Z coordinates in meters |
| VELOCITY | TYPE_FOR_VELOCITY | Scalar | The velocity of an aircraft in meters per hour. |
| OUTPUT_COMPONENT | TYPE_FOR_OUTPUT_COMPONENT | Composite | A formatted message with the following components:<br>■ X coordinate<br>■ Y coordinate<br>■ Z coordinate<br>■ velocity |

(b) Constants

| Name of Constant | Value | Description |
|---|---|---|
| CALIBRATION_FACTOR_Z | 139.0 | Factor used to calibrate the information field of a message received in format Z from a communications channel |
| METERS_TO_FEET | 0.305 | Factor used to convert a coordinate reading in meters to feet |
| KILOMETER/HOUR_TO_MILES/HOUR | 0.620 | Factor used to convert a velocity value in kilometers per hour to miles per hour |

(c) Scalar Types

| Name of Data Type | Category | Permissible Values | Decimal Places/Increment of Coarseness |
|---|---|---|---|
| TYPE_FOR_COORDINATE | Real | -1000.00 to +1000.00 | two/0.1 |
| TYPE_FOR_VELOCITY | Integer | 50 to 350 | |

TABLE 9-2. *(continued)*

**(d) Array Types**

| Name of Data Type | Dimension | Indices per Dimension | Component Type |
|---|---|---|---|
| TYPE_FOR_POSITION | 1 | 3 | TYPE_FOR_COORDINATE |

**(e) Record Types**

| Name of Data Type | Name of Each Component | Name of Type for Each Component |
|---|---|---|
| TYPE_FOR_OUTPUT_COMPONENT | X_COORDINATE<br>Y_COORDINATE<br>Z_COORDINATE | TYPE_FOR_COORDINATE |

definition of the data structure based on the formulation of design requirements for processing. As source statements for the design are written and tested, the hidden data structure is extended and refined.

## 9.2.5    Step 5: Review and Refine the Design

Once an initial version of a design has been specified, a natural and necessary part of the design process is to review, modify, and refine the design. To do so, the designer can make several different checks.

### Requirements Traceability

To check the extent to which program requirements have been accounted for in a design, a design review team can generate a matrix that relates the contents of a software requirements specification to the contents of a software design specification. This matrix is a two-way check because any requirements not accounted for in the software design will be identified and any design features without corresponding specified requirements will also be identified. For requirements not yet accounted for in the design, expansion to the design will be necessary. Any expansion most likely will result in additions to the design for specific independent packages. It is possible, although less likely, that an additional independent package will be needed. For design features not accounted for in the software requirements specification, requirements have to be expanded as necessary to form a baseline for the development of acceptance test procedures. Acceptance test procedures are typically written as a function of the contents of the software requirements specification.

### High-Level Architectural Assessment

Part of the design review process is to go over the architectural structure of the large computer program. For example, the design review team can assess the following:

- the extent to which the independent packages model the problem
- the independence of the independent packages
- the cohesion inherent in the independent packages
- the extent of coupling between the independent packages

As argued in Chapter 3, the closer we *model the problem* with the independent packages that reflect real-world entities, the more understandable the design will be. Programmers, system engineers, and other personnel involved in a software development project will not have to make a mental transformation from the problem to the design. As also argued in Chapter 3, *independence* among the independent packages promotes flexibility in the large computer program, making it responsive to ever changing requirements. This independence is accomplished by hiding the operation and the internal state of an independent package, making them not accessible to other independent packages.

*Cohesion* should be a natural fallout of selecting independent packages to model the problem, because a cohesive package performs operations only for the the real-world entity services it is modeling. This is in contrast with a noncohesive Ada package that would provide a set of operations not necessarily highly related or unique to a single real-world entity.

As addressed in Chapter 4, *coupling* is a measure of interconnection between independent packages. The best form of coupling is none at all. In a design, several of the independent packages should not interact in any way. This means that not only are data entities not to be passed between such packages, but also that data entities are not to be shared through a global data structure. Where coupling must exist, it should be constrained to the passing of data entities that are the quantitative results of operations performed within the independent package (and not variables, types, or flags used in the formulation of the operations).

Another check of the design for the architectural structure of a computer program is to compare requirements assigned to each of the independent packages to see if common attributes and services exist. As suggested in Chapter 7, if a number of the attributes and services assigned to two or more independent packages are held in common, it might be possible to establish independent packages as a class of common attributes and services to be shared by other packages as members of the class.

### Assessing the Size and Scope of Each Independent Package

Another check in the design review process is to reexamine the internal design of each independent package. At a *high level*, the design review team can assess whether the design requirements for the visible data structure, operations, or hidden data structure are clear and easily comprehesible by the average programmer. If one or more of the design entities are not clear and understandable, the problem needs to be corrected. This may necessitate improving the formulation of the data structures or operational requirements or possibly partitioning an independent package that is too large and complicated (with respect to services, data structures, or both). For example, suppose package-size estimates derived from the design are as follows:

- `ICU_COMMUNICATION_LINES`—5,300 source statements
- `ICU_DATA_MANAGER`—2,500 source statements
- `ICU_MESSAGES`—14,000 source statements
- `ICU_CONSOLE`—5,200 source statements

The designer might be pleased with all these projected sizes for the package implementations except the implementation of the data structure and operations to be encapsulated in the package `ICU_MESSAGES`. If this is the case, the designer might attempt to identify smaller independent packages to replace the package `ICU_MESSAGES`.

At the other extreme, an independent package should not be trivial. If a package is trivial, the designer should consider combining it with another package, which will simplify interpackage communication (i.e., the amount of data to be passed between packages will decrease because the data passage will be internal to a package implementation). Too many small packages can result in unnecessarily complex communication between independent package implementations, with several parameters flowing from one package implementation to another.

### Assessing the Internal Design of an Independent Package

Once the size and scope of an independent package have been approved, more specific checks of the internal design can be made. For example, the program units to be used to implement an independent package can be checked for cohesion, interface complexity, and modular construction.

A *cohesive program unit* essentially performs only a single task. A spectrum of cohesion given by Roger Pressman in his book *Software Engineering, A Practitioner's Approach* (1987) is shown in Figure 9-11. Pressman argues that a designer should strive for high cohesion, although cohesion in the mid-range of the cohesion spectrum may be acceptable. As indicated in the figure, program units to implement processing that is loosely related are said to be coincidentally cohesive. Program units to implement processing that is related logically are said to be logically cohesive. Program units to

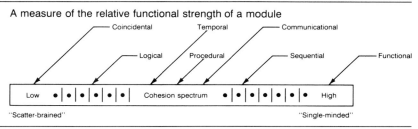

A measure of the relative functional strength of a module

FIGURE 9-11. Cohesion spectrum. Reprinted with permission from Roger S. Pressman, *Software Engineering, A Practitioner's Approach.* New York: McGraw-Hill, 1977.

implement processing related by the fact that it is to be executed in the same time period are said to be temporally cohesive. Program units to implement processing that is related and must be executed in a specific order are said to be procedurally cohesive. Program units to implement processing that concentrates on one part of a data structure are said to be communicationally cohesive.

*Interfaces* between program units internal to an independent package should be designed to pass information consistent with the purpose of the program unit. Passing of seemingly irrelevant data indicates low cohesion and should be corrected, because interface complexity can lead to implementation errors.

As a very basic consideration, each program unit should have been designed consistent with the spirit of *structured programming*, with only one entry point and one exit point. The logic and operations in a program unit are usually considered easier to understand when they are so structured (as discussed in Chapter 2).

## 9.4 Key Concepts

- The specific engineering steps that can be used to design a large computer program to be implemented in Ada are as follows:
    1. Identify and define a set of packages that partition the program into independent parts.
    2. Specify logical concurrency among the independent packages.
    3. Define interfaces for the independent packages.
    4. Specify a design for the set of independent packages.
    5. Review and refine the design.

- When selecting independent packages for a large computer program and assigning software requirements to these packages, a designer should keep in mind such things as the roles the packages are to play, the things they are to remember, the organizations and locations they should have knowledge of, the entities they are to interact with, the entities and devices they are to control, and the entities and devices they are to use. The designer should keep in mind that requirements defining a package should be easy to understand, compile, and test and should be related and consistent (e.g., requirements for database management should not be mixed with requirements for statistical processing and display).
- When a program is designed from a system engineer's point of view, the independent packages selected and their interactions can be thought of as establishing an operational model of real-world entities found in program requirements. From a software engineering point of view, the independent packages selected can be thought of as software entities needed to solve the problem at hand. It is in software design that we must bridge the gap between the system engineer's view of the system and the software engineer's view. From a software design point of view, we must make the transition from system requirements to an abstracted design representation of the computer program.
- To specify an internal design of a package, we can specify (a) a visible data structure applicable to data entities to be received and exported, (b) operations to be undertaken, and (c) a hidden data structure applicable to variables, flags, and types unique to the package and used in the formulation of processing operations.
- To review a design, designers can check for traceability between requirements and the design. They can also check to make sure that the design establishes packages that are (a) relatively easy to understand, implement, compile, and test, (b) model the problem space, (c) are cohesive, and (d) are not unnecessarily coupled with other packages.

## 10.1   Introduction

This chapter suggests steps for designing a software system as a set of computer programs that are to execute in a distributed manner within a single processor.

## 10.2   Steps for Designing a Software System

A set of engineering steps for designing a software system are as follows:

1. Assess requirements for the software system.
2. Declare Ada tasks to establish logical concurrency for a set of computer programs.
3. Define interfaces between interacting computer programs and between each of the computer programs and the outside world.
4. Design the computer programs in accordance with the steps delineated in Chapter 9.
5. Refine the design.

These steps for designing a software system are addressed in an example given next.

## 10.3   Design Example

For an example of a software system, let's develop a design for a hypothetical earth-orbiting space station. The software system is to include two or more computer programs for (a) collecting and processing experimental data, (b) monitoring sensors, (c) directing solar panels, and (d) testing processing hardware periodically.

### 10.3.1  Assess Requirements for the Software System

For our example, let's assume that an aerospace company has entered into a contract with a space agency for the development of a space station. The terms of the contract call for the aerospace company to subcontract the development of the space station's software system. The contract requires that among other things the software subcontractor is to specify a design as part of its deliverable products. (Other deliverable products are to include a software requirements specification, source statement listings, formal test procedures, and magnetic tapes containing object code.) As the first step in the design of the space station software system, requirements for the system are defined and assessed.

### Customer Requirements

To gain a general conceptual view of what the software system is to accomplish, engineers from the aerospace company hold a series of technical meetings with representatives of the space agency. They reach a general agreement as to the scope of processing requirements, which is that a computer is to interface with (a) system operators, (b) the earth mission center, (c) sensors , and (d) ports associated with space-unique experimentation, as shown in Figure 10-2.

The specific requirements agreed to are delineated in Table 10-1. As these requirements indicate, space station software is to monitor sensors that measure power and general environmental conditions within the space station. The software is to collect and process experimental data, properly align solar panels, and periodically test the system.

### Requirements Specification

After assessing the processing requirements, the subcontractor software engineers prepare a software requirements specification that presents their interpretation of requirements for the space station software system. Part of this specification is shown in Figure 10-3. The specification is delivered to the space agency and the aerospace company for review. Two months later, the software subcontractor

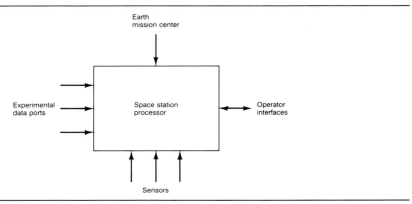

FIGURE 10-2. Space station processor interfaces

*TABLE 10-1.* Conceptual View of Space Station Processing

| Item | Requirements |
| --- | --- |
| Experimental collection and storage | The program shall collect data for three experiments and assemble data samples. The data samples shall be stored in a historical database. The system operator shall be able to initiate the calculation of a data sample's mean, standard deviation, and normal or Poisson distribution. The results of these calculations shall be displayed at a workstation. |
| Solar panel | The program shall calculate factors associated with the optimum alignment of solar panels. The factors shall provide control information to solar panel servomechanisms used to align the solar panel. |
| Sensor interface and checks | The program shall interface with sensor hardware providing power, temperature, and pressure readings. Limits for acceptable sensor readings shall be established by operator inputs. Sensor readings shall be compared to the acceptable limits and an alarm generated if a reading is out of bounds. |
| Processor tests | A test shall be run to monitor the fitness of the computer processor. The test shall exercise the computer processor instruction set, memory, and peripherals. Unexpected results shall be reported to system operators. |

meets with the space agency and the aerospace contractor to formally receive comments on the contents of the software requirements specification.

## 10.3.2 Establish Concurrency for a Set of Computer Programs as a Software System

Upon agreement among the space agency, the aerospace contractor, and the software subcontractor as to the contents of the software requirements specification, the software subcontractor continues the design of the space station software system.

### Establishing Concurrency

As the second step in the design of the space station software system, the design team selects three computer programs to execute concurrently:

3.0   Space Station Processing

3.1   *Workstations*

3.1.1   *Workstation A.* The processing system shall receive operator requests for sensor processing from a workstation to be referred to as Workstation A, and shall generate system outputs in response to the requests.

3.1.2   *Workstation B.* The processing system shall receive operator requests for the processing of experimental data from a workstation to be referred to as Workstation B, and shall generate system outputs in response to the requests.

3.2   *Experimental Data Collection, Storage and Processing*

3.2.1   *Experimental Data Requests.* Upon request by an operator, the Space Station Computer Program shall read values at experimental ports, to be referred to as Port 1, Port 2, and Port 3.

3.2.2   *Data Sample Size.* As a normal (default) value, 1000 readings shall be collected together to form a sample. An identification number shall be assigned to each sample.

3.2.3   *Operator Interface.* The following operator requests shall be accommodated: (a) designation of the number of readings to be used to form a sample, (b) request for sample identification numbers that have been established for a specified port number, (c) deletion of a sample designated by its identification number and port, (d) display the readings of a data sample, (e) calculate statistical parameters for a designated sample, and (f) establish a statistical distribution for a designated sample.

3.2.3.1   *Statistical Parameters Calculation.* Upon request for statistical parameters, the program shall calculate the mean value of a sample and its standard deviation.

3.2.3.2   *Statistical Distribution Calculation.* Upon request for a statistical distribution, the program shall calculate either the normal or poisson distribution as requested.

3.3   *Sensor Checking*

3.3.1   *Space Station Temperature Check.* The space station temperature sensor shall be sampled to ensure that it is within permissible limits. The normal limits are 18 to 22°C. If a temperature reading lines outside these limits, an alarm message shall be sent to the operator interface.

3.3.2   *Space Station Pressure Check.* The space station pressure sensor shall be sampled to ensure that it is within permissible limits. The normal limits are 0.85 to 1.05 atmospheres. If a pressure reading lies out of these limits, an alarm message shall be sent to the operator interface.

3.3.3   *Space Station Power Check.* The current value for space station power consumption shall be sampled to ensure that it is below a nominal value. The normal upper limit for power shall be 20 kilowatts. If the power level exceeds the limit, an alarm shall be sent to the operator interface.

---

*FIGURE 10-3.*   System specification processing requirements for the space station

2. A request for the current value of a sensor in SENSOR_READING _REQUEST (via entry READING_REQUEST_ENTRY), where the value of POWER_SENSOR_VALUE is to indicate that the current reading of the power sensor has been requested, the value TEMPERATURE_SENSOR_VALUE is to indicate that the current reading of the temperature sensor has been requested, and the value PRESSURE_SENSOR_VALUE is to indicate that the reading of the pressure sensor has been requested. To complete this rendezvous, the value of the requested sensor is to be returned in SENSOR_READING.

3. A command to change the limits of acceptable values for a sensor in LIMITS_SETTING_COMMAND (via the entry LIMITS_COMMAND _ENTRY). The command is to specify the subject sensor and its new upper and lower boundaries. In response, the text LIMITS MODIFIED is to be returned in COMMAND_CONFIGURATION to complete this rendezvous.

**Task** EXPERIMENT_DATA

The computer program implemented in the task EXPERIMENT_DATA is to interact with experimental data ports and workstation B. As shown in Figure 10-6, through rendezvous with the experimental data ports, the task EXPERIMENT_DATA is to receive PORT_1_ READING via its entry PORT_1_RECEIVE; PORT_2_READING via its entry PORT_2_RECEIVE; and PORT_3_READING via its entry PORT_3_RECEIVE. Also, through rendezvous with workstation B, the task EXPERIMENT_DATA is to receive various requests/commands, as follows:

1. A command to initiate or stop the collection of experimental data in DATA_COLLECTION_REQUEST (via the entry DATA_REQUEST _ENTRY).

2. A command to change the size of samples in DATA_SAMPLE_ SIZE (via the entry SAMPLE_SIZE_ENTRY).

3. A request for a set of sample identification numbers for a designated experiment port in DATA_IDs_REQUEST (via the entry IDs_REQUEST_ENTRY), where the value of PORT_1 is to indicate port number 1, a value of PORT_2 is to indicate port number 2, and a value of PORT_3 is to indicate port number 3. To complete this rendezvous, the requested sample identification numbers are to be returned in SAMPLE_IDs.

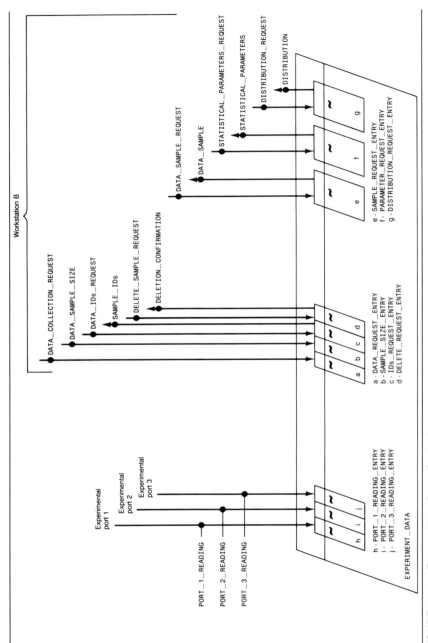

FIGURE 10-6. External interfaces for task EXPERIMENT_DATA

4. A request to delete a sample from the experimental historical database in DELETE_SAMPLE_REQUEST (via entry DELETE_REQUEST_ENTRY), where the sample's identification number and port number are to be provided in DELETE_SAMPLE_REQUEST. In response, the text SAMPLE DELETED is to be returned in DELETION_CONFIRMATION to complete the rendezvous.

5. A request for the retrieval and display of a data sample from the experimental historical database in DATA_SAMPLE_REQUEST (via the entry SAMPLE_REQUEST_ENTRY), where the request is to indicate the sample's identification number and port number. In response, a set of readings for the designated sample is to be returned in DATA_SAMPLE to complete the rendezvous.

6. A request for the calculation and display of statistical parameters for a designated data sample in STATISTICAL_PARAMETERS_REQUEST (via the entry PARAMETER_REQUEST_ENTRY), where the request is to indicate the sample's identification number and port number. In response, a mean and standard deviation for the designated sample is to be returned in STATISTICAL_PARAMETERS to complete the rendezvous.

7. A request for the calculation and display of a normal or Poisson distribution for a designated data sample in DISTRIBUTION_REQUEST (via the entry DISTRIBUTION_REQUEST_ENTRY), where the request is to indicate the sample's identification number and port number and whether a normal or Poisson distribution is required. In response, a set of values for the requested distribution is to be returned in DISTRIBUTION to complete the rendezvous.

### Task SOLAR_PANEL

The computer program implemented in the task SOLAR_PANEL is to interact with workstation B and the earth mission center. Through rendezvous with the earth mission center, the task SOLAR_PANEL is to receive angular rotation pairs in ROTATION_PAIRS (via its entry MISSION_CENTER_INTERFACE) and return an optimum orientation vector in OPTIMUM_VECTOR. Also, through rendezvous with workstation B, the task SOLAR_PANEL is to receive a request for the orientation of the solar panel in SOLAR_PANEL_ORIENTATION (via its entry WORKSTATION_B_INTERFACE). In response to this request, the task SOLAR_PANEL is to return the optimum vector and angular rotation pairs of the solar panel in SOLAR_PANEL_OPTIMUM_VECTOR and SOLAR_PANEL_ROTATION_PAIRS, respectively, to complete the rendezvous.

## 10.3.4 Design the Computer Programs

The fourth step in the design of the space station software system is preparation of a design for each computer program. The following section describes this effort, which applies the computer program design steps introduced in Chapter 9, which are referred to as substeps 4-1, 4-2, and so forth.

### Substep 4-1: Identify the Independent Packages

First, the design team assesses the requirements for each program to identify independent packages. They examine the requirements assigned to the *solar panel orientation* computer program, which is to calculate an optimum orientation for the space station's solar panel and initiate robotic motion to reorient the panel in accordance with the optimum orientation. As shown in Figure 10-7, the identified independent packages are as follows:

- a *solar panel* package, which is to receive directional data from the process task and calculate an optimum panel vector
- a *robot* package, which is to use the optimal panel vector to generate signals for motors that initiate the motion necessary to reorient the solar panel

Second, the design team assesses the requirements assigned to the *station monitor* computer program, which is to check sensor panels and computer processing equipment periodically. As shown in Figure 10-8, identified independent packages are as follows:

| SOLAR_PANEL | |
|---|---|
| *Data* | *Operation* |
| Rotation matrix ($R_T$) | Update solar panel reference vector |
| Reference vector ($x_0$, $y_0$, $z_0$) | |
| Optimum panel vector ($x_1$, $y_1$, $z_1$) | |

| ROBOT | |
|---|---|
| *Data* | *Operation* |
| Optimum panel vector ($x_1$, $y_1$, $z_1$) | Move solar panels into position |

*FIGURE 10-7.* Independent packages selected for the Solar Panel computer program

| SENSORS | |
|---|---|
| *Data* | *Operations* |
| Power reading | Read sensors |
| Temperature reading | Check validity |
| Pressure reading | Generate alarms |
| Upper power limit | Respond to operator requests |
| Lower power limit | |
| Upper temperature limit | |
| Lower temperature limit | |
| Power sensor state | |
| Temperature sensor state | |
| Pressure sensor state | |

| BUILT_IN_TEST | |
|---|---|
| *Data* | *Operations* |
| State of memory | Test computer memory |
| State of CPU | Test CPU |
| State of peripherals | Test peripherals |

*FIGURE 10-8.* Independent packages selected for the STATION MONITOR computer program

- A *sensors* package, which is to receive sensor values and determine if the values are within an acceptable range. If a value is out of bounds, an alarm is to sound and an error message is to be displayed at both workstations.
- A *built-in-test* package, which is to periodically exercise the space station's processor to check its central processing unit, memory, and peripherals. Any problems detected are to be reported to workstation B, so appropriate maintenance action can be initiated.

Third, the design team assesses requirements assigned to the *experimentation* computer program, which is to collect experimental data and, upon request from workstation B, statistically analyze the data. As shown in Figure 10-9, the identified independent packages are as follows:

- A *data samples* package, which is to receive port readings and assign them to samples by port number. When the number of readings assigned to a sample reaches a designated number, an

| DATA_SAMPLES | |
|---|---|
| *Data* | *Operations* |
| Port readings | Receive readings |
| Data samples (Exp. 1) | Receive deletion requests |
| Data samples (Exp. 2) | Receive sample sizes |
| Data samples (Exp. 3) | Establish data samples |
| Sample ID number | Export data samples |
| | Export deletion requests |

| DATA_MANAGER | |
|---|---|
| *Data* | *Operations* |
| Data sample port 1 | Store samples in database |
| Data sample port 2 | Retrieve samples |
| Data sample port 3 | Delete samples |
| Sample ID number | |

| STATISTICS | |
|---|---|
| *Data* | *Operations* |
| Sample values | Calculate mean |
| Mean of sample | Calculate standard deviation |
| Standard deviation of sample | Calculate normal distribution |
| Normal distribution | Calculate Poisson distribution |
| Poisson distribution | |

*FIGURE 10-9.* Independent packages selected for the EXPERIMENTATION computer program

identification number is to be assigned to the sample. Then the sample is to be exported for storage in an experimental historical database.

- A *data manager* package, which is to receive a data sample and insert it into a database keyed by the port number and a sample identification number. Upon request from workstation B, the package is to retrieve a designated sample from the historical database or delete it from this database.

- A *statistics* package, which is to respond to requests from workstation B for (a) a set of reading values for a designated sample, or (b) statistical processing of a designated sample to calculate its mean, standard deviation, and normal or Poisson distribution.

***Substep 4-2: Specify Logical Concurrency
among the Independent Packages***

For the *solar panel orientation* computer program, the requirements for the solar panel package are to be implemented by program units encapsulated in the package SOLAR_PANEL. The requirements for the panel robot package are to be implemented by program units encapsulated in the package ROBOT.

Upon reviewing the requirements for these packages, the design team decides that they are to execute in a sequential manner. That is, the package SOLAR_PANEL is to first calculate an optimal panel vector, and then the package ROBOT is to reorient the solar panel. To accomplish this end, the design specifies that the procedure OPTIMUM _ORIENTATION is to be visible in the package SOLAR_PANEL (to receive orientation data from the earth mission center via the task SOLAR_PANEL) and that procedure MOTION is to be visible in the package ROBOT (to receive parameters designating panel movement), as shown in Figure 10-10(a). Also, the package SOLAR _PANEL is to have access to the package ROBOT via an Ada with clause.

For the *station monitor* computer program, the requirements for the sensor-checking package are to be implemented by program units encapsulated in the package SENSORS. The requirements for the built-in-testing object are to be implemented in program units encapsulated in the package BUILT_IN_TEST.

Upon reviewing the requirements for these packages, the design team decides that they are to execute in a logically concurrent manner. That is, the package SENSORS may receive sensor readings or an operator request at the same time it is to check out the processing system. Accordingly, the design team specifies that visible tasks are to be declared in both packages to carry out logically concurrent execution. Specifically, as shown in Figure 10-10(b), the design team specifies that the package SENSOR_PROCESSOR is to contain the visible task RECEIVE_SENSOR_READING, which is to rendezvous with the process task STATION_MONITOR to receive sensor readings.

The design team also specifies that the package SENSORS is to contain the visible tasks SENSOR_STATE, CHECK_SENSORS, and SET_LIMITS. The task SENSOR_STATE is to respond to a request for the state of a designated sensor (i.e., whether the sensor is enabled or disabled). The task CHECK_SENSORS is to receive and check sensor readings. The task SET_LIMITS is to receive new limits on sensor values designated as acceptable. Furthermore, the design

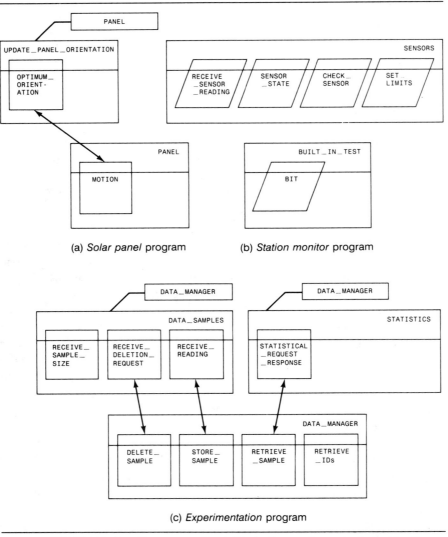

(a) *Solar panel* program  (b) *Station monitor* program

(c) *Experimentation* program

FIGURE 10-10. Program units visible in the packages selected for the software system

team specifies that the package BUILT_IN_TEST is to contain the visible task BIT. It is to periodically check the fitness of processing equipment and rendezvous with the task STATION_MONITOR to report the results of the check to workstation A. Because the package SENSORS and the package BUILT_IN_TEST are independent, program units in one do not call program units in the other (thus, the Ada with clause is not used).

For the *experimentation* computer program, the requirements for data collection and reduction are to be implemented by program units encapsulated in the package DATA_SAMPLES, the package DATA_MANAGER, and the package STATISTICS. Upon reviewing the requirements for these packages, the design team decides they are to execute in a sequential manner at the discretion of the task EXPERIMENT_DATA. Accordingly, the design team specifies that visible procedures are to be declared in these packages. Specifically, as shown in Figure 10-10(c), the procedures RECEIVE_SAMPLE_SIZE, RECEIVE_DELETION_REQUEST, and RECEIVE_READING are to be visible in the package DATA_SAMPLES. The procedures DELETE_SAMPLE, STORE_SAMPLE, RETRIEVE_SAMPLE, and RETRIEVE_IDs are to be visible in the package DATA_MANAGER. The procedure STATISTICAL_REQUEST_RESPONSE is to be visible in the package STATISTICS. Both the DATA_SAMPLES and STATISTICS packages are to access the package DATA_MANAGER (thus, the Ada with clause applies to both packages).

### Substep 4-3: Establish Interfaces for the Independent Packages

Having selected a set of independent packages, the design team breaks into three groups, one for each computer program. Each group proceeds with the design of the computer program it is responsible for.

For an example of one of these efforts, let's follow the results of the group assigned to the *experimentation* computer program. Calls to procedures and data flow associated with these calls are shown in Figure 10-11. As shown, the task EXPERIMENT_DATA is to make calls to three different procedures in the package DATA_SAMPLES, which in turn is to call two procedures in the package DATA_MANAGER. The task EXPERIMENT_DATA is to make calls to two different procedures in the package DATA_MANAGER and one call to one procedure in the package STATISTICS, which in turn is to make a call to a procedure in the package DATA_MANAGER.

Specifically, the design specifies the following for the package DATA_SAMPLES:

- Procedure RECEIVE_READING is to receive an experimental reading in READING and a port number in PORT_NUMBER and enter them into a buffer established for the applicable port. When this buffer fills up with a designated number of readings, it is to establish a sample and assign an identification number to the sample. The sample then is to be forwarded to the package DATA_MANAGER in SAMPLE_VALUES

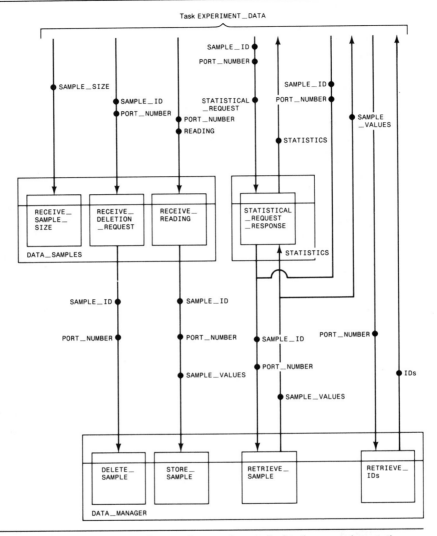

*FIGURE 10-11.* Data flow and procedure calls for the *experimentation* program

via a call to the procedure STORE_SAMPLE, along with the applicable port number in PORT_NUMBER and the sample identification number in SAMPLE_ID. The procedure STORE_SAMPLE is to enter the sample into a experimentation historical database by port and sample identification number.

- The procedure RECEIVE_SAMPLE_SIZE is to receive in SAMPLE_SIZE an operator's designation of the number of readings to be included in a sample.
- The procedure RECEIVE_DELETION_REQUEST is to receive a designation for a sample to be deleted from the historical database. The procedure RECEIVE_DELETION_REQUEST, in turn, calls the procedure DELETE_SAMPLE of the package DATA_MANAGER, which removes the sample from the database.

The design team specifies that data entities are to be passed to the package STATISTICS from the user interaction task via the procedure STATISTICAL_REQUEST_RESPONSE. This procedure is to receive a sample designation in SAMPLE_ID, a port number in PORT_NUMBER, and a request for statistical data in STATISTICAL_REQUEST. STATISTICAL_REQUEST_RESPONSE in turn calls the procedure RETRIEVE_SAMPLE of the package DATA_MANAGER to obtain a data sample in SAMPLE_VALUES. It then calculates the mean, the standard deviation, and the normal distribution of the sample, or the mean and the Poisson distribution of the sample.

The design team specifies the following for the package DATA_MANAGER:

- The procedure RETRIEVE_IDs is to receive a port number in PORT_NUMBER. It returns in IDs (for the designated port) a list of sample identification numbers, the time/date the first reading of that sample was received, and the time/date the last reading of that sample was received.
- The procedure RETRIEVE_SAMPLE is to receive a sample designation in SAMPLE_ID and PORT_NUMBER. It returns a set of readings for the designated sample in SAMPLE_VALUES.
- The procedure STORE_SAMPLE is to receive a sample in SAMPLE_VALUES and store it as a function of the sample's identification number (received in SAMPLE_ID) and the applicable port number (received in PORT_NUMBER).
- Procedure DELETE_SAMPLE is to receive the identification number of a sample to be deleted from the database in SAMPLE_ID, along with the applicable port number in PORT_NUMBER.

As Figure 10-11 shows, data entities passed between the independent packages account for data samples, storage, operator requests, and the results of statistical calculations. However, variables, flags, and types used to implement the operations unique to each independent package (e.g., those used to establish a database and the statistical calculations) are not passed. Because of this, the Ada packages are essentially independent of each other, which is a primary design goal. Because the packages are independent, changes can be made to the implementation of one Ada package without affecting the others. This simplifies development testing and, even more important, future maintenance.

### Substep 4-4: Establish the Internal Design of the Independent Packages

The design group assigned to the *experimentation program* next addresses the internal design of each independent package. For each package, they specify (a) a visible data structure applicable to the data entities to be received and exported, (b) the segmentation of operations among program units and the specific operations to be undertaken in each program unit, and (c) a hidden data structure to be used in the formulation of processing operations. The following paragraphs describe how the design group addresses the internal design of the package STATISTICS.

**Specify Descriptors for the Visible Data Structure of the Package** STATISTICS. The design group specifies the visible data structure for the package STATISTICS, as shown in Table 10-2. Specifically, section *a* of this table lists descriptors for variables, section *b* provides descriptors for a record type, section *c* provides descriptors for array types, and section *d* lists descriptors for scalar data types.

**Specify Processing Operations in the Package** STATISTICS. The design group distributes processing operations into the *program units* shown in Figure 10-12. As shown, the procedure STATISTICAL _REQUEST_RESPONSE declares the procedures MEAN, STANDARD_ DEVIATION, NORMAL_DISTRIBUTION, and POISSON_DISTRIBUTION. The procedure STANDARD_DEVIATION declares the function SQUARE_ ROOT, while the procedure NORMAL_DISTRIBUTION declares the function ESTABLISH_EXPONENTIAL, and the procedure POISSON _DISTRIBUTION declares the function FACTORIAL. The function SQUARE_ROOT declares the function LOG.

Next, the design group specifies *interaction* between these program units, as shown in Figure 10-13. As indicated, the visible procedure STATISTICAL_REQUEST_RESPONSE calls the procedure

TABLE 10-2. Descriptors for Visible Data Structure in Package Statistics

(a) Variables

| Name of Data Entity | Type | | Description |
|---|---|---|---|
| | Name | Category | |
| SAMPLE_ID | TYPE_FOR_SAMPLE_ID | Scalar | A numeric code used to identify a sample. |
| PORT_NUMBER | TYPE_FOR_PORT_NUMBER | Scalar | The following integers:<br>• 1 for experimental port number 1<br>• 2 for experimental port number 2<br>• 3 for experimental port number 3 |
| STATISTICAL_REQUEST | TYPE_FOR_STATISTICAL_REQUEST | Scalar | Operator-generated requests for the mean, standard deviation, normal distribution, or Poisson distribution |
| SAMPLE_SIZE | TYPE_FOR_SAMPLE_SIZE | Scalar | The number of readings to be included in a sample (N) |
| STATISTICS | TYPE_FOR_STATISTICS | Composite | The output record generated by the package STATISTICAL_PROCESSOR |

(b) Record Types

| Name of Data Type | Name of Each Component | Name of Type for Each Component |
|---|---|---|
| TYPE_FOR_STATISTICS | MEAN_SETTING | TYPE_FOR_MEAN_SETTING |
| | STD_DEV_SETTING | TYPE_FOR_STD_DEV_SETTING |
| | PROBABILITY_SETTINGS | PROBABILITY_SETTINGS_TYPE |
| | X_VECTOR_SETTINGS | X_VECTOR_SETTINGS_TYPE |

TABLE 10-2. (continued)

(c) Array Types

| Name of Data Type | Dimensions | Indices per Dimension | Components Type |
|---|---|---|---|
| PROBABILITY_SETTINGS_TYPE | One | 20 | DIST_COMP_TYPE |
| X_VECTOR_SETTINGS_TYPE | One | 20 | TYPE_FOR_X |

(d) Scalar Types

| Name of Data Type | Category | Permissible Values | Decimal Places |
|---|---|---|---|
| TYPE_FOR_SAMPLE_ID | Integer | 1 to 99,000 | |
| TYPE_FOR_PORT_NUMBER | Integer | 1, 2, or 3 | |
| TYPE_FOR_STATISTICAL_REQUEST | Enumeration | MEAN_REQUEST STANDARD_DEVIATION_REQUEST NORMAL_DISTRIBUTION_REQUEST POISSON_DISTRIBUTION_REQUEST | |
| TYPE_FOR_SAMPLE_SIZE | Integer | 100 to 1,000,000 | |
| TYPE_FOR_MEAN_SETTING | Real | 0.0 to 2000.0 | One |
| TYPE_FOR_STD_DEV_SETTING | Real | 0.0 to 2000.0 | One |
| DIST_COMP_TYPE | Real | 0.0 to 2000.0 | Two |
| TYPE_FOR_X | Real | 0.00 to 2000.00 | Two |

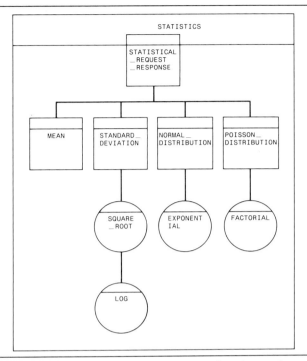

FIGURE 10-12. Program units internal to the package STATISTICS

RETRIEVE_SAMPLE to retrieve a data sample and then makes calls to program units hidden in the package STATISTICS to calculate statistics for the sample. Specifically, the design group specifies that the procedure STATISTICAL_REQUEST_RESPONSE is to (1) call the procedure MEAN to establish a mean for the data sample, and possibly (2) call the procedure STANDARD_DEVIATION to establish a standard deviation for the data samples. In addition, STATISTICAL_REQUEST_RESPONSE may call the procedure NORMAL_DISTRIBUTION to establish a normal distribution as a function of the mean and the standard deviation, or it may call the procedure POISSON_DISTRIBUTION to establish a Poisson distribution as a function of the mean. The procedure STANDARD_DEVIATION is to use the function SQUARE_ROOT, which in turn is to use the function LOG. The procedure NORMAL_DISTRIBUTION is to use the function EXPONENTIAL, while the procedure POISSON_DISTRIBUTION is to use the function ESTABLISH_EXPONENTIAL, plus the function FACTORIAL.

Then the design group specifies the *design of each program unit* by defining the flow of data entities between program units and

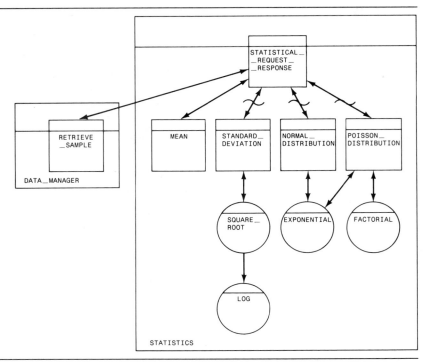

*FIGURE 10-13.* Interaction of program units internal to the package
STATISTICS

the logic and processing operations to be performed within each
program unit. As shown in Figure 10-14, the visible procedure
STATISTICAL_REQUEST_RESPONSE is to receive a command in
STATISTICAL_REQUEST for processing of a designated sample. The
sample is designated by its identification number, port number, and
size, which are received by the procedure STATISTICAL_REQUEST
_RESPONSE in SAMPLE_ID, PORT_NUMBER, and SAMPLE_SIZE. The
designated sample is to be retrieved from the historical database via
a call to the procedure RETRIEVE_SAMPLE of the package DATA
_MANAGER. The statistical request in STATISTICAL_REQUEST can
be MEAN_REQUEST, STANDARD_DEVIATION_REQUEST, NORMAL_
DISTRIBUTION_REQUEST, or POISSON_DISTRIBUTION_REQUEST.
The data flow associated with each request is to be as follows:

- When the value furnished in STATISTICAL_REQUEST is MEAN
  _REQUEST, then the procedure STATISTICAL_REQUEST_

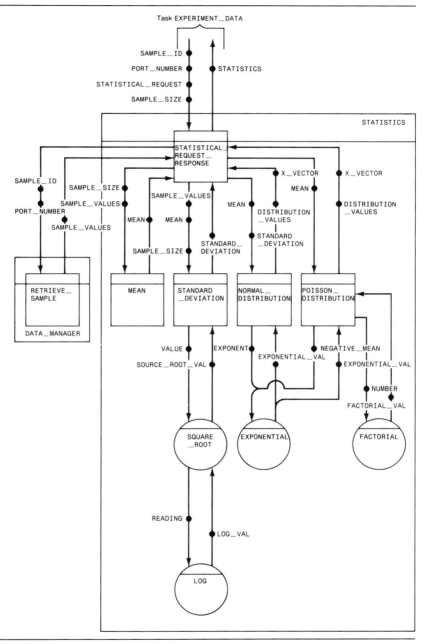

*FIGURE 10-14.* Data flow for the thread of program units internal to the package STATISTICS

RESPONSE is to call the procedure MEAN. In doing so, the procedure STATISTICAL_REQUEST_RESPONSE is to forward to the procedure MEAN a set of sample readings in SAMPLE_VALUES and the size of the sample in SAMPLE_SIZE. It is to receive in return the mean value of the sample readings in MEAN.

- When the value furnished in STATISTICAL_REQUEST is STANDARD _DEVIATION_REQUEST, the procedure STATISTICAL_REQUEST _RESPONSE is to call the procedure MEAN to establish the sample's mean. Then it is to call the procedure STANDARD_DEVIATION and forward to it a set of sample readings in SAMPLE_VALUES, the mean of these values in MEAN, and the size of the sample in SAMPLE_SIZE. In return, it is to receive the standard deviation for these readings in STANDARD_DEVIATION. STANDARD_ DEVIATION is to use the function SQUARE_ROOT to calculate a square root, which in turn is to use the function LOG, to establish a logarithm to the base e.

- When the value furnished in STATISTICAL_REQUEST is NORMAL _DISTRIBUTION, the procedure STATISTICAL_REQUEST_ RESPONSE is to call the procedure MEAN to obtain the mean of a designated sample and the procedure STANDARD_DEVIATION to obtain the standard deviation of the designated sample. It then is to call the procedure NORMAL_DISTRIBUTION and forward to it the mean in MEAN and the standard deviation in STANDARD_ DEVIATION. In return, STATISTICAL_REQUEST_RESPONSE is to receive a set of values for a normal distribution in DISTRIBUTION_VALUES. When establishing the normal distribution, the procedure NORMAL_DISTRIBUTION is to use the function EXPONENTIAL to calculate the exponential.

- When the value furnished in STATISTICAL_REQUEST is POISSON _DISTRIBUTION, the procedure STATISTICAL_REQUEST_ RESPONSE is to call the procedure MEAN to obtain the mean of a designated sample. It then is to call the procedure POISSON _DISTRIBUTION and forward to it the mean in MEAN. In return, STATISTICAL_REQUEST_RESPONSE is to receive a set of values for a Poisson distribution in DISTRIBUTION_VALUES. When establishing the Poisson distribution, the procedure POISSON_ DISTRIBUTION is to use the function EXPONENTIAL to calculate an exponential and the function FACTORIAL to calculate the factorial of a number to be instantiated as a real number.

Having established the data flow between program units, the design group next specifies in an abstracted manner *operations to be undertaken within each program unit*. Figure 10-15 presents the pseudocode for the processing to be undertaken by the procedure STATISTICAL_REQUEST_RESPONSE. As the pseudocode indicates, this procedure is to receive a request for statistical processing of a sample in STATISTICAL_REQUEST. When a mean has been requested, the procedure MEAN is called. Figure 10-16 presents pseudocode for the processing to be undertaken by the procedure MEAN. When a standard deviation has been requested, the procedure STANDARD_DEVIATION is called. Figure 10-17 presents the pseudocode for processing to be undertaken by the procedure STANDARD_DEVIATION. When a normal distribution has been requested, then the procedures MEAN, STANDARD_DEVIATION, and NORMAL_DISTRIBUTION are called, in that order. Figure 10-18 presents the pseudocode for the processing to be undertaken by the procedure NORMAL_DISTRIBUTION. When a Poisson distribution has been requested, the procedures MEAN and POISSON_DISTRIBUTION are called. Figure 10-19 presents the pseudocode for the processing to be undertaken by the procedure POISSON_DISTRIBUTION.

The procedure STANDARD_DEVIATION uses the function SQUARE_ROOT. Figure 10-20 presents the pseudocode for the processing to be undertaken by the function SQUARE_ROOT. Figure 10-21 presents the pseudocode for the processing to be undertaken by the function LOG. Figure 10-22 presents the pseudocode for the processing to be undertaken by the function EXPONENTIAL. (The procedures NORMAL_DISTRIBUTION and POISSON_DISTRIBUTION use the function EXPONENTIAL.) Figure 10-23 presents the pseudocode for the processing to be undertaken by the function FACTORIAL. (The function EXPONENTIAL uses the function FACTORIAL.)

**Establish the Data Structure Internal to the Package**
STATISTICS. The design group next defines the hidden data structure applicable to the processing to be undertaken by the independent package STATISTICS. Data entities found in data flow diagrams and the pseudocode are collected and assessed. Then data structure descriptors are defined. The results are shown in Table 10-3. Section *a* of the table lists descriptors for variables, section *b* lists descriptors for constants, section *c* for record types, section *d* for array

```
┌─────────────────────────────────────────────┐
│ Procedure STATISTICAL_REQUEST_RESPONSE        │
└─────────────────────────────────────────────┘
```

*Abstract:* Responds to an operator request for a statistical calculation of the mean value of sample readings and/or the standard deviation, normal distribution, or Poisson distribution of the sample readings.

*Pseudocode:*

Begin Procedure STATISTICAL_REQUEST_RESPONSE ─────────────────

    Receive a request for the statistical processing of a sample in
       STATISTICAL_REQUEST, plus the sample's port
       number in PORT_NUMBER, its identification
       number in SAMPLE_ID, and the number of
       readings in the sample in SAMPLE_SIZE.

    Declare procedures MEAN, STANDARD DEVIATION,
       NORMAL_DISTRIBUTION, and POISSON_DISTRIBUTION.

    Call Procedure RETRIEVE_SAMPLE of Package
       DATA_MANAGER to fetch a sample.

    Receive a set of sample readings from Procedure
       RETRIEVE_SAMPLE in SAMPLE_VALUES.

    Determine the statistical processing to be undertaken as follows:

If STATISTICAL_REQUEST is MEAN_REQUEST, then
    • Call Procedure MEAN to calculate the mean value
      of a set of sample readings
    • set standard deviation to zero
    • set distribution values to zero ──────────────────────────────┐
elsif STATISTICAL_REQUEST is STANDARD_DEVIATION_REQUEST then       │
    • call Procedure MEAN to calculate the mean value             │
      of a set of sample readings                              │
    • call Procedure STANDARD_DEVIATION to calculate the          │
      standard deviation of a set of sample readings           │
    • set distribution values to zero ──────────────────────────┐ │
elsif STATISTICAL_REQUEST is NORMAL_DISTRIBUTION then             │ │
    • call Procedure MEAN to calculate the mean value           │ │
      of a set of sample readings                            │ │
    • call Procedure STANDARD_DEVIATION to calculate the        │ │
      standard deviation of a set of sample readings         │ │
    • call Procedure NORMAL_DISTRIBUTION to establish           │ │
      a normal distribution as a function of the mean        │ │
      and the standard deviation ──────────────────────────┐  │ │
else                                                           │  │ │
    • call procedure MEAN to calculate the mean value        │  │ │
      of a set of sample readings                         │  │ │
    • call procedure POISSON_DISTRIBUTION to establish       │  │ │
      a Poisson distribution as a function of the mean    │  │ │
    • set standard deviation to zero                         │  │ │
end if ────────────────────────────────────────────────────────┘  │ │
Return an Ada record in STATISICS containing the mean setting,
    the standard deviation setting, and the setting for distribution values
End procedure STATISTICAL_REQUEST_RESPONSE ──────────────────
```

FIGURE 10-15. Pseudocode for the procedure STATISTICAL_REQUEST_RESPONSE
```

---

Procedure MEAN

*Abstract:* Calculates the mean value of a set of numbers as follows:

$$MEAN = \frac{1}{N} \sum_{i=1}^{N} x_i \tag{10-1}$$

where in the pseudocode to follow, $N$ is given by SAMPLE_SIZE and $x_i$ is a sample reading supplied in the input SAMPLE_VALUES (i.e., a vector with multiple values $x_1, x_2, \ldots x_N$)

*Pseudocode:*
Begin Procedure MEAN
       Receive a set of sample readings $x_i$
       in SAMPLE_VALUES and the number of
       readings in a sample in SAMPLE_SIZE

       Calculate the mean of the readings as follows:

           MEAN = 0
           for $i$ = 1 to SAMPLE_SIZE loop
             MEAN = MEAN + $x_i$
           end loop
           MEAN = MEAN/SAMPLE_SIZE
       Return MEAN
End Procedure MEAN

---

*FIGURE 10-16.* Pseudocode for the procedure MEAN_CALCULATION

types, and section *e* for scalar types. This establishes an initial version of the hidden data structure. Upon review, revision, and refinement of the design and as a result of coding activity, the data structure will be expanded and refined.

### Substep 5: Refine the Design

For the fifth step, the design group reviews the design for consistency and correctness, traceability to requirements, and adherence to the design strategy. As a result of this review, the group decides that the mathematical functions SQUARE_ROOT, LOG, EXPONENTIAL, and FACTORIAL should be used from an existing Ada package named MATH_ALGORITHMS. This package includes the set of visible Ada functions shown in Figure 10-24.

Also as part of the review, the group assesses the technique specified for interaction with the sensors for power, temperature, and pressure in the *experimentation* computer program. The members of the design team decide that the space station processing system should respond to these sensors in a timely manner. Originally,

Procedure STANDARD_DEVIATION

*Abstract:* Calculates a standard deviation as follows:

$$\text{STANDARD\_DEVIATION} = \sqrt{\frac{1}{N}\sum_{i=1}^{N}(x_i - \text{MEAN})^2}$$  (10-2)

where in the pseudocode, AV_SQUARE_SUM is equal to

$$\frac{1}{N}\sum_{i=1}^{N}(x_i - \text{MEAN})^2$$

*Pseudocode:*
Begin Procedure STANDARD_DEVIATION
    Receive a set of sample readings $x_i$
    in SAMPLE_VALUES and the number of
    readings in a sample in SAMPLE_SIZE

Receive the mean of the sample readings
    in MEAN_VALUE

    Calculate the standard deviation of the readings as follows:

        SQUARE_SUM = 0
        for $i$ = 1 to SAMPLE_SIZE loop
            SQUARE_SUM = SQUARE_SUM + $(x_i - \text{MEAN})^2$
        end loop

        AV_SQUARE_SUM = SQUARE_SUM / SAMPLE_SIZE

    Apply Function SQUARE_ROOT as follows:
    STANDARD_DEVIATION = SQUARE_ROOT (AV_SQUARE_SUM)

    Return STANDARD_DEVIATION

End Procedure STANDARD_DEVIATION

*FIGURE 10-17.* Pseudocode for the procedure STANDARD_DEVIATION

readings from the sensors were to be received via acceptance statements associated with entry points in the task STATION_MONITOR. As shown in Figure 10-5, these entry points were to be conditional in the sense that if a call was not pending when an acceptance statement was reached, the next acceptance statement in a seqence would be immediately executed. This design was considered inadequate, since a whole series of acceptances (and processing incurred after each acceptance) could take place before the acceptance statement for the sensors was reached. Because of this, the team moves the sensor entry points into separate tasks, one for each sensor, as shown in Figure 10-25.

For the same reasons, entry points for receiving experiment readings in the task EXPERIMENT_DATA are moved into separate tasks, one for each experimentation port. If the readings to be received from each experimentation port are of the same nature (with respect to format and frequency of arrival), a task type could be used, as shown in Figure 10-26. Possible instances of the task type are shown in Figure 10-27.

As a third example of the results of the design review, the design group assesses design considerations for the storage and retrieval of data samples. The design specifies a data sample is to consist of a set of experiment readings stored as an array. The contents of each sample are to be moved to a database maintained by the DATA _MANAGER package through a call to the STORE_SAMPLE procedure. The design group decides that this operation may be unnecessarily time consuming, especially for a sample with a large number

---

Procedure NORMAL_DISTRIBUTION

*Abstract:* For an evenly incremented set of values over a range of sample readings, calculate a normal distribution as follows:

$$f(x) = \frac{1}{\sigma\sqrt{2\pi}} e^{-\frac{1}{2}\left(\frac{x-\mu}{\sigma}\right)^2} \qquad (10\text{-}3)$$

where $\mu$ is the mean and $\sigma$ is the standard deviation for the readings of a sample. In the pseudocode, FACTOR is equal to $\frac{1}{\sigma\sqrt{2\pi}}$ and EXPONENT is equal to $-\frac{1}{2}\left(\frac{x-\mu}{\sigma}\right)^2$.

*Pseudocode:*
Begin Procedure NORMAL_DISTRIBUTION ───────

Receive the mean for a sample in MEAN ($\mu$), the sample's standard deviation ($\sigma$) in STANDARD_DEVIATION, and its values in SAMPLE_VALUES.

Calculate the normal distribution as follows:
  Establish the upper and lower values for the distribution X(INITIAL), X(FINAL)

  Establish the increment of distribution values, $\Delta$X

  FACTOR = $\dfrac{1}{\sigma\sqrt{2\pi}}$
  Set $x$ = X(INITIAL)
    while $x$ ≤ X(FINAL) loop ───────────
  EXPONENT = $-((x - \text{MEAN}) / \text{STANDARD\_DEVIATION})^2 /2$
  Use Function EXPONENTIAL as follows:
  DISTRIBUTION_VALUE($x$) = FACTOR * EXPONENTIAL(EXPONENT)

  $x$ = $x$ + $\Delta$x

  end loop ───────

Return $\bar{x}$ and distribution values
for $\bar{x}$ = $\bar{x}$(INITIAL), x(INITIAL) + $\Delta$x, ... x(FINAL)

End Procedure NORMAL_DISTRIBUTION ───────

---

*FIGURE 10-18.* Pseudocode for the procedure NORMAL_DISTRIBUTION

---

| Procedure POISSON_DISTRIBUTION |

*Abstract:* For an evenly incremental set of values over a range of sample readings, calculates a Poisson distribution as follows:

$$f(x) = \frac{\mu^2 e^{-\mu}}{x!} \qquad (10\text{-}4)$$

In the pseudocode, NUMERATOR is equal to $\mu^2 e^{-\mu}$. DENOMINATOR is equal to x!.

*Pseudocode:*
Begin Procedure POISSON_DISTRIBUTION ──────────────────────

Receive the mean for a sample in MEAN

Calculate the Poisson distribution as follows:

   Establish the upper and lower values for the distribution x(INITIAL), x(FINAL)

   Establish the increment of distribution values, Δx

   NEGATIVE_MEAN = -MEAN
   Use Function EXPONENTIAL as follows:
     NUMERATOR = MEAN * MEAN * EXPONENTIAL(NEGATIVE_MEAN)

   Set x = x(INITIAL)

   while x ≤ x(FINAL) loop ──────────────────

   Use Function FACTORIAL as follows:
     NUMBER = integer equivalent of x
     DENOMINATOR = FACTORIAL(NUMBER)

   DISTRIBUTION_VALUE(x) = NUMERATOR/DENOMINATOR

   x = x + Δx

   end loop ──────────────────

Return $\bar{x}$ and distribution values for $\bar{x}$ = x(INITIAL), x(INITIAL) + Δx,
...x(FINAL)

End Procedure POISSON_DISTRIBUTION ──────────────────

---

FIGURE 10-19.   Pseudocode for the procedure POISSON_DISTRIBUTION

of experiment readings. To make the design more time efficient, they assign a pointer to each sample in a variable SAMPLE_POINTER through the use of an Ada *access type*. Specifically, they specify TYPE_FOR_SAMPLE_POINTER as an access type, and declare the variable SAMPLE_POINTER to be of type TYPE_FOR_SAMPLE_POINTER. That is,

| Name of Data Entity | Type Name | Type Category | Comment |
|---|---|---|---|
| SAMPLE_POINTER | TYPE_FOR_SAMPLE_POINTER | Access | Points to a data sample |

*Abstract:* Calculates the square root of a number as follows:

$$\sqrt{x} = 1 + \frac{1}{2}(\log_e x) + \frac{1}{8}(\log_e x)^2 + \frac{1}{48}(\log_e x)^3 \tag{10-5}$$

*Pseudocode:*

Begin Function SQUARE_ROOT ──────────────────────

Receive READING

Use Function LOG as follows:
  FACTOR = LOG(READING)

SQUARE_ROOT = 1 + FACTOR/2 + FACTOR$^2$/8 + FACTOR$^3$/48

Return SQUARE_ROOT_VAL

End Function SQUARE_ROOT ──────────────────

*FIGURE 10-20.* Pseudocode for the function SQUARE_ROOT

Function LOG

*Abstract:* Calculates the log to the base *e* of a number as follows:

$$\log_e x = \frac{x-1}{x} + \frac{1}{2}\left(\frac{x-1}{x}\right)^2 + \frac{1}{3}\left(\frac{x-1}{x}\right)^3 + \frac{1}{4}\left(\frac{x-1}{x}\right)^4 \tag{10-6}$$

In the pseudocode, LOG is equal to $\log_e x$ and FACTOR is equal to $(x-1)/x$.

*Pseudocode:*

Begin Function LOG ──────────────────

Receive READING

FACTOR = (READING − 1)/READING

LOG = FACTOR + FACTOR$^2$/2 + FACTOR$^3$/3 + FACTOR$^4$/4

Return LOG_VAL

End Function LOG ──────────────

*FIGURE 10-21.* Pseudocode for the function LOG

Then, as shown in Figure 10-28, SAMPLE_POINTER is passed from the DATA_SAMPLES package to the DATA_MANAGER package via the call to the STORE_SAMPLE procedure. The pointer in SAMPLE_POINTER is entered into the database keyboard on (i.e., as a function of) the sample identification number in SAMPLE_ID and the experiment port number in PORT_NUMBER.

Correspondingly, as also shown in Figure 10-28, the retrieval of samples by the STATISTICS package from the DATA_MANAGER package is accomplished by returning a pointer rather than the large

Function EXPONENTIAL

*Abstract:* Calculates the exponential of a number as follows:

$$e^x = 1 + x + x^2/2! + x^3/3! = x^4/4! \tag{10-7}$$

In the pseudocode, EXPONENTIAL is equal to $e^x$, TWO_FACTORIAL is 2!, THREE_FACTORIAL is 3! and FOUR_FACTORIAL is 4!

*Pseudocode:*

```
Begin Function EXPONENTIAL
Receive READING

   EXPONENTIAL = 1 + READING
                   + READING²/TWO_FACTORIAL
                   + READING³/THREE_FACTORIAL
                   + READING⁴/FOUR_FACTORIAL

Return EXPONENTIAL_VAL

End Function EXPONENTIAL
```

FIGURE 10-22.   Pseudocode for the function EXPONENTIAL

Function FACTORIAL

*Abstract:* Calculates the factorial of a number as follows:
$$N! = 1 * 2 * 3 * \ldots * N \tag{10-8}$$

*Pseudocode:*

```
Begin Function FACTORIAL

Receive NUMBER

FACTORIAL = 1

For N = 2 to NUMBER loop
   FACTORIAL=FACTORIAL*N
end loop

Return FACTORIAL_VAL

End Function FACTORIAL
```

FIGURE 10-23.   Pseudocode for the function FACTORIAL

amount of data in a sample. Specifically, the call to the RETRIEVE _SAMPLE procedure returns the appropriate pointer value in SAMPLE_POINTER.

Upon making these and other changes to the design, the design group formally documents the design in a design specification. This document is delivered to the prime contractor and the space agency for their review and approval prior to the coding phase of the

TABLE 10-3. Descriptors for the Hidden Data Structure in the Package STATISTICS

(a) Variables

| Name of Data Entity | Type | | Description |
| --- | --- | --- | --- |
| | Name | Category | |
| DISTRIBUTION_VALUES | TYPE_FOR_DISTRIBUTION_VALUES | Composite | Values of f(x), where $f(x) = \frac{1}{\sigma\sqrt{2\pi}} E^{-\frac{1}{2}\left(\frac{x-\mu}{\sigma}\right)^2}$ for an evenly incremented set of values for x (Figure 10-18) |
| AV_SQUARE_SUM | TYPE_FOR_AV_SQUARE_SUM | Scalar | Input to the Ada function SQUARE_ROOT (Figure 10-20) |
| SQUARE_ROOT_VAL | TYPE_FOR_SQUARE_ROOT | Scalar | The value returned upon execution of the function SQUARE_ROOT (Figure 10-20) |
| READING | TYPE_FOR_READING | Scalar | Input to the Ada function LOG (Figure 10-21) |
| LOG_VAL | TYPE_FOR_LOG | Scalar | The value returned upon execution of the function LOG (Figure 10-21) |
| EXPONENT | TYPE_FOR_EXPONENT | Scalar | The exponent $-\frac{1}{2}\left(\frac{x-\mu}{\sigma}\right)^2$ in equation 10-3 (Figure 10-18) |
| EXPONENTIAL_VAL | TYPE_FOR_EXPONENTIAL | Scalar | The value returned upon execution of the function EXPONENTIAL (Figure 10-22) |
| NEGATIVE_MEAN | TYPE_FOR_NEGATIVE_MEAN | Scalar | The exponent $-\mu$ in equation 10-4 (Figure 10-19) |
| NUMBER | TYPE_FOR_NUMBER | Scalar | The value of x in equation 10-4 |
| FACTORIAL_VAL | TYPE_FOR_FACTORIAL | Scalar | The factorial x! in equation 10-4 |
| MEAN | TYPE_FOR_MEAN | Scalar | The mean value of the readings of a sample (i.e., $\mu = \frac{1}{N}\sum_{i=1}^{N} x_i$) (Figure 10-16) |

*TABLE 10-3.* (continued)

### (a) Variables (continued)

| Name of Data Entity | Type | | Description |
|---|---|---|---|
| | Name | Category | |
| STANDARD_DEVIATION | TYPE_FOR_STANDARD_DEVIATION | Scalar | The standard deviation of the readings of a sample (i.e., $\sigma = \sqrt{\frac{1}{N}\sum_{i=1}^{N}(x_i - \mu)^3}$ |
| I,J | TYPE_FOR_INDEX | Scalar | Indexes |
| FACTOR | TYPE_FOR_FACTOR | Scalar | The value of FACTOR in equation 10-3, $FACTOR = \frac{1}{\sigma\sqrt{2\pi}}$ (Figure 10-18) |
| SAMPLE_VALUES | TYPE_FOR_SAMPLE_VALUES | Composite | The readings of a sample |
| X | TYPE_FOR_X | Scalar | Variable in equation 10-3 (Figure 10-18) |
| X_INITIAL | TYPE_FOR_X | Scalar | Lowest value of x (Figure 10-18) |
| X_FINAL | TYPE_FOR_X | Scalar | Highest value of x (Figure 10-18) |
| DELTA_X | TYPE_FOR_X | Scalar | Increment (Figure 10-18) |
| SQUARE_SUM | TYPE_FOR_SQUARE_SUM | Scalar | The sum of x – MEAN squared in equation 10-2 (Figure 10-17) |
| X_VECTOR | TYPE_FOR_X_VECTOR | Composite | Set of sample readings used in a normal or Poisson distribution (i.e., $\bar{x}$ in Figures 10-18 and 10-19) |

TABLE 10-3. (continued)

## (b) Constants

| Name of Constant | Value | Description |
|---|---|---|
| SQUARE_ROOT_2PI | $\sqrt{2\pi}$ | The $\sqrt{2\pi}$, which is used in equation 10-3 in the calculation of a normal distribution (Figure 10-18) |
| ONE-EIGHTH | $\frac{1}{8}$ | Factor used in equation 10-5 in calculating the square root of a number (Figure 10-20) |
| ONE-FORTY-EIGHTH | $\frac{1}{48}$ | Factor used in equation 10-5 in calculating the square root of a number (Figure 10-20) |
| ONE-HALF | $\frac{1}{2}$ | Factor used in equation 10-5 in calculating the square root of a number and in equation 10-6 in calculating the log of a number (Figures 10-20 and 10-21) |
| ONE-THIRD | $\frac{1}{3}$ | Factor used in equation 10-6 in calculating the log of a number (Figure 10-21) |
| ONE-QUARTER | $\frac{1}{4}$ | Factor used in equation 10-6 in calculating the log of a number (Figure 10-21) |
| TWO_FACTORIAL | $2! = 2$ | Factor used in equation 10-7 in establishing the exponential of a number (Figure 10-21) |
| THREE_FACTORIAL | $3! = 6$ | Factor used in equation 10-7 in establishing the exponential of a number (Figure 10-21) |
| FOUR_FACTORIAL | $4! = 24$ | Factor used in equation 10-7 in establishing the exponential of a number (Figure 10-21) |

## (c) Record Types

| Name of Data Type | Name of Each Component | Name of Type for Each Component |
|---|---|---|
| TYPE_FOR_DISTRIBUTION_VALUES | X_VECTOR | TYPE_FOR_X_VECTOR |
| | PROBABILITY | TYPE_FOR_PROBABILITY |

TABLE 10-3. (continued)

(d) Array Types

| Name of Data Type | Dimension | Indices per Dimension | Components Type |
|---|---|---|---|
| TYPE_FOR_X_VECTOR | One | 20 | TYPE_FOR_X (see Table 10-2) |
| TYPE_FOR_PROBABILITY | One | 20 | DIST_COMP_TYPE (see Table 10-2) |
| TYPE_FOR_SAMPLE_VALUES | One | 1000 | TYPE_FOR_X (see Table 10-2) |

(e) Scalar Types

| Name of Data Type | Category | Permissible Values | Decimal Places |
|---|---|---|---|
| TYPE_FOR_MEAN | Real | 1.0 to 2000.0 | One |
| TYPE_FOR_STANDARD_DEVIATION | Float | | |
| TYPE_FOR_AV_SQUARE_SUM | Float | | |
| TYPE_FOR_SQUARE_ROOT | Real | 0.0 to 2000.0 | One |
| TYPE_FOR_READING | Float | | |
| TYPE_FOR_LOG | Float | | |
| TYPE_FOR_EXPONENT | Float | | |
| TYPE_FOR_EXPONENTIAL | Float | | |
| TYPE_FOR_NEGATIVE_MEAN | Real | −2000.0 to 0.0 | One |
| TYPE_FOR_NUMBER | Integer | 2 to 2000 | |
| TYPE_FOR_FACTORIAL | Float | | |
| TYPE_FOR_INDEX | Integer | 1 to 100 | |
| TYPE_FOR_FACTOR | Real | 0.00 to 1.00 | Two |
| TYPE_FOR_SQUARE_SUM | Float | | |

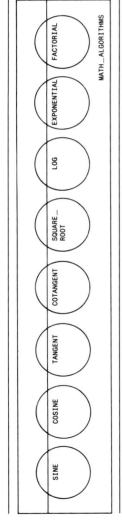

*FIGURE 10-24.* Package of mathematical functions

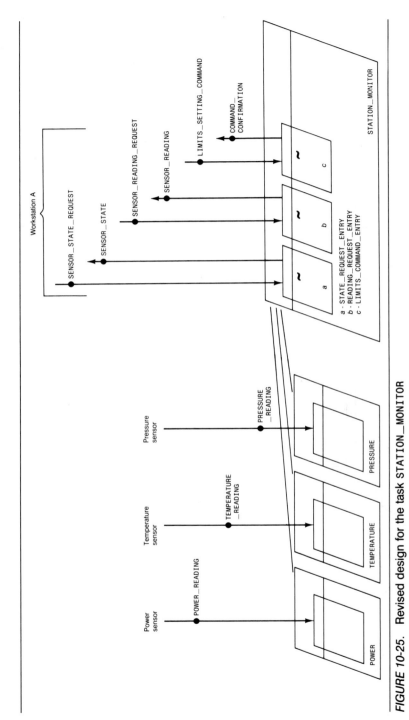

*FIGURE 10-25.* Revised design for the task STATION_MONITOR

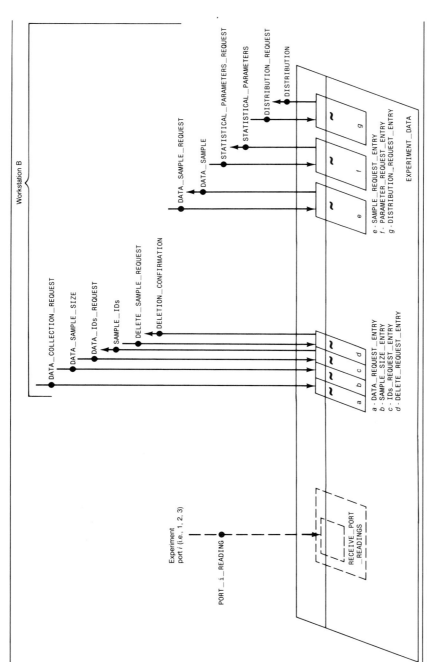

*FIGURE 10-26.* Revised design for the task EXPERIMENT_DATA: introducing task type

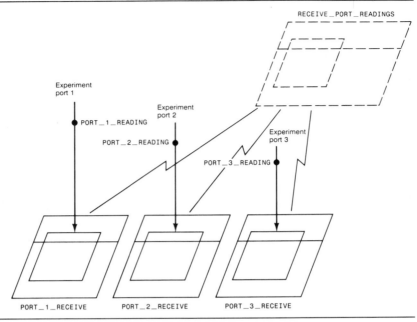

*FIGURE 10-27.* Revised design for the task EXPERIMENT_DATA: instances of task type

software development project. Once approved, the design is turned over to programmers who will develop Ada source statements that will implement the design. At the same time, the software requirements and the design are turned over to test engineers, who will prepare procedures for acceptance testing of the space station software system.

## 10.4 Key Concepts

- A set of computer programs can execute in a distributed manner within a large processor as a software system.
- In Ada, the concurrent execution of programs can be logically accomplished using Ada tasks.
- Steps for the design of a software system as a set of concurrently executing computer programs are as follows:

  1. Assess requirements for the software system.

2. Declare Ada tasks to establish logical concurrency for a set of the computer programs.
3. Define the interfaces between interacting computer programs and between each of the computer programs and the outside world.
4. Design the computer programs.
5. Refine the design.

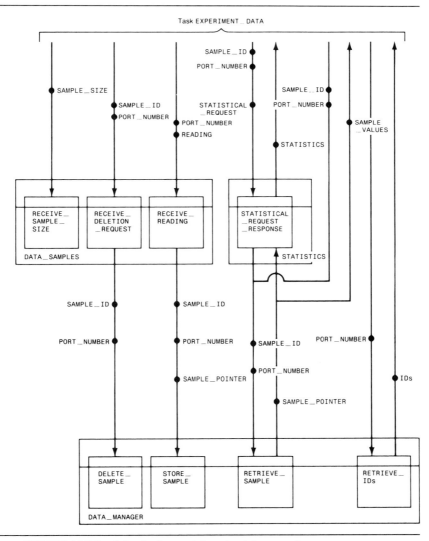

*FIGURE 10-28.* Introducing pointers to data samples

## 10.5 Exercises

1. Specify a design for the package UPDATE_PANEL_ORIENTATION of the *solar panel* process of the hypothetical space station software system. In the design, specify requirements for data structures and segment operations.

2. Specify a design for the package SENSORS of the *station monitor* process of the space station software system. In the design, specify requirements for the hidden data structure, identify program units to be used to segment operations, and specify the variables that pass between the program units.

3. Categorize the independent packages selected in the design of the earth-orbiting space station as interaction, tangible objects, roles, incidents, or data specifications, where interaction accounts for user and interface requests, tangible objects are physical entities, roles are played by persons or organizations (e.g., supervisors, owners, divisions, subdivisions), incidents represent an occurrence or event (e.g., experiment, built-in-test), and data specifications account for such things as model number, size, and rating (e.g., in inventory).

# PART IV

# The Relationship of Design to Risk, Implementation Issues, and Life Cycle Costs

*The fourth part of this book addresses how a design can help control risk, implementation problems, and life cycle costs in the development of a large software system. These factors are important because in the real world of engineering, an important bottom line for judging the merit of design technique is its effect on the economics of a system's life cycle.*

*Chapter 11 assesses the extent to which our design approach helps control risk and implementation problems. This chapter points out that design can help engineers and programmers perform software development work in a systematic manner. Design can also help managers comprehend a large and complex software problem by providing understandable independent packages. Managers can measure and monitor progress in the development of the packages.*

*Chapter 12 assesses the economics of applying our design approach. This chapter points out that designing a large software system with independent parts can help control software development and maintenance costs if the design is adhered to over the life cycle of the software system.*

# CHAPTER 11

# Controlling Risk and Implementation Problems through Design

In this book, software engineering has been addressed in the context of general engineering. As such, software engineering has been considered a process for developing software systems in a practical and cost-effective manner. Software design is an important part of the software engineering process. If done with cost and risk control in mind, proper design can make a significant economic contribution to the development of a software system.

## 11.1  Introduction

The development of a set of large computer programs as a software system encompasses several activities, including requirements analysis, design, and source statement development. Chapters 2 and 7 addressed the analysis and specification of requirements. Chapters 3 through 10 addressed the design of computer programs for large and complex software systems. This chapter examines how the design approach suggested can help control risk and potential implementation problems. Risk is discussed in the context of changing requirements and the possible adverse effects on software performance when changes are made. Implementation issues are discussed in the context of compilation/recompilation, incremental development, reuse of existing packages, and integration of independent packages. In each case, the use of our design approach for a set of independent packages lays a foundation for accomplishing these tasks in an efficient and cost-effective manner. However, if a proper design is not prepared and adhered to during the development of a software system, the exact opposite effect may well take place.

## 11.2 Control of Risk Inherent in Changing Requirements

### 11.2.1 Control of Requirements Changes

An obvious approach to the control of change is to eliminate change itself. Some software engineers and analysts argue that in the development of large software systems, the responsible software development organization should establish firm and fixed requirements in specifications and submit them to the customer for approval before programming is begun. Then, using the "frozen" requirements as a baseline, the large software system can be designed, coded, and tested so that it conforms to the frozen requirements.

In practice, the precise definition of what a large system should do is difficult, and the comprehensive transformation of system performance into detailed requirements specifications is even more difficult. Thus, the initial version of a large software system often does not conform exactly to the customer's needs. In the view of some software engineers and analysts, this problem is generally fundamental to the acquisition of a large and complex software system. Therefore, establishing frozen requirements for a large and complex computer program is difficult.

### 11.2.2 Software Prototype

To help a customer formulate requirements for a large and complex computer program, some designers have proposed the development of a prototype of the software system. The customer can operate the prototype system to identify missing capabilities and other performance anomalies. This knowledge can then be used to establish more comprehensive operational requirements. Classically, a software prototype can be defined as a model of an operational software system meant to demonstrate the functions performed by the software and the human engineering associated with user interfaces. As such, a prototype typically generates system output in response to operator input. The output can be, for example, system responses in a predetermined scenario using a subset of processing capabilities.

In the development of a prototype, the high-level architectural structure of the software system is usually formulated first. As part of this effort, packaged tasks for computer programs and independent packages within each computer program are identified. The computer programs are then implemented with respect to servicing external users, while modeling or stubbing the independent packages. The development effort may be undertaken without extensive documentation, without regard to execution speed and possibly without regard to source code reliability and general quality. Modeled packages can emulate, for example, typical responses to a user request, perhaps including only a subset of possible responses. Stubbed packages may satisfy interface requirements by simply returning "canned" responses, perhaps consuming memory, mass storage, and CPU time (e.g., through the use of loops).

In some cases, certain packages of the prototype may be designed, coded, and tested with production or near-production quality. These package implementations can then be exercised under both nominal and extreme conditions to determine the technical feasibility of processing associated with questionable requirements, to evaluate alternative implementation techniques, and to establish memory requirements and execution speed.

Thus, a prototype of a software system can be used to assess the user interfaces of the program and critical program capabilities. Based on the results of trial applications of the program by the customer and by analysts, feedback on performance may be used early in the development cycle to improve the quality of software requirements, before full-scale development efforts begin. In this way, the number of changes that must be made to the requirements once development is fully underway can be reduced, thus controlling to a certain extent the problem of change.

### 11.2.3 Design in Anticipation of Requirements Changes

The Ada design approach introduced in this book is meant to lay the foundation for the development of a flexible software system which is a means for controlling adverse side effects that may result when a program is changed. Adverse side effects may be encountered in a software system after changes are made, usually to repair bugs and in response to changes in system requirements.

With the Ada design approach, a software system is compartmentalized into independent packages, which can be thought of as "armor-plated" black boxes. Many of the independent packages do not interact; those that do, do so only in a limited way. Since the independent packages behave like armor-plated black boxes, ripple effects and side effects in performance due to changes cannot propagate beyond the walls of the independent packages. Therefore, changes to one part of a software system should not affect other parts of the system. A software system derived from a design developed using this approach can be thought of as elastic, amenable to change if the design has been adhered to during the life cycle of the software system.

## 11.3 Control of Risk Inherent in Software Development through Design

The sections that follow analyze the relationship of a design to the problems inherent in implementing a software system. Specifically, we discuss how a design that specifies an architectural structure of independent packages helps facilitate timely compilation/recompilation, incremental development, reuse of existing packages, and integration test of a large program.

### 11.3.1 Compilation/Recompilation

Application of our design approach results in a general topology of independent packages that help control compilation/recompilation problems inherent in the development of a software system. During development, the independent packages of the software system can be individually designed, coded, and tested. The test of an independent package actually begins at compilation time, where static aspects of Ada's strong typing are checked. For example, information passed between program units is checked for consistency in both parameter name and kind. Upon successful compilation, the performance of a package implementation has to be tested further by observance of its performance in a set of trial runs.

For each trial run, the programmer can use a debugger to step through the source statements that implement the operations of the package. The debugger allows the programmer to set break points at which execution is halted, so that program results can be compared to those expected. Deviations from expected results flag errors in logic, data manipulation, algorithm performance, or the data structure. The reason for an error can be identified and corrected by changing the original Ada source statements. The resulting source statements can then be recompiled and the trial runs reexecuted. This error detection and correction process may have to be repeated several times before the trial runs appear to execute successfully.

Each iteration of the checkout process may require compilation of all or part of a program, so let's discuss what is involved in compilation/recompilation with Ada. Because we are dealing with a large number of source statements, and because an Ada compiler is relatively slow compared to compilers for other simpler languages, the time required to complete each recompilation of a program can become an issue. Design, however, can help make recompilation more timely.

### Compilation Units

An Ada compiler can translate Ada source code into a form that is executable in a target processor for one or more compilation units. The following are compilation units:

- subprogram declaration
- subprogram body
- package declaration
- package body
- generic declaration
- generic instantiation
- subunit

(Note, a task specification cannot be compiled since tasks can be declared only within subprograms or packages.) In accordance with ANSI/MIL-STD-1815A (*the Ada Language Reference Manual*), Ada compilation units are compiled subject to the following order:

- the specification of a package or a subprogram before its body
- a program unit's body before any subunit in the body
- the specification of a package before any unit that refers to the package
- the body of a generic (and any of its subunits) before every instantiation of the generic

Every Ada with clause in a compilation also must be satisfied. Otherwise, semantic errors will occur for the program unit having the with clause.

An Ada linker forms an executable program out of separately compiled Ada compilation units. Specifically, it combines object code of compilation units, the Ada run-time and I/O libraries, and a full tasking kernel. An Ada linker finds the main program in a user-constructed library and locates the run-time library, the tasking kernel, and the source code debugger. The typical sequence of linking events is as follows:

1. Find all libraries associated with the program
2. Check that all required program units are available and have been compiled in the Ada-defined order
3. Assemble code to elaborate the program
4. Link the modules

The compilation units establish a library. A library manager can be used to store and retrieve information characterizing the compilation units. For example, for each compilation unit, library information may include (a) the date/time of syntax/semantic checking and the date of code generation, (b) program units that must be compiled to complete the compilation of a program unit, (c) the names of source files and object files associated with the program unit, (d) the program unit kind (e.g., package body, subprogram body, or generic), (e) the names of units withed by the program unit, and (f) the names of program units that with the program unit.

### *Assessing Compilation/Recompilation*

During development of a software system and later as part of maintenance, the extent of program recompilation depends on where modifications have been made. If the body of an independent package is changed, then only that body may need to be recompiled. If the specification of an independent package is changed, then both the specification and the body of the package must be recompiled, along with all dependent compilation units. Dependent compilation units include the program units listed in an Ada with clause for the independent package to be changed. Because of this, the extent of recompilation necessary in a program is driven by the program's architectural structure and where a change is made.

In the Ada design approach introduced in this book, the topology of a software system consists of the main Ada procedure, packaged tasks, the independent packages, and the program units within the independent packages, as illustrated in Figure 11-1. In practice, changes should be restricted to the bodies of the independent packages so that only the body of a modified package has to be recompiled. If the specification of an independent package changes, then the recompilation effort grows to encompass the specification and the body of the modified package, and the specifications and the bodies of the independent packages that interact with the modified package. For this case, a design that constrains coupling between

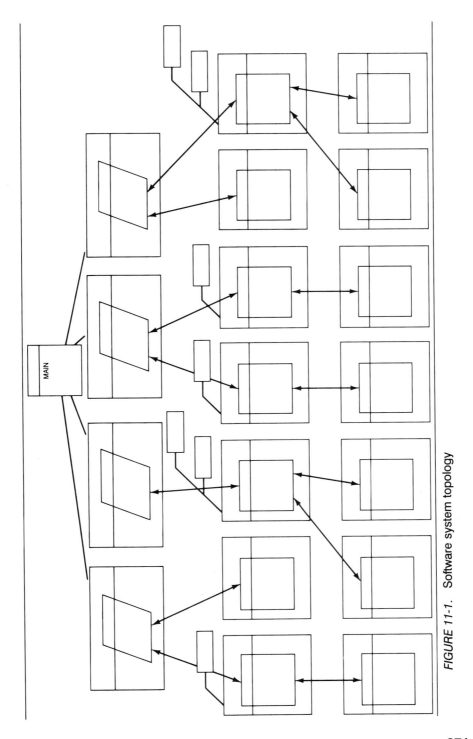

*FIGURE 11-1.* Software system topology

independent packages typically necessitates recompiling only two or three independent packages within a program.

During the development and/or maintenance of a software system, problems may be encountered if the original design was faulty or if the integrity of a "good" design is not kept in place. In the later case, the original design for a software system may have specified independence between architectural packages and may have controlled coupling between the packages. However, this independence and loose coupling may not be kept intact.

Over the course of development and maintenance, the original design may begin to break down as individual developers (and later maintainers) introduce dependencies and coupling not originally called for by the design, as illustrated in Figure 11-2. For example, during maintenance programmers may gain access to one independent package from a second independent package simply by adding an Ada with clause in front of the second package and recompiling. In this way, package coupling can be extended beyond that called for by the original design.

Modification of a design not only may lead to problems in executing the software system, it may also increase the extent of recompilation necessary. As indicated previously, Ada's compilation rules require that a change to a portion of a large Ada computer program necessitates the recompilation of the changed portion and everything that depends on that changed portion. For a large software system with a degraded design, the time to recompile may take hours (or longer when extensive interprogram coupling has been introduced). Since recompilation undoubtedly will have to be repeated several times during development and maintenance operations (even for one change), good productivity necessitates a design (and adherence to that design) that encourages acceptable time frames for recompilation and relinking.

Care should be taken to not introduce unnecessary coupling not called for by the original design, especially coupling across programs. For example, the Ada with clause should be used only where explicitly permitted in the original design.

## 11.3.2 Incremental Development

Following our design approach results in a set of independent packages, which lend themselves well to incremental development. A

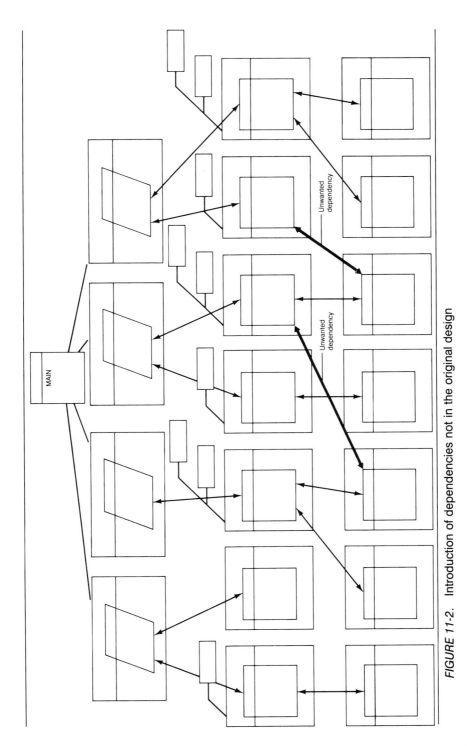

MAIN

Unwanted dependency

Unwanted dependency

*FIGURE 11-2.* Introduction of dependencies not in the original design

core system of independent packages can be implemented to establish basic operations of the software system. Then additional packages can be implemented and incrementally added to the software system as a series of software "builds." The initial builds may add independent packages that extend the basic capabilities of the core set of compilation units. Later builds may introduce independent packages associated with advanced capabilities. Because each package implementation is essentially unique and independent, the addition of new package implementations should not disrupt the core system and other package implementations already integrated with the core system.

Incremental development of a large software system can be undertaken with different teams of programmers working in parallel. One team can work on one package implementation, while other teams work on other package implementations. Incremental development is especially appropriate for software development teams that include inexperienced programmers. In effect, a software development job can be subdivided into a series of small and relatively independent jobs. The poor performance of one package implementation should not seriously disrupt other package implementations at integration time, if sufficient independence between package implementations has been maintained.

Since incremental development of an Ada design can be accomplished as a series of different and relatively independent jobs, the overall software development costs should decrease (when compared to software development costs for a software system that is one large aggregation of highly coupled components). This decrease in cost is due, first, to the fact that the development of a small software entity is more efficient from both a time and a cost point of view (software development costs increase exponentially with size). Second, the integration of independent packages is time and cost effective since the introduction of one independent package does not disrupt other package implementations already integrated and properly executing.

### 11.3.3 Reuse of Existing Ada Packages

Adherence to our design approach facilitates the reuse of existing independent packages. This approach to software development was discussed in Section 7.3.2, and is reviewed and extended in the following paragraphs.

### Basic Concepts

A key rationale for the design of the Ada language was the concept of software reusability. It is desirable that certain processing encapsulated in Ada packages have multiple applications in different software systems. Reusable Ada packages can facilitate processing, for example, in such things as I/O device drivers, network protocols, special-purpose processing algorithms, database management systems, and other applications. Reusable Ada packages also can be used to encapsulate reusable modules, including routines for data structure manipulation (e.g., stacks, queues, and linked lists).

As discussed in Chapter 7, reusable independent packages can be added to a system of independent packages without disturbing the processing being undertaken in any independent package of the system. A reusable Ada package can be constructed as an independent package with its own unique data structure and operations. As such, a reusable Ada package will not use the variables and flags found in other independent packages of the software system and will not permit other independent packages of the software system to access its internal formulation. Accordingly, changes to other parts of the software system will not affect a reusable independent package or its performance, and changes to a reusable independent package will not affect the performance of other parts of the software system.

Reusing existing code is not without risk, however. To reuse code, we need to know exactly what the code does, what information it expects and in what form, how it outputs information, and so on. We also must be sure that the software will work with high reliability for all extremes of its possible reapplication. In addition, the issue of portability arises when an independent package developed to operate on one particular machine is to be reapplied on another machine.

### Porting of Reusable Packages

Ideally, reusable Ada packages are applicable to multiple computers. Ada promotes such porting of a reusable package from one computer to another, although special design and implementation steps may have to be taken to address porting issues. With Ada, the U.S. Department of Defense requires that all compilers must be validated to ensure that they adhere to the requirements of ANSI/MIL-STD–1815A. This eliminates the possibility of several different versions of Ada. In the past, porting of software written in languages other than Ada was complicated by multiple versions of the languages and their associated compilers.

Nevertheless, Ada code is subject to porting problems that may arise due to language implementation liberties allowed by ANSI/MIL-STD-1815A. In general, the design and implementation of a reusable Ada package must address variations in the performance of language constructs when it is to execute on different machines (due to such things as variations in timing, precision, order of execution). In addition, portable Ada packages must address variations in (a) processing machine speed and storage capacity, (b) I/O processing techniques (due to such factors as variations in terminal screens and keyboards), and (c) run-time performance (due to such things as differences in applicable operating systems from one processor to another, e.g., variations in utilities, library routines, and the implementation of logical concurrency).

Special steps have to be taken in the implementation of reusable Ada packages. Specifically, the parts of the software in the body of the reusable package that are not portable have to be clearly isolated and flagged as such and inserted into a customizable Ada package that can be accessed (e.g., through the Ada with clause). This second package then has to be reimplemented for the specific applicable processor. Each version of the second package can have a specification identical to that of other versions, with only the package's body varying from one version to another. To control the potential adverse effects of variation from one version to another, each customizable second Ada package should be constructed as an independent package, with its own unique data structure and processing operations that are not accessible to external entities. A reusable Ada package should have access to the second customizable Ada package only through limited means declared in the specification.

Thus, several issues have to be addressed in the generation of reusable program units. However, the proper use of Ada packages in an independent manner and effective documentation schemes will lay the foundation for resolving problems and facilitating an Ada package industry.

### 11.3.4 Integration of Independent Packages

Following our design approach will result in a set of independent packages that can be readily integrated. Our approach calls for partitioning a software system into a set of independent packages at a coarser level of granularity than that of a top-down design. In our design approach, the first level breakdown of a computer program was into Ada packages ranging in size from about 3000 to 7000 source statements. In a traditional top-down design, a computer program is decomposed into small program units of less than 200 source statements. Because of this, the number of software entities to be integrated are far fewer than the multitude of small program units inherent in a traditional top-down design. The following paragraphs address the issues associated with the integration of independent packages. Two points are made. First, using the design approach introduced in this book results in a set of independent packages that can be readily integrated and thus development can be completed in a timely and cost-effective manner. Second, testing can be undertaken by introducing additional "test-unique" independent packages.

### Basic Concepts

A test team can run tests to verify that integrated independent packages satisfy design and system requirements. From a design point of view, test cases can verify the proper interaction of the independent packages. From a system point of view, test cases can verify that packages integrated together as a whole perform in accordance with system requirements (e.g., for system state transitions and activities/data flow within each state). To run test cases for either point of view, test stimuli can be generated to exercise a set of integrated independent packages under both nominal and stress conditions. The performance of the independent packages can be measured by recording the parameters that are passed between packages and between the packages and the outside world. The recorded data can then be compared to expected values.

### Test Software

Test software can include test drivers, an environmental simulator, and data-recording software. Data-recording software can be used to record the performance of integrated independent packages that execute in response to a test driver or environmental simulator stimuli. Test drivers generate static stimuli, typically used for one isolated test case. An environmental simulator generates dynamic stimuli, which vary over time. An environmental simulator can be used for complex dynamic interaction between independent packages.

As part of the framework for testing the interaction of independent packages, an Ada package can be developed to generate test-driver stimuli. With such a package, various test cases can be initiated under operator control. For example, a task declared in the specification of a test package can simulate test-driver stimuli. During task rendezvous, the stimuli can be passed to a process task, as illustrated in Figure 11-3, where the test-driver package is shaded to distinguish it from the application software.

To test the interaction of independent packages in a realistic and dynamic manner, an environmental simulator package can be developed, capable of generating a sequence of stimuli over time. The Ada task in the specification of the environmental simulator package can respond to feedback received from the independent packages under test. Such an environmental simulator package can be programmed offline by a test engineer (to establish the sequence of stimuli to be generated). An example of this test configuration is shown in Figure 11-4, where again test software is shaded to distinguish it from the application software.

When tests are run, data recording program units can be called just prior to the passing of data. As shown in Figure 11-4, a call to a recording program unit can be made conditional. Through the setting of conditionable flags, appropriate conditions can be set prior to test execution, defining what data passage is to be recorded and what data passage is not to be recorded. In this way, the amount of test data generated for a given test case can be limited to only that needed.

### Acceptance Testing of a Software System

An integrated set of independent packages can be tested for acceptability through the execution of test cases. The steps for each test case are specified in a test procedure. Documentation for the test procedure presents test cases, the objective of each test case, the test steps, and the expected system response for each test step.

Test cases should encompass both nominal and stress testing of packages integrated together as a whole. *Nominal testing* introduces stimuli and operating conditions typical of those to be experienced by the software in an operational real-world environment. Nominal testing is designed to exercise the software under expected conditions, to ensure that all package implementations are performing as required under such conditions.

*Stress testing* introduces stimuli and operating conditions that will subject the software to possible extreme conditions. Stress testing makes maximum, overload, or even erroneous demands on object implementations. It can include simulated breakdown of interfacing hardware and other unexpected conditions that could occur in the operational environment. Attention can be given to unusual combinations of events that should have been anticipated in the

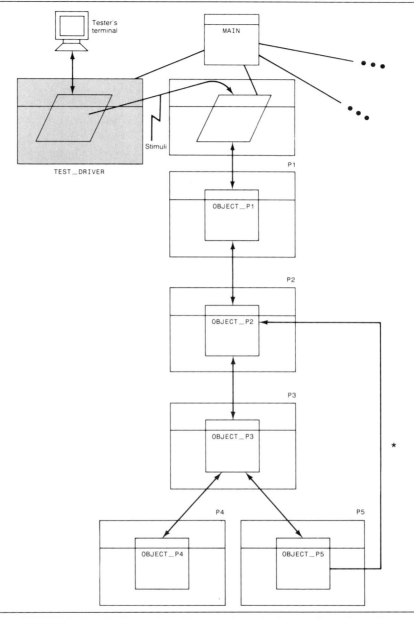

*FIGURE 11-3.* Adding a test-driver package to the configuration of independent packages

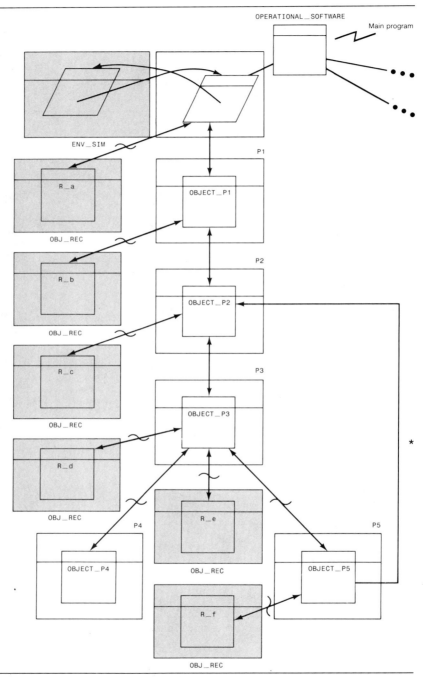

FIGURE 11-4. Adding an environmental simulator package to the configuration of independent packages

design. These extreme values of stimuli can be generated by either the test-driver package or the environmental simulator package. The environmental simulator package can stress integrated independent packages with respect to the frequency at which stimuli are presented to them.

In addition to nominal and stress testing, endurance tests can be run to verify that the large computer program can perform correctly over time. Such testing is especially applicable to exercising critical interaction of independent packages (e.g., packages associated with life-dependent events). Performance endurance testing can exercise the independent packages over their full range of input values. Test cases should be selected to incorporate in a dynamic manner both nominal and extreme conditions and can include many combinations of representative input values. Tests results can be analyzed manually or with the aid of statistical analysis tools to identify performance patterns and detect anomalies and biases in overall performance. Graphs and tables of results can be prepared to draw conclusions from program performance. Results may indicate special situations that require additional testing. Results can also be used to define the range of missions that can be successfully accomplished by the large computer program and to compare the performance of different versions of the large computer program.

### Lower-Level Tests

Lower-level tests can be run if incorrect performance is detected during testing of an integrated set of independent packages. Lower-level tests can be used to determine a faulty independent package and to further isolate the problem to the internal structure of the faulty package. A possible configuration for such testing is shown in Figure 11-5. Classical computer programmer testing can be used to test the levels of interacting program units within a faulty independent package. Such testing can be accomplished with a debugger and other test tools provided in an Ada programming support environment. For example, parameters passed between subprograms can be checked, internal branching within each subprogram verified, and data generated in arrays or records checked. Breakpoints can be set at specific ports in the software (with a debugger), and values of parameters at that point can be reviewed.

The testing of several interacting Ada tasks (if used in the internal structure of a package implementation) is not as straightforward as interacting procedures because of the concurrency associated with task execution. Although classical techniques using a debugger can

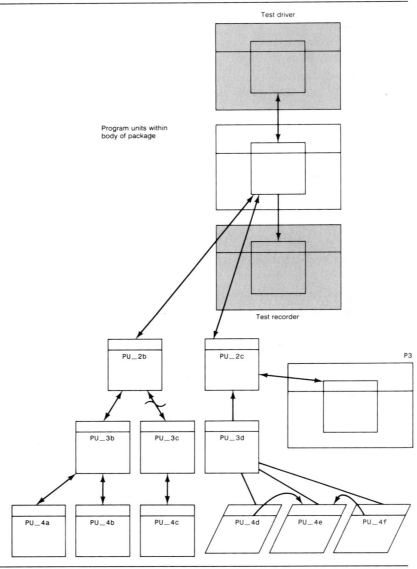

*FIGURE 11-5.* Testing the program units in the body of an Ada package

be applied to assess task performance to a certain extent, other time-dependent tests typically have to be conducted to check the temporal aspects of task execution. To establish time-dependent tests, the environmental simulator package can generate a sequence of stimuli in a predetermined manner and over a specific time period.

The data-recording package can collect and assess data passed between tasks, and to check the validity of the parameter values and if they are passed in a timely manner, in compliance with mission requirements.

As shown in Figure 11-6, the recording package can contain a set of procedures. Calls can be made to the procedures from acceptor tasks, as part of their accept statements. With this recording capability, a record of parameter values passed during task rendezvous and the time of task rendezvous can be established. The calls to recording procedures can be made conditional. In this way, the tester can establish the conditions needed to provide the test recording needed for the particular test case being run.

The temporal aspects of task rendezvous make such testing much more complicated than the testing of sequential procedure calls. In addition, with complex sets of task calls, timing problems can occur because certain tasks may have to wait longer than is acceptable for their entry points to be called, or a called entry point may not become available to complete a rendezvous in a timely manner. In the design approach introduced in this book, Ada tasks are used to establish logical concurrency between programs and independent packages, but internal to packages only where necessary to reduce complexity.

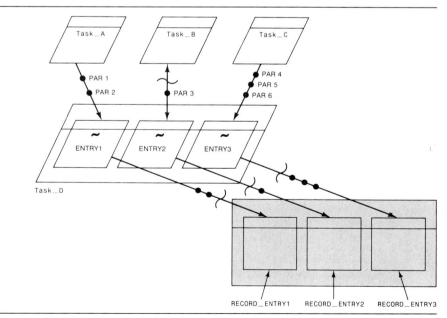

FIGURE 11-6. Task rendezvous recording package

Extensive use of Ada tasks can be dangerous because of potential timing and test problems. In general, a designer can keep a design and its implementation simple by not introducing unnecessary complexity into a design.

## 11.4 Key Concepts

- Risks inherent in the development of a software system can be controlled by using design that leads to flexible software, capable of change without introducing side effects that degrade overall performance.
- A prototype of a software system can be developed to assess the requirements for that software system. A prototype can be used to evaluate both user interfaces and critical program capabilities. Feedback received after operation of a prototype can be used to improve requirements for the software system.
- Design can facilitate timely compilation and recompilation of Ada units. During development and maintenance, the number of compilation units that have to be recompiled depends on the location of changes in the computer program. For example, if the body of an independent package is changed, then only that body needs to be recompiled. However, if the specification of an independent package is changed, then the specification as well as the body of the package must be recompiled, along with all dependent compilation units linked to the specification. Because of this, programs with extensive coupling between independent packages may take hours to recompile when one or more package specifications are modified. Therefore, good productivity necessitates a design that calls for limited coupling between independent packages and adherence to that design during the life cycle of a software product.
- A computer program as a set of independent packages can include existing, reusable packages. A reusable package that is independent and self-sufficient will not use variables and flags found in other parts of the software system and will not permit other parts of the software system to access its internal formulation. Changes to the other parts of the software system will not affect a reusable independent package, and changes to the reusable independent packages will not affect the performance of other parts of the software system.

- A design for a software system as a set of independent packages can be made into Ada source statements in an incremental manner. Initially, a core set of independent packages can be implemented to establish basic operations of the large computer program. Additional packages then can be implemented and integrated, as a series of software "builds." Builds may add packages that extend the basic capabilities of the core set, eventually integrating packages associated with advanced capabilities.

- A design for a computer program as a set of independent packages results in a set of software entities that can be systematically integrated and tested. A test team can run tests to verify that package implementations integrated in a build satisfy design and system requirements. Test stimuli can be generated to exercise integrated independent packages under both nominal and stress conditions. The performance of the package implementations can be measured by recording the parameters passed between interacting package implementations and between the package implementations and the program tasks declared in the main program. The recorded data can then be compared to expected values. If, during testing, a faulty package implementation is detected, lower-level tests can further isolate the problem to the internal structure of the package implementation. For example, parameters passed between subprograms can be checked, internal branching within each subprogram verified, and data generated in arrays or records checked.

- Our design approach does not promote extensive use of Ada tasks with levels of rendezvous. This is because the testing of levels of interacting Ada tasks is not as straightforward as the testing of levels of subprograms, due to concurrency associated with task execution. Although techniques used to test subprograms can be applied to assess task interaction to a certain extent, additional tests typically have to be conducted to check the temporal aspects of task execution. Timing problems can occur because certain tasks may have to wait longer than is acceptable for their entry points to be called, or a called entry point may not become available to complete rendezvous in a timely manner.

## 11.5  Exercises

1. How can a prototype be used to evaluate the requirements for a software system?

2. How does the design for a software system support the incremental development of that software system? What are the advantages of incremental development?
3. How can design facilitate the introduction of existing independent packages into a software system? How can design facilitate the portability of reusable packages?
4. What determines the extent of recompilation that must be undertaken when a change is made to a program? How can design be used to limit the time required to complete recompilation?
5. How can a design based on partitioning a software system into a set of independent packages help control software integration and test costs? How does this relate to incremental development?
6. To what extent do you recommend the introduction of Ada tasks into a design? Why?

# CHAPTER 12

# Control of Software Life Cycle Costs

We have defined software engineering as an engineering discipline that can be used to develop and maintain software in an economical manner. Although the economics of a software product are fundamental to its engineering, it is typically not addressed in books on software engineering. However, our basic objective has been just this—to develop a strategy for designing a software system that is easy to understand and apply in an economical manner.

## 12.1  Introduction

This chapter focuses on costs and their control during the development and maintenance of a software system. The ability of a design approach to lay a foundation to control software life cycle costs is a major criterion on which a design approach should be judged.

## 12.2  Qualitative Assessment of Life Cycle Costs

Life cycle costs for a software system include the cost to develop the system, install it at a site location and maintain the system over the years of its operation.

### 12.2.1 Development Costs

The cost to develop a software system encompasses the labor costs incurred by the team involved in the development effort. In addition to software engineers and programmers, the team may include project managers, system engineers, test engineers, configuration management personnel, and quality assurance personnel.

*Project managers* plan and direct the software development effort. The planning activity encompasses establishing budgets and schedules; identifying needed personnel, development facilities, and other resources; and determining how and when the needed resources will be applied. The directing activity includes supervision of personnel, approving documentation, checking progress, identifying problems, and instigating changes to budgets and schedules that reflect resolution of identified problems.

*System engineers* collect, define, and document system requirements and identify the requirements to be implemented in the software. Their activities include defining concepts of operation, system states, and transition from one state to another; defining system inputs and outputs and operations on inputs to produce outputs; specifying performance precision, accuracy, reliability, and allowable processing time; specifying interfaces with other systems, information flow, and data rates; specifying man-machine interfaces with displays and man-machine dialogs; and defining constraints on architecture, memory, algorithms, processing time, and costs.

*Software engineers* are responsible for mapping software-related system requirements into software design representations. The design must clearly specify the architectural structure of a software system and the distribution of data structures across independent packages. The design must specify concurrency among the independent packages and the internal design of each package.

*Programmers* develop source statements to carry out the processing specified in the design requirements. Programmers compile the source statements, execute the source statements in several trial runs, and locate and correct program errors. Initially, they develop individual program units and later integrate those units in independent packages.

*Test engineers* verify that a software system as an integrated set of independent packages executes in accordance with system requirements. Using a set of test cases, test engineers evaluate the transition between the states of the software system and the activity within each state. The test cases measure the performance under both nominal and stress conditions. Test case data are compared to expected values, either directly or after data reduction (i.e., transformation of data from one form to another to facilitate comparison to expected results).

*Quality assurance (QA)* and *independent verification and validation (IV&V)* personnel check software products (e.g., source code and design documentation) to ensure compliance with contractual requirements. QA personnel are part of a contractor's project team, but IV&V personnel typically report directly to the customer and are independent of the development contractor.

*Configuration management* personnel assign the major components of a software system to configuration items and control changes to software components or products associated with each configuration item. Once a system is under configuration control, changes to a software product usually are not made without approval of an engineering change proposal (ECP) by a configuration management board. The board typically consists of configuration m n-agement specialists and key development personnel. In an Ada development effort, configuration management personnel can complement quality assurance personnel in maintaining the integrity of design.

If the different project personnel perform their tasks efficiently, the costs to develop a software system can be controlled. If not, problems can set in, and progress may be erratic, as discussed in Chapter 1. The design of a software system as a set of independent packages provides a framework for project personnel to complete project tasks in a timely and efficient manner. With respect to *project management*, the independent packages of a software system provide an ideal set of software entities to monitor. For example, a large program consisting of, say, 200,000 source statements might encompass 40 independent packages. A project manager can readily monitor progress in the development of each package (as opposed to monitoring thousands of small program units associated with a top-down design) by reviewing such things as (a) changes in the number of implementing source statements, (b) progress in meeting milestones, (c) changes in requirements, (d) testing progress, and (e) open-action items for problems to be resolved.

With respect to *engineering*, the independent packages can be systematically designed, implemented, and tested. Software engineers can carefully assess requirements and "optimize" the architectural structure of a software system by laying the foundation for developing flexible software, that is, software that is responsive to changes in requirements. Test engineers can efficiently devise procedures to systematically test the software system as a set of independent packages.

With respect to *programming*, proper design helps control the time required to compile and recompile. Also, the set of independent packages can be implemented in an incremental manner and integrated as a set of builds. Senior personnel can be assigned to the development of complex independent packages, or independent packages that are important with respect to performance or schedule. Also, existing Ada packages can be reused and integrated into systems without affecting the performance of other packages in the system.

With respect to *quality assurance* and *configuration management*, steps can be taken to make sure that the integrity of a design is kept over the long and arduous development process. It is important that unnecessary dependencies between Ada packages are not introduced into the software system—they can lead to compilation problems and later on to implementation and maintenance problems. For example, it is paramount that coupling between Ada packages in different programs is not introduced due to unwise use of the Ada with clause or global types not called for in the design.

## 12.2.2 Installation and Initial Operation Costs

The cost to install a software system includes the labor costs incurred by system engineers, software engineers, programmers, and test engineers in the initial trial application of the software system in a real-world environment. A software system derived from an Ada design and adherence to that design will help facilitate effective site installation.

If effective design steps have not been used to produce flexible software, site-unique changes might result in problems often referred to as program "bugs." Fixing a program bug may introduce a new bug worse than the original bug, and more and more time has to be spent fixing the secondary problems. New bugs may degrade the structure of a large program, introducing undesirable dependencies between program units, variables, and types. Extensive retesting of a computer program in its entirety has to be undertaken to ensure that such side effects have not degraded overall performance (referred to as "regression testing"). However, if a software system consists of a set of programs that have been partitioned into independent packages, the effect of a change to fix a bug is trapped within the changed package. Thus, only the package that has been changed needs to be retested, and extensive regression testing should not be necessary.

### 12.2.3 Maintenance Costs

The cost to maintain a software system includes the labor costs incurred by programmers and others associated with making changes to specific programs of the system over the years of operation of the software system. Changes are made for different reasons, including

- to correct errors
- to improve performance
- to make programs interface with hardware (e.g., telecommunications facilities)
- to change databases
- to enhance program capabilities

A computer program is maintainable to the extent it can be changed to correct defects, and enhance performance and capabilities.

Historically, software maintainability has been assumed to be a function of the documentation available, the accessibility of that information, and the tools available to support making changes and testing the changes. Indeed, these resources are important. However, the maintainability of a large and complex software system is in large part driven by the ability of that system to respond to change. As we have argued in this book, Ada software can be made more responsive to change through the use of appropriate design to control complex dependencies between program units, variables, and types.

#### Significance of Maintenance

Through the years, the costs attributed to maintaining a computer program have grown. In the 1950s and 1960s, programs were small and easy to maintain. Change in a given program unit typically had only minimal and understandable effects on other program units used to construct the small program. When changes were made, the small computer program could be recompiled and reexecuted in a matter of minutes. Since there were not a great number of program units to change and since each program unit tended to be unique and independent of other program units, the ramifications of a change could be readily comprehended by a programmer. Therefore, small computer programs tended to be flexible, subject to change without undesirable side effects on overall performance, and therefore main-tainable at a relatively low cost. As shown by the shaded areas in Figure 12-1, the cost of maintenance during the life cycle of a small program in the 1960s typically was relatively small when compared to the cost of other life cycle activities.

As processing capacity increased and the size of computer pro-grams grew, software maintenance began to increase in cost, as illustrated by the shaded areas in Figure 12-2. In fact, maintenance costs at times have typically run more than development costs.

### Conceptual View of Software Maintenance

Conceptually, the software life cycle might be viewed as separated into two different planes, one for documentation and one for imple-mentation, as illustrated in Figure 12-3. The view from the bottom plane can be very different from the view from the top plane. If special steps have not been taken in design and the documentation of a design, it may be difficult for a maintenance programmer to relate the documentation plane to the implementation plane. When this is the case, maintenance of code may be undertaken exclusively in the lower plane, where computation semantics are explicit but the original design intent may be obscure. In a worst case situation, the design may become essentially lost during the maintenance of code. If this happens, code maintenance becomes difficult because of the mental reverse-engineering process a programmer must go through to uncover a design from a source statement listing. For each change request, a programmer must be able to comprehend enough of the current design to relate it to the change request. Using reverse engineering to uncover design from code is time consuming and error prone. As a result, the change request could be termed "not feasible"; worse, it could be undertaken blindly, which could result in the introduction of undesirable dependencies between program units, variables, and types among independent package. The main-tenance programmer may not understand the independence between

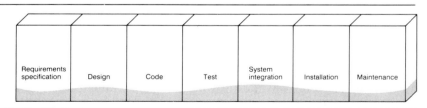

*FIGURE 12-1.* Software life cycle costs in the 1960s

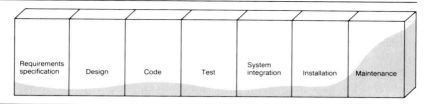

*FIGURE 12-2.* Software life cycle costs in the 1970s

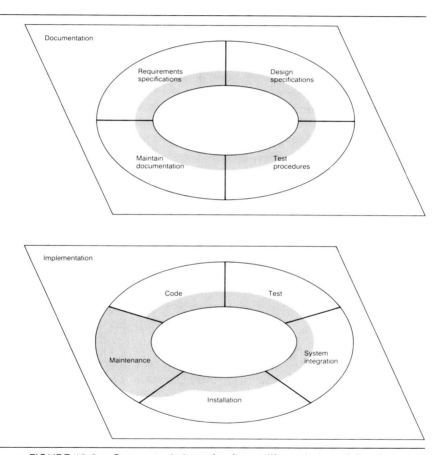

*FIGURE 12-3.* Conceptual view of software life cycle in activity planes

architectural components and data structures because it may not be self-evident in the implementing code.

In this book, we have introduced design steps that can be used to promote flexible software systems. We have directly addressed the question of maintenance by providing a mechanism for making a large program responsive to change, which is the primary activity of maintenance. In addition, we have established and applied a design notation that can be used to represent directly the architectural aspects of a design in a concise manner and as a direct abstraction of Ada itself. This notation can be used to bridge the gap between the documentation plane and the implementation plane. If kept up to date, design views can bring maintenance programmers rapidly up to date on the architectural structure of a large computer program and other design considerations. Design views also can be used as a mechanism for clearly recording any changes made to the design.

Quality assurance personnel and configuration management personnel can help ensure that the design views are kept up to date. QA personnel can review the updated design views to check that the integrity of a design is being kept during maintenance. For example, quality assurance personnel can check that undesirable dependencies are not introduced between independent packages. Configuration management personnel can review each change and not approve any changes that introduce excessive coupling between independent packages or dependencies not called for by the design.

## 12.3 Quantitative Assessment of Life Cycle Costs

Various aspects of our design approach should help control the life cycle costs of a software system in many ways for several different reasons. In this section, we address in a quantitative manner the cost savings that can be expected when a software system is partitioned into a set of independent packages, one specific aspect of our design approach. Specifically, we apply existing cost-estimating algorithms to demonstrate the savings that can be realized through the use of independent packages as the main architectural component of a software system.

### 12.3.1 Cost-Estimating Algorithms

Cost models have been developed empirically to relate the cost of software development to the size of a computer program and the factors characterizing its development. As a general relationship, the cost to develop a computer program has been related to the size of the program and other factors as follows:

$$software\ costs\ =\ C^1 * C^2 * C^3 * \ldots\ C^n * size^E \qquad (12\text{-}1)$$

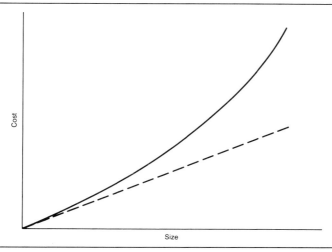

*FIGURE 12-4.* Nonlinear increase in software costs versus the size of a computer program

where *size* is raised to some power $E$ and the coefficients $C_n$ $(n = 1, 2, \ldots, N_{max})$ account for such things as product attributes, development personnel, programming practices to be used, and schedule considerations. The exponent accounts for the fact that software development costs have increased at a more than linear rate versus size, as illustrated in Figure 12-4.

## 12.3.2 The Constructive Cost Model (COCOMO)

To demonstrate software cost savings through the use of independent packages, let's apply the constructive cost model, or COCOMO. The formulation and calibration of this model has been derived from data collected from software efforts at TRW, Inc., and is presented by Barry Boehm in his book *Software Engineering Economics*.* Different versions of the COCOMO model have been formulated with different degrees of accuracy. Basic COCOMO predicts software development costs as a function of the expected size of the software product in source instructions.

Other versions of COCOMO predict software costs as a function of attributes of the software development effort, as well as the number of source statements to be developed. These versions can be

---

*Barry W. Boehm, *Software Engineering Economics*, © 1981, pp. 57–144. Adapted by permission of Prentice Hall, Inc., Englewood Cliffs, New Jersey.

used to estimate the cost of the total software package or of components of the total software package. Each version of COCOMO distinguishes between modes of software development that differ in scope and intrinsic difficulty. These modes are referred to as organic, embedded, and semidetached. The *organic mode* applies to small- to medium-size in-house projects undertaken by persons familiar with the application and experienced in developing software for related applications. The *embedded mode* refers to the development of a strongly coupled complex of hardware and software that is difficult to change or fix, that consists of new architecture, and that is tightly constrained by reliability, memory, and speed of execution. The *semidetached mode* includes projects halfway between a familiar, in-house organic project and an unfamiliar, innovative embedded project.

COCOMO cost projections account for design, code, test, and integration activities in developing a software product. The algorithms of COCOMO predict the number of man-months required to complete these activities (a man-month is defined as 152 hours of working time). COCOMO estimates assume that the project management by both the developer and the customer is good and that the requirements specification is not substantially rewritten during the development effort.

### The Formulation of Basic and Intermediate COCOMO

*Basic COCOMO* uses the following algorithm to estimate the effort to develop software in units of man-months (*MM*):

$$MM = K(DSI/1000)^E \tag{12-2}$$

where *DSI* is the number of source statements projected to implement a design. Values of the coefficient $K$ and the exponent $E$ are given in Table 12-1. As indicated in the table, unique values for $K$ and $E$ are selected as a function of the mode of software development.

TABLE 12-1.  Coefficients and exponents of the COCOMO estimation algorithms

| Development mode | Basic COCOMO | | Intermediate COCOMO | |
|---|---|---|---|---|
| | K | E | K | E |
| Organic | 2.4 | 1.05 | 3.2 | 1.05 |
| Semiattached | 3.0 | 1.12 | 3.0 | 1.12 |
| Embedded | 3.6 | 1.20 | 2.8 | 1.20 |

*Intermediate COCOMO* also estimates software development costs as a function of the projected source statement count and the development. However, the algorithm of intermediate COCOMO also includes coefficients that account for characteristics of the development effort as follows:

$$MM = (C_1 * C_2 * \ldots C_{15})K(DSI/1000)^E \qquad (12\text{-}3)$$

where the coefficients $C_n$ are functions of attributes ratings (e.g., high, nominal, low).[1] Values of $K$ and $E$ are those given in Table 12-1.

COCOMO has been found to work reasonably well in estimating the cost to implement a software system in Ada, and a version of COCOMO has been tailored for Ada. In the tailored version, the

---

[1]The first three coefficients of COCOMO are functions of attributes that account for the characteristics of the *software product*:

$C_1$ = required software reliability

$C_2$ = database size

$C_3$ = product complexity

The next four coefficients are functions of the attributes that account for the *computer used*:

$C_4$ = execution time constraint

$C_5$ = main storage constraint

$C_6$ = virtual machine volatility

$C_7$ = computer turnaround time

The next five coefficients are functions of the attributes that account for the *development personnel*:

$C_8$ = analyst capability

$C_9$ = applications experience

$C_{10}$ = programmer capability

$C_{11}$ = virtual machine experience

$C_{12}$ = programming language experience

The next two coefficients are functions of the attributes that account for programming considerations:

$C_{13}$ = use of modern programming practices

$C_{14}$ = level of tool support

The final coefficient is a function of an attribute that accounts for schedule constraints:

$C_{15}$ = schedule constraint

values of the coefficients have been calibrated to Ada development efforts using data collected over large Ada projects at TRW.

### 12.3.3 Control of Software Development Costs

In this section, we apply COCOMO to demonstrate the control of costs in the development of a software system. Using the design approach presented in this book, we partition a software system into a set of independent packages. Since each package is to be independent and to interact in a limited manner with only a few other packages, we can assume that the costs to develop a software system is essentially the sum of the costs to develop the individual packages, plus the cost to integrate the packages. This is given in the following relationship:

$$\textit{system cost software} = \left\{ \sum_{CP=1}^{\#CPs} \sum_{IP=1}^{\#IPs(CP)} cost(CP, IP) \right\}$$
$$+ \; \textit{integration costs} \qquad (12\text{-}4)$$

where $cost(CP, IP)$ is the cost to develop the $IP$th independent package of the $CP$th computer program, $\#CPs$ is the number of computer programs in the software system, and $\#IPs(CP)$ is the number of independent packages in the $CP$th computer program. Let's apply COCOMO to estimate the two principal factors in this equation to estimate the cost of a software system consisting of 10 programs, with each program containing five independent packages, which on the average can be implemented by 5,000 source statements. Let's also compare the resulting cost estimate to an estimate of the cost for developing the same size system in a traditional top-down manner.

For the traditional top-down approach, we would assume that the program has been designed as a hierarchy of subprograms ranging in size from 100 to 200 source statements and that COCOMO can be directly applied using equation 12-2, as follows:

$$\begin{aligned} MM(\textit{software system}) &= K(DSI/1000)^E \\ &= 3.6(250{,}000/1{,}000)^{1.2} \\ &= 2715.4 \end{aligned}$$

For our design approach, the cost to develop package $i$ can be calculated using equation 12-2, as follows:

$$MM(package\ i) = K(DSI/1000)^E$$
$$= 3.6(5000/1000)^{1.2}$$
$$= 24.8$$

In both cases, we have assumed that the embedded mode is applicable, with the coefficient $K$ equal to 3.6 and the exponent $E$ equal to 1.2 (from Table 12-1). The cost to develop each program with five packages is then assumed to be five times the cost to develop a single package, or 124 man-months. Therefore, the cost to develop the software system as ten programs is 1,240 man-months. This results in a cost saving of 1475.4 man-months.

Repeating these calculations for different size software systems (assuming five independent packages per program) and plotting the results lead to the cost curve shown in Figure 12-5, where the cost of a software system is plotted against size. In this figure, the lower curve accounts for the cost required to develop the independent packages of a software system using the strategy of partitioning the software system into independent packages. If the independent packages are in fact independent (i.e., they do not pass variables, flags, and types used in the formulation of their unique operations) and are loosely coupled, then integration costs will be low and the difference in the curves shown in Figure 12-5 will essentially indicate the expected savings attributable to partitioning aspects of our design strategy. However, the difference in the curves will decrease if the independence between packages is weak and coupling is high.

We can conclude that during design and system development, the extent to which independence and coupling are introduced and maintained determines the extent to which savings can be expected. For designs with high package independence and little coupling, significant savings should be realized. For designs with high package dependence and extensive coupling, savings may be minimal.

In practice, a software system developed from a traditional top-down design of small program units might be considered a high-risk situation where costs could be worse than the upper curve shown in Figure 12-5 as predicted by COCOMO. This is because when changes are made to a software system that consists of highly dependent and coupled program units, the system may become less and less ordered due to strange side effects caused by the changes. In a worst-case scenario, the system can reach a point where developers cease to gain ground. Progress bogs down or represses, since each change

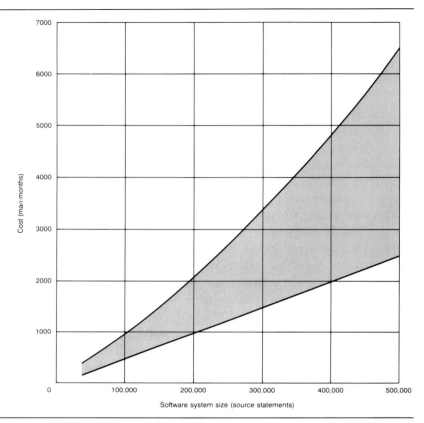

*FIGURE 12-5.* Development costs

may introduce new and significant problems. Changes to correct
bugs may produce new bugs, perhaps worse than the original bugs.
As a result, the project can reach the disaster stage, and recoup may
have to be undertaken. The recoup effort will require extensive
redesign to decrease dependence and coupling between independent
packages, the necessary prerequisite to developing a software system in a cost-effective and low-risk manner.

### 12.3.4 Control of Software Maintenance Costs

The cost to maintain a software system may far exceed development
costs. These costs typically have been found to run two to five times
more than development costs and have been measured at as much as
50 times development costs. Such high maintenance costs may be

caused in large part by high dependence and coupling across program units. To demonstrate cost savings in maintenance that can be realized with partitioning of a software system into independent packages, let us establish an algorithm that quantifies the savings. Again, we will contrast the costs for software systems with highly independent and loosely coupled packages to the costs for software systems developed from a traditional top-down design (based on decomposition with small, highly coupled program units and not independent packages).

For a software system designed as a set of loosely coupled independent packages, assume that during maintenance only the modified package has to be regression tested. With this assumption, we can quantify annual Ada maintenance costs using the following algorithm:

*maintenance cost packages approach = (rework cost + regression test (single package)) \*#changes per year*

(12-6)

For a computer program to be designed in a traditional top-down manner, assume that the entire software system will have to be regression tested to verify the effects of a package modification. With this assumption, we can quantify annual maintenance costs using the following algorithm:

*maintenance cost traditional approach = (rework cost + regression test (entire program)) \*#changes per year*

(12-7)

Cost savings with our design approach relative to a traditional approach are as follows:

*cost saving = maintenance cost traditional approach − maintenance cost packages approach*

*= (rework cost + regression test (entire package)) \*#changes per year*
*− (rework cost + regression test (single package)) \*#changes per year*

*= (regression test (entire package)) − regression test (single package))\*#changes per year*

The regression test of a single Ada package with 5,000 source statements can be calculated using equation 12-2 multiplied by the

TABLE 12-2. Values of P(i) (fraction of the total software development effort for a specific subeffort)

| Mode | i | | P(i) | | | | |
|------|---|--|------|------|------|------|------|
| | | | 2 KDSI | 8 KDSI | 32 KDSI | 128 KDSI | 512 KDSI |
| Organic | 1 | High-level design | .16 | .16 | .16 | .16 | |
| | 2 | Detailed design | .26 | .25 | .24 | .23 | |
| | 3 | Code and unit test | .42 | .40 | .38 | .36 | |
| | 4 | Integration and test | .16 | .19 | .22 | .25 | |
| Semidetached | 1 | High-level design | .17 | .17 | .17 | .17 | .17 |
| | 2 | Detailed design | .27 | .26 | .26 | .24 | .23 |
| | 3 | Code and unit test | .37 | .35 | .33 | .31 | .29 |
| | 4 | Integration and test | .19 | .22 | .25 | .28 | .31 |
| Embedded | 1 | High-level design | .18 | .18 | .18 | .18 | .18 |
| | 2 | Detailed design | .28 | .27 | .26 | .25 | .24 |
| | 3 | Code and unit test | .32 | .30 | .28 | .26 | .24 |
| | 4 | Integration and test | .22 | .25 | .28 | .31 | .34 |

fraction of the software development life cycle attributed to test (i.e., P(4) in Table 12-2) and by 0.1 as follows:

*regression test (single package)*
$$= 0.1*.25*3.6(5{,}000/1{,}000)^{1.2}$$
$$= .62 \text{ man-month}$$

The factor 0.1 is applied because we are assuming that the cost of each regression test is equal to 10 percent of the original software integration test cost. The regression test of a software system with 250,000 source statements can be calculated in the same manner, as follows:

*regression test (entire program)*
$$= 0.1*.31*3.6(250{,}000/1{,}000)^{1.2}$$
$$= 84.17 \text{ man-months}$$

Assuming 10 changes per year, the annual cost saving would be as follows:

*cost saving* $= (841.7 - 6.2)*10 = 835.5$ man-months

Repeating this calculation for different size software systems and assuming that such maintenance activity takes place over 10 years results in the range of savings shown in Figure 12-6.

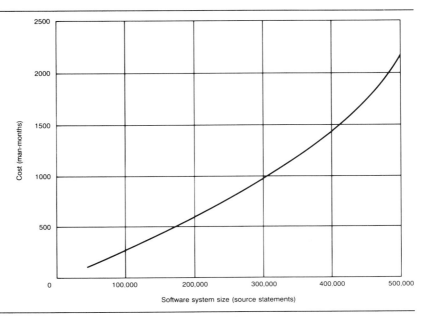

*FIGURE 12-6.* Annual maintenance savings.

In practice, regression-testing costs for a large computer program designed with a traditional top-down approach could be even more than our projections. As we have said, changes may degrade the structure of a large program, each change possibly introducing new dependencies between program units, variables, and types. Because of this, regression testing may uncover severe new problems that are very expensive to find and correct. In extreme cases, a large software system can reach a point where extensive rewrite is necessary. Thus, with traditional approaches to maintenance, there always is the reality of very expensive regression testing costs and the possibility of costly rework of the software system.

## 12.3.5 Conclusions

As the size of software systems has grown, high development costs have proved to be the rule and not the exception. In addition, the maintenance of software systems over 10 years or so costs significantly more than development costs. The high maintenance costs in the past are due in part to possible adverse effects on the performance of a program caused by changes made to the program. Because of this, maintenance necessitates expensive regression testing.

The design approach introduced in this book directly addresses the question of maintenance by providing a means for making a large program responsive to change. In addition, the SMART design notation introduced here can be used to represent in a concise manner selected architectural aspects of a large software system. This design representation can be used and maintained by maintenance programmers so that they can readily understand the general topology of the software system, eliminating the mental reverse engineering process necessary to discover the architectural structure from code. With this knowledge, dependencies between independent packages can be avoided during maintenance, thus keeping the software system flexible and responsive to change.

In this chapter, we demonstrated the magnitude of the costs associated with developing and maintaining a large computer program. The cost projections made were meant to demonstrate the savings possible using our design approach when compared to a traditional top-down design approach. Although we can argue as to exactly what these cost projections should be, most will agree that "bulk is bad" and extensive dependencies are not desirable.

Accordingly, we have suggested use of a design approach whereby a software system is partitioned into a set of independent packages. Each package is to be sufficiently small to be easily understood, developed, and maintained, yet at a much higher level of granularity than that associated with a traditional top-down design. By controlling dependencies and coupling between independent packages, maintenance activity essentially is reduced to making changes to individual independent packages. This is not an expensive proposition if the implementation of each independent package is not excessively large (nominally less than 10,000 source statements) and the effect of a change is trapped in the implementation of that package. When this is the case, extensive regression testing is not necessary and maintenance costs can be controlled. In this way, our design approach can help control maintenance costs. These savings, when coupled with savings in the development of a software system, should result in significant overall life cycle cost savings.

# Bibliography

Aho, A. V., Hopcroft, J. E., and Ullman, J. D. *The Design and Analysis of Computer Algorithms*. Reading, MA: Addison-Wesley, 1974.

Barnes, J. G. P. *Programming in Ada*. Workingham, England: Addison-Wesley, 1989.

Bauer, F. L., "Software Engineering," *Information Processing* 71:530, 1972.

Ben-Ari, M. *Principles of Current Programming*. Englewood Cliffs, NJ: Prentice Hall, 1982.

Berlinski, D. *On Systems Analysis: An Essay Concerning the Limitations of Some Mathematical Methods in the Social, Political, and Biological Studies*. Cambridge, MA: MIT Press, 1976.

Birkhoff, G., and Bartee, T. C. *Modern Applied Algebra*. New York: McGraw-Hill, 1970.

Bobrow, L. S., and Arbib, M. A. *Discrete Mathematics: Applied Algebra for Computer and Information Science*. Washington, DC: Hemisphere Publishing, 1974.

Boehm, B. W. *Software Engineering Economics*. Englewood Cliffs, NJ: Prentice Hall, 1981.

Booch, G. *Software Engineering with Ada*. Menlo Park, CA: Benjamin Cummings, 1983.

Brooks, F. P. *The Mythical Man-Month, Essays on Software Engineering*. Reading, MA: Addison-Wesley, 1975.

Bryan, D. L., and Mendel, G. O. *Exploring Ada*. Englewood Cliffs, NJ: Prentice Hall, 1990.

Buhr, K. J. A. *System Design with Ada*. Englewood Cliffs, NJ: Prentice Hall, 1984.

Churchman, C. W. *The Systems Approach*. New York: Dell Publishing, 1968.

Cleaveland, J. C. *An Introduction to Data Types*. Reading, MA: Addison-Wesley, 1986.

Cox, B. J. *Object-Oriented Programming: An Evolutionary Approach*. Reading, MA: Addison-Wesley, 1986.

Crawley, J. W., and McArthur, W. Q. *Structured Programming Using PASCAL*. Englewood Cliffs, NJ: Prentice Hall, 1988.

Dahl, O. J., Dijkstra, E. W., and Hoare, C. A. R. *Structured Programming*. London: Academic Press, 1972.

Deo, N. *Graph Theory with Applications to Engineering and Computer Science*. Englewood Cliffs, NJ: Prentice Hall, 1974.

DeMarco, J. *Structured Analysis and System Specification*. Englewood Cliffs, NJ: Yourdon Press, 1978.

Dijkstra, E. W. *A Discipline of Programming*. Englewood Cliffs, NJ: Prentice Hall, 1976.

Dorchak, S. F., and Rice, P. B. *Writing Readable Ada: A Case Study Approach*. Lexington, MA: D. C. Heath, 1989.

Ellul, J. *The Technological System*. New York: Continuum, 1980.

Freedman, R. S. *Programming Concepts with the Ada Language*. New York: Petrocelli, 1983.

Gehani, N. *Ada: An Advanced Introduction*. Englewood Cliffs, NJ: Prentice Hall, 1983.

Gannet, G. H. *Handbook of Algorithms and Data Structures*. Reading, MA: Addison-Wesley, 1984.

Habermann, A. N., and Dewayne, E. P. *Ada for Experienced Programmers*. Reading, MA: Addison-Wesley, 1983.

Halstead, M. H. *Elements of Software Science*. New York: North Holland, 1977.

Howden, W. E. *Functional Program Testing and Analysis*. New York: McGraw-Hill, 1987.

Jeffry, S., and Linden, T. A. "Software Engineering is Engineering." Proceedings of the Computer Science and Engineering Curricula Workshop, The Institute of Electrical and Electronic Engineers, 1977.

Johnson, P. I. *Ada: Applications and Administration: An Introduction to the Ada Programming Language and Structured System Technology*. New York: McGraw-Hill, 1990.

Keller, J. *The Ada Challenge: Strategies, Risks, and Payoffs*. Pasha Publications, 1988.

Kernighan, B. W., and Plauger, P. J. *Software Tools*. Reading, MA: Addison-Wesley, 1976.

Koffman, E. B. *Problem Solving and Structured Programming in PASCAL*. Reading, MA: Addison-Wesley, 1981.

Korsch, J. F., and Garett, J. J. *Data Structures, Algorithms, and Program Style Using C*. Boston: PWS-Kent, 1988.

Lilienfeld, R. *The Rise of System Theory: An Ideological Analysis*. New York: John Wiley, 1978.

Martin, J., and McClure, C. *Software Maintenance: The Problem and Its Solution*. Englewood Cliffs, NJ: Prentice Hall, 1983.

Maurer, H. H. *Data Structures and Programming Techniques*. Englewood Cliffs, NJ: Prentice Hall, 1977.

Meyer, B. *Object-Oriented Software Construction*. Hertfordshire, England: Prentice Hall International, 1988.

Meyers, G. J. *Composite/Structured Design*. New York: Van Nostrand Reinhold, 1978.

Mohnkern, G. L., and Mohnkern, B. *Applied Ada*. Blue Ridge Summit, PA: TAB Books, 1986.

Peters, L. J. *Software Design: Methods & Techniques*. Englewood Cliffs, NJ: Yourdon Press, 1981.

Pressman, R. S. *Software Engineering: A Practitioner's Approach*. New York: McGraw-Hill, 1987.

Pyle, I. C. *Developing Safety Systems: A Guide to Using Ada*. Engelwood Cliffs, NJ: Prentice Hall, 1990.

Schildt, H. *Advanced C*. Berkeley, CA: Osborne McGraw-Hill, 1988.

Schlaer, S., and Mellor, S. J. *Object-Oriented System Analysis: Modeling the World in Data*. Englewood Cliffs, NJ: Yourdon Press, 1988.

Schumate, K. *Understanding Ada: With Abstract Ada Types*. New York: John Wiley, 1989.

Schumate, K. *Understanding Concurrency in Ada*. New York: McGraw-Hill, 1988.

Sodhi, J. *Managing Ada Projects Using Software Engineering*. Blue Ridge Summit, PA: TAB Books, 1989.

Stanat, D. F., and McAllister. *Discrete Mathematics in Computer Science*. Englewood Cliffs, NJ: Prentice-Hall, 1977.

Trembly, J., DeDourek, J. M., and Friesen, V. J. *Programming in Ada*. New York: McGraw-Hill, 1990.

Trembly, J., and Sorenson, P. G. *An Introduction to Data Structures with Applications*. New York: McGraw-Hill, 1976.

Wiener, R., and Sincovec, R. *Software Engineering with Modula-2 and Ada*. New York: John Wiley, 1984.

Wirth, N. *Algorithms + Data Structures = Programs*. Englewood Cliffs, NJ: Prentice Hall, 1976.

Young, S. J. *An Introduction to Ada*. West Sussex, England: Ellis Horwood Ltd., 1983.

Yourdan, E. *Techniques of Program Structure and Design*. Englewood Cliffs, NJ: Prentice Hall, 1975.

# Index

conditional task acceptance, SMART
  view of, 168, 172, 173
configuration management, role of,
  289, 290
constructive cost model (COCOMO),
  295–299
control logic, 107
  establishing, 107–108
costs
  algorithms to assess, 294–295
  constructive cost model (COCOMO),
    295–299
  controlling development, 298–300
  controlling maintenance, 300–303
  development, 288–290
  installation, 290–291
  maintenance, 291–294
  operation, 290–291

data dictionary, 28
data flow, SMART view of, 160,
  163–166
data flow diagram, 25, 29–30
data manager package, 190, 191
data structure
  clarity of, 103
  concepts of, 85–90
  descriptors of, 181
  design considerations, 97
  graphic representation of, 149
  hidden, 98–99
  representation of, 178, 180
  specifications for, 91–97
  visible, 93–96, 198
Defense Department, 3, 16
delta reserved word, 88n
development cost, 288–290
  controlling, 298–300
digits reserved word, 88n
do keyword, 70n, 80n
documentation, software, 13–14
dynamic allocation, 101

else keyword, 108n, 116
elsif keyword, 116
encapsulation, 48, 49
end keyword, 63, 70n, 77n
end if reserved words, 108n, 116
end record reserved words, 90n

endurance testing, 281
entry keyword, 70n, 80n
enumeration type, 88, 121
environmental simulation, 277–278
exception handling, 112
exit keyword, 109n
external interfaces, documentation of,
  33

fixed point type, 121
floating point type, 121
flowchart, 35–37
for clause, 108n, 182
function, 80–81
  graphic representation of, 147, 148
  syntax for, 77, 78
function keyword, 77n
functionality, documentation of, 32

generic keyword, 133n
generic package, 130–136
  SMART view of, 172–178
generic subprogram, 120–121
generic type definition, 121
geometric representation of program
  units, 147–149
granularity, 61

hardware interfaces, documentation of,
  33
hidden program unit, 204–206
high-level architecture, assessment of,
  210–211

if keyword, 116
if statement, 107–108, 183
  types of, 182
in keyword, 77n, 79n
in out keyword, 79n
independent package, 6, 60–62, 65–67
  Ada typing and, 102–103
  cohesion of, 211
  concurrency in, 69, 233–235
  coupling of, 78–79, 211
  data flow between, 197
  design of, 112–121
  exception handling in, 112
  generic, SMART view of, 172–178
  graphic representation of, 147, 148

implemented by Ada package, 86–87
independence of, 210–211
integration of, 276–277
interaction among, 73–75, 195–197
interface specification, 193–194
interfaces for, 235–238
internal design of, 198–210,
    211–213, 238–247
in large program, 188–190
operations of, 107–111
program units internal to, 198–208
reusable, 130–136, 274–284
segmenting operations in, 112–116
size and scope of, 211–212
SMART view of, 150
in software system, 230–247
syntactic structure of, 64
testing of, 277–284
independent verification and validation
    (IV&V), 289
integer type, 87, 121
interface, 46, 213
    between independent packages,
        193–194
    documentation of, 33
    for independent package, 235–238
    specification of, 224–229
interface control unit (ICU), 25–28
    concurrency and, 72, 192
    design of, 189–191
    state transition diagram for, 32
is keyword, 63n, 70n, 77n
iteration, 107

Jeffrey, S., 5

library units, SMART view of, 166, 167
life cycle costs
    development costs, 288–290,
        298–300
    installation costs, 290–291
    maintenance costs, 291–294,
        300–303
    operation costs, 290–291
    qualitative assessment of, 287
    quantitative assessment of, 294–303
limited private type, 101–102
Linden, T.A., 5
linked list, 85, 86

logic. *See* control logic
logical concurrency, 44–45, 47, 69,
    72–73, 192, 221–224, 233–235
loop statement, 108, 183

maintenance
    conceptual view of, 292–294
    cost control, 300–303
    costs of, 291
    documentation of, 33
    importance of, 291–292
matrix, 85
messages package, 190, 191
Meyer, Bertrand, 49
modeling, 61–62
module
    reusable, 116–121
    segmenting operations in, 112–116
multiple demands, servicing, 193–194

nested iterations, 107
new keyword, 103n, 110n, 134n
nominal testing, 278

object-oriented design, 45
    concepts of, 48–50
one-dimensional array, 89n
operating system, 217
operation, representation of, 180, 182
operations
    concepts of, 107
    costs of, 290–291
operator console package, 190, 191
out keyword, 79n

package body keyword, 63n
package keyword, 63n
package. *See* independent package
parameter passing, 79, 81
    SMART representation of, 166
PDL, Ada as, 146
    defined, 146
performance constraints,
    documentation of, 33
pointer, implementation of, 100–101
policy, documentation of, 33
pool keyword, 100
portability, 33, 275–276
Pressman, Roger, 49–50, 212

private type, 101–102
private keyword, 102n
procedure, 79
    graphic representation of, 147, 148
    syntax for, 78
procedure keyword, 77n
processing capabilities, documentation
    of, 32–33
program
    adverse effects of changing, 56–59
    characterized, 8–9
    granularity of structure, 61
    modeling for, 61–62
    packaging of, 60–67
    prototype, 59, 266–267
    SMART view of, 218
program design language, 146
program unit call
    representation of, 184
    SMART view of, 154, 158–160
program unit declaration, SMART view
    of, 151–152, 154
program units
    cohesiveness of, 212–213
    design of, 202–207
    hidden, 204–206
    hierarchy of, 41–42, 43
    interdependency of, 58–59
    SMART view of, 147–149
    SMART view of data flow between,
        160, 163–166
    specification of, 198–202
    visible, 203–204
programmer, role of, 288, 290
project manager, role of, 288, 289
pseudocode, 37–38, 180, 182

quality assurance (QA), 289, 290

range reserved word, 87n
real type, 87
recompilation, 268–269
    assessment of, 270–272
record, 90
    pointer to, 100–101
    using, 111
record reserved word, 90n
recursive calls, SMART view of,
    163–165

reliability, documentation of, 33
rendezvous, 72, 75
    SMART view of, 166–169
requirements
    anticipating changes in, 267–268
    changes in, 266
    for data structure, 91–97
    documentation of, 31–33
    instability of, 59–60
    for programs with complex data
        structures, 124–129
    scope of, 23–24
    for software system, 219–221
    specification of, 22, 220–221
    traceability of, 210
return keyword, 77n
reusable module, 116–121
    design of, 121
    generic subprograms, 120–121
reusable package, 130–136, 274–284
    concept of, 275
    integration of, 276–284
    porting of, 275–276
robotics, 3

scalar variable, 85, 86
    types of, 87–88
    using, 109–110
semicolon, 63n, 70n, 77n, 79
separate keyword, 154
services, 127
small computer program. See program
SMART Ada, 147
    view of data flow, 160, 163–166, 197
    view of generic package, 172–178
    view of generic procedures, 170–172
    view of independent package, 150,
        151
    view of main program, 218
    view of subprogram, 151–166, 167
software
    controlling cost of, 298–303
    development costs of, 3, 288–290,
        298–300
    documenting requirements, 31–33
    installation and initial operation
        costs, 290–291
    life cycle costs of, 287–303
    life cycle of, 23

maintenance costs, 3, 291–294,
  300–303
prototype, 59, 266–267
quality assurance of, 289, 290
representing requirements, 24–31
requirements, 23–24
for testing, 277–278
software design
  Ada typing and, 102–103
  application of technology, 50
  class-member relationships,
    129–136, 139
  data structures, 91–103
  data-driven, 48
  as data structure, 48
  history of, 34–37
  incremental development, 272, 274
  independent package, 112–121
  with independent packages, 64
  levels of, 34
  logical concurrency in, 44–45, 47,
    72–73, 192
  need for, 15–16
  object-oriented, 45–50
  program design, 230–260
  refinement, 247–260
  representation for, 17–18
  requirements changes and, 266–268
  reusable module, 121
  risk control through, 268–285
  SMART Ada, 147–184
  steps in, 188–213
  structured programming in, 37–38
  subprograms, 81
  system design, 217–260
  task types, 137–138
  top-down, 39–44
software engineering
  defined, 4–5
  product development, 6–8
  requirements specification, 22
  role of, 288, 289
software ICs, 130
software system
  acceptance testing of, 278, 281
  concurrency in, 221–224
  cost control in, 287–303
  development of, 9–12
  documentation for, 13–14

independent packages in, 230–232
interfaces in, 224–229, 235–238
maintenance of, 291–294
package design for, 238–247
program design in, 230–260
progress of, 12
refinement of, 247–260
requirements for, 219–221
size of, 13–14
steps for designing, 219
topology of, 271
specification, of requirements, 31–33
state transition diagram, 28, 30–31
states, documentation of, 32
stress testing, 278
structured English, 28
structured programming, 37–38, 213
subprogram, 68–69, 76–77
  generic, 120–121
  graphic representation of, 147, 148
  SMART view of, 151–166
subtype keyword, 102n
systems engineer, role of, 288, 290

tasks
  acceptor, 168
  caller, 166
  execution of, 70
  graphic representation of, 147, 148
  priority setting, 71
  receiver, 72
  rendezvous among, 72, 75, 166–169
  sender, 72
  SMART view of, 178, 179
  source statements for, 74–75, 80
  states of, 71
  structure of, 70
  syntactic structure of, 71
  types, 137–138
task acceptance, SMART view of, 169,
  174
task body keyword, 70n
task entry point, graphic representation
  of, 148, 168
task keyword, 70n
test engineer, role of, 288–289
testing
  acceptance, 278, 281
  debugging, 281–282

testing (*cont'd*)
    endurance, 281
    environmental simulation, 277–278
    lower-level, 281–284
    nominal, 278
    software for, 277–278
    stress, 278
    time-dependent, 282–283
then keyword, 108n, 116
top-down design, 39–41
    considerations in, 41–42
    example of, 42–44
two-dimensional array, 85, 89n–90n
type
    array, 89, 121
    composite, 89–90
    defined, 86
    enumeration, 88, 121
    fixed point, 121
    floating point, 121
    generic definition, 121
    integer, 87, 121
    limited private, 101–102
    private, 101–102
    real, 87
    record, 90

variable
    multi-valued, 85
    single-valued, 85
    *See also* array; record; scalar; vector
vector, 85, 86
visible data structure, descriptors of,
    198
visible program unit, 203–204

while clause, 109n, 182
with clause, 129, 269
    SMART Ada representation of, 150